Disadvantaged Post-Adolescents:
Approaches to Education and Rehabilitation

Special Aspects of Education

A series of books edited by Roy Evans, Roehampton Institute, London, UK, and Herman Green, Northern Illinois University, De Kalb, Illinois, USA.

Volume 1
Disadvantaged Post-Adolescents:
Approaches to Education and Rehabilitation
Reuven Kohen-Raz

Volume 2
Israelis in Institutions:
Studies in Child Placement, Practice and Policy
Eliezer D. Jaffe

Volume 3
Parental Participation in Children's Development and Education
Sheila Wolfendale

Other volumes in preparation

ISSN: 0731-8413

Disadvantaged Post-Adolescents: Approaches to Education and Rehabilitation

REUVEN KOHEN-RAZ

The Hebrew University

GORDON AND BREACH SCIENCE PUBLISHERS
New York London Paris Montreux Tokyo

Gordon and Breach, Science Publishers, Inc.
One Park Avenue
New York, NY 10016

Gordon and Breach Science Publishers Ltd.
42 William IV Street
London WC2N 4DE

Gordon & Breach
58, rue Lhomond
75005 Paris

Gordon and Breach Science Publishers S.A.
P.O. Box 161
1820 Montreux 2

Gordon and Breach, Science Publishers, Inc.
48-2 Minamidama, Oami Shirasato-Machi
Sambu-Gun
Chiba-Ken 229-32

Library of Congress Cataloging in Publication Data

Kohen-Raz, Reuven.
    Disadvantaged post-adolescents.

    (Special aspects of education, ISSN 0731-8413 ; v. 1)
    Bibliography: p.
    Includes indexes.
    1. Socially handicapped youth—Israel.   2. Socially handicapped youth—Israel—
Rehabilitation.   I. Title.   II. Series.
HQ799.8.I75K63 1983   371.96'7'095694   83-9029
ISBN 0-677-06010-6

3-13-87

To Zdeny, our beloved and loving mother

Contents

Introduction to the Series   ix

Preface   xi

Introduction — Definition of the Problem   1

PART I   **Psychodynamics of Post-Adolescence**

Chapter 1   Post-Adolescence as a Developmental Stage   7

Chapter 2   Psychodynamics of Normal Post-Adolescence   15

Chapter 3   Psychodynamics of the Disadvantaged
Post-Adolescent   40

PART II   **Models of Normal and Abnormal Mental Development
at Adolescence and Problems of the Curriculum**

Chapter 4   Rey's Model of Practical Intelligence   67

Chapter 5   Frankenstein's Psychodynamic Theory
of Intelligence   83

Chapter 6   Psychobiological Aspects of Mental
Development at Adolescence   90

Chapter 7   The Role of Context in Mental Development   105

Chapter 8   The Traditional Curriculum as a Source of
School Failure of Disadvantaged Adolescents   112

PART III   **Current Projects of Rehabilitation of Disadvantaged
Post-Adolescents in Israel**

Chapter 9   Feuerstein's Program of Instrumental
Enrichment   121

Chapter 10 Frankenstein's Model of Rehabilitative
Teaching   133

Chapter 11 Smilansky's Boarding School Fostering
Program   145

Chapter 12 The Curriculum of Contextual Learning
Units   153

Chapter 13 The Structure and Content of the
Curriculum of Contextual Learning Units   159

Chapter 14 Evaluation of the Program of Contextual
Learning Units   190

Concluding Remarks   198

References   202

Author Index   212

Subject Index   216

Introduction to the Series

Increasingly in the last 10 to 15 years the published literature within the field of care and education has become more specialised and focused: an inevitable consequence of the information explosion and the improved standards of theoretical and practical knowledge being required of students in both the traditional and developing areas of professional training. Students within initial and post-initial training evidently need to have ready access to specialist theoretical and pedagogical resources relevant to the context of future professional involvements which also develop special aspects of an area of study in a critically evaluative way.

In the study of education and pedagogy, the analytical and experimental approaches of psychology, philosophy, sociology, social anthropology, etc., have provided insights to teaching and learning, to schooling and education. Historically these disciplines have focused their attention on relatively homogeneous populations. Increased worldwide mobility has created a need for a more pluralistic approach to education – particularly in Western countries – and a more broadly based concern for educational issues related to particular contexts. Hence, *further* literature has developed in recent years which is concerned with the pedagogical and curriculum issues raised, for example, in connection with the "urban school", minority ethnic groups, disadvantaged and handicapped groups, and children who live apart from their families.

What is frequently missing from discipline orientated studies is a real appreciation of context beyond the "general". What is often not present in the contextual study is an interdisciplinary analysis of the issue, to provide a framework for practice.

The present series – *Special Aspects of Education* – is intended to bridge the gap between the problems of practice as perceived in a variety of contexts, and the theory as derived from a variety of disciplines. Books accepted or commissioned for inclusion in the series will be expected to manifestly acknowledge the interdisciplinary nature of issues and problems in the field of education and care, and in addressing themselves to particular contexts, provide a conceptual framework for identifying and meeting special educational needs.

ROY EVANS
HERMAN GREEN

Preface

This book has been written in an attempt to offer a contribution to one of Western culture's most urgent problems: the disadvantaged post-adolescent — the problem of youth between the ages of 15 and 20 from underprivileged socio-economic and ethnic groups who have only marginally adjusted to the demands of socialization, education and vocational formation, imposed by contemporary and technological or, more exactly, post-technological society.

The first reason for reviewing and summarizing some recent experiences and experiments in Israel stems from its precarious political situation; it has been forced to seek solutions more urgently and more drastically than other countries with less internal and external political pressures. Thus, whatever the limits of the *ad hoc* empirical findings and the restricted validity of local results, it seems worthwhile to present them and to attempt to provide a theoretical framework which will facilitate the elucidation of generally valid aspects.

The second reason for writing this book in its present form was personal experience with marginal youth in the framework of a project called "The Program of Contextual Learning Units". This project was carried out during the last six years in close collaboration with the Pedagogical Department of the Bureau for Manpower Training and Development of the Israeli Ministry of Labour and Social Affairs. This department is largely responsible for marginal and drop-out youth after all other institutions and services ceased to function as effective socializing agents. The project is a common effort of scientific investment, pedagogical initiative and administrative courage, and since it is in the forefront of rehabilitative and re-educational activity, it has accommodated obstacles and unforeseen circumstances.

The project still appears to fill an important gap in the continuum of other rehabilitation projects described in the third part of this book. I hope the detailed description of its learning units in the later chapters will provide valuable information for the interested reader. In this context I wish to acknowledge the co-authorship and co-direction of Mrs Miryam Bar-Lev in the "Contextual Learning Units" project and the efficient collaboration of Mr Yitzchak Sochen, who heads the organization and implementation of the program. I extend my gratitude to Mr Beni Levinson, Director of the Pedagogical Department, who has been involved in the program since its inception and is contributing to its continual expansion and future growth.

I also wish to thank Theresina Rey, André-Louis-Rey, Geneva, the authors, D. Dulit, R. Feuerstein, P.C. Wason, P.N. Johnson-Laird, P. Legrenzi, R.D. Odom and the publishers Delachaux & Niestlé, Neuchâtel; Alcan/Presses Universitaires de France, Paris; Academic Press and Plenum Publishing Corporation, New York; University Park Press, Baltimore and Batsford, London for their authorisation to reproduce materials under their copyrights.

REUVEN KOHEN-RAZ

INTRODUCTION

Definition of the Problem

The general educational problems of 'disadvantaged pupils' have stimulated a plethora of basic and applied research, as well as generated a vast number of intervention and enrichment programs. However, the focus of educational experimentation has been early prevention at preschool age of the ill effects of socio-cultural deprivation *in statu nascendi*. While these effects are assumed to be reversible, the preschool period is still considered to be a critical period for children's growth (Deutsch, 1967; Passow *et al.*, 1967, 1972; Riessman, 1976; Rutter and Madge, 1976).

There has been relatively little concern, however, for disadvantaged groups beyond the age of sixteen, i.e. the period of 'post-adolescence, generally defined as the developmental stage which starts *after* physiological puberty, characterized by psychosomatic and hormonal disequilibrium, and which terminates with the attainment of adult social and vocational status at the beginning of the third decade of life (Blos, 1962). (The psychodynamics and various psychosocial aspects of this developmental period will be discussed in detail in the first part of this book). This restriction of systematic efforts to investigate and to treat the problems of disadvantaged post-adolescents appears to be based on the assumption that successful early childhood and preschool enrichment programs lead intrinsically to normalization at later ages, while, on the other hand, there seem to be only limited prospects to rehabilitate emotional and intellectual retardation at post-adolescence (Kohen-Raz, 1977a).

This assumption is derived from two models of human development. One, the model of *cumulative effects* explains that early enrichment generates steadily growing intellectual progress and emotional maturation, while, on the other hand, early deprivation

1

creates a vicious circle of retardation, scholastic failure, frustration and social maladjustment (Deutsch, 1967). The second model emphasizes the deceleration of intellectual growth during the second decade of life, approaching asymptotically the ceiling of adult mental level. According to this model, it is also tacitly assumed that mental growth potential, as well as the flexibility and plasticity of mental abilities, diminishes as adulthood approaches (Bloom, 1964; Guidford, 1967; Thurstone and Ackerman, 1929).

Theoretically, it is surely worth contemplating whether these two models should be maintained as a frame of reference for educational research with the disadvantaged, or whether they should be complemented or replaced by recent theories postulating delayed emergence of genetically or constitutionally determined hidden potentials before and beyond puberty (Kohen-Raz, 1981b; Wilson, 1974a, b; 1981).

From a purely pragmatic point of view, the crude fact has to be faced — that there is a considerable number of disadvantaged adolescents whose problems have not been solved by existing programs of early enrichment, mainstreaming, compensatory education, etc. That is to say, these boys and girls have been enroled formally in the elementary and post-elementary school system, but generally have not gathered more than four years of scholastic experience, not mastered reading, writing and arithmetic and not acquired rudimentary knowledge in basic school subjects such as history, geography, the natural sciences, and so on. They frequently abscond from school and when they reach post-adolescence they are illiterate, unemployed, wayward and delinquency-prone, having lost all motivation to study and to work (Kitsis, 1974; Halper, 1978). The situation is further aggravated by the weakness and insufficient organization and coordination of educational, social and vocational guidance services supposed to be responsible for the re-education and rehabilitation of these youngsters. Their numbers cannot be accurately reported for a number of reasons. Firstly, they may be formally enroled in schools because their principals and parents are reluctant to admit the failure to ensure their compulsory school attendance. Secondly, they may have passed the age of compulsory education and no governmental institution or service is keeping track of them. Finally, they may not be reported among the officially unemployed as they may work only sporadically. Rough estimates of the number of these youngsters in Israel is about 40,000, which is about 13% of the population between the ages 12 to 18.

Numerous attempts in Israel and elsewhere have been undertaken to solve this urgent problem The basic re-educational policy has been to establish schools, hostels or centers where supervised indoor or outdoor work (mostly unskilled or semi-skilled) is combined with some schooling, consisting essentially of a 'last hour' attempt to teach basic school subjects at the level of the second to fifth elementary school grade (Cull and Hardy, 1975; Feuerstein, 1980; Kohen-Raz, 1979, 1980, 1981a).

Generally, it may be stated that most of these rehabilitation projects and programs have met with only limited success and the amount of yet unresolved issues is still greater than the few encouraging positive results of the pioneer work done in this area.

It is the aim of this book to offer various points of view of the problem of the disadvantaged post-adolescent from a theoretical as well as practical perspective, including a critical overview of some ongoing programs in Israel. In order to integrate these various aspects of the problem the book has been organized along the following lines.

A theoretical part in which the psychodynamics of post-adolescents in general, and of disadvantaged post-adolescents in particular, will be described. Specific aspects and characteristics of cognitive retardation and emotional-social maladjustment of disadvantaged post-adolescents will then be analyzed in greater detail. This will be followed by a discussion of the objectives and rationales of the general school curriculum and the probable reasons why it has failed to meet the educational, cognitive and emotional needs of disadvantaged youth.

The second aspect of the problem, i.e. the possibilities of re-education and rehabilitation, will be presented first from a theoretical point of view, describing the Piagetian approach (Inhelder and Piaget, 1959; Piaget, 1971; 1972), Rey's model of Practical Intelligence (Rey, 1935) and Frankenstein's Depth Analysis of cognitive malfunctioning under conditions of 'externalisation' (Frankenstein, 1968; 1979). We shall also report on some recent psychobiological studies on the relationship between physiological and mental maturation in normal and disadvantaged adolescents which open new perspectives on the chances of 'late' intervention programs. (Douglas and Ross, 1964; Ljung, 1965; Kohen-Raz, 1977b).

Finally, the role of *context* as a critical determinant of cognitive and mental development will be discussed in juxtaposition with the Piagetian model of mental schemata (Karplus, 1981; Linn and Rice, 1979; Wason and Johnson-Laird, 1972). The practical part describes four local projects of rehabilitation of disadvantaged post-adolescents in Israel which we assume have enough generally valid aspects to merit the attention of educators and psychologists in other countries (Feuerstein, 1980; Frankenstein, 1979; Kohen-Raz, 1979, 1980; Smilansky, 1979). We also hope that the background of theoretical considerations presented in the first part of the book will enable the reader to interpret the meaning of local findings and to examine their validity and applicability in different socio-cultural contexts and educational situations.

The Curriculum of Contextual Learning Units successfully used with disadvantaged populations in Israel for the last six years (Kohen-Raz, 1979; 1980; 1981a) will be described in detail.

While we do not want to underestimate the seriousness of the problem, we hope that the confrontation of the theoretical analysis with the experiments carried out in the field will leave an impression of mild optimism, create an atmosphere of encouragement for seeking new methods, and mobilize additional efforts to bring back to the road of life a group of young human beings on the verge of despair and deterioration.

PART I

Psychodynamics of Post-Adolescence

CHAPTER 1

Post-Adolescence as a Developmental Stage

The exploration of post-adolescence, also called 'late adolescence' or 'youth', as a separate developmental stage is a relatively recent pursuit (Keniston, 1975). Generally, this period, roughly spreading between ages 16 to 20, has been treated under the heading of 'adolescence' — a period, supposed to embrace a rather extended life-span from the beginning of pubertal physical changes until 'the attainment of emotional, social and other aspects of adult maturity' (Strang, 1957, p. 180). Obviously, a developmental stage which is demarked at its upper end by the rather vague criterion of 'adult maturity' will be defined differently by various psychological and sociological theories of human development. Consequently, there is a large number of definitions of adolescence, some putting its onset as early as eight years, and some its termination as late as 25 (Manaster, 1977, p. 5). Some clinically-oriented scientists speak of certain types of immature and emotionally disturbed adults as 'eternal adolescents', irrespective of their chronological age†.

In spite of this variety of definition, there is a considerable consensus on the following points:

1) 'Adolescence' is to be clearly differentiated from 'puberty', 'pubescence' or the 'pubertal period'. The latter is defined as a process of physiological changes, transforming the infantile organism into an adult human being capable of sexual reproduction and ready to endure the physical stress required for independent survival. In this respect, many similarities can be found between humans and mammalian species. On the other

---

†Compare Jung's concept of the "puer aeternus" (Jung, 1952).

hand, *adolescence* is a typically human psycho-social process, extending well beyond the pubertal period, and during which social roles and skills already acquired during early and late childhood are supposed to be transformed and adapted to roles and tasks which are mastered by adults living in the actual social environment.

2) The stress, tension and turmoil experienced by the adolescent during this period is a function of the *discrepancy* between the type and content of his childhood experiences and between the type and content of the adult roles which he is expected to assume (Benedict, 1953).

3) In well-off socio-economic strata of affluent societies, adolescents up to their 20s need not work and are economically supported by their parents. Thus, a period of transition is granted, enabling the 'teenager' to experiment with social and economic roles without constraint and commitment. This transitory phase has been defined by Erikson as 'a moratorium' (Erikson, 1963). On the other hand, some authors claim that in 'primitive societies' and at lower socio-economic levels, there is no moratorium'. Subsequently, there are no changes of experimentation and little changes will be expected in the 'externalized style of life' from adolescence to adulthood in these populations (Frankenstein, 1968).

4) The type and duration of adolescence is a function of the type of socio-cultural environment, as well as a function of the historical changes in socio-cultural norms and styles of life (Keniston, 1975; Muchov, 1962). In eras of rapid and drastic changes of social, economic and political conditions, as witnessed after World War II, patterns of adolescence will differ from decade to decade.

5) It is plausible to subdivide adolescence into three main substages

a) *Pre-adolescence*, described as the age-span between the beginning of pubertal changes (increased secretion of adrenal androgenes, first signs of the pre-adolescent growth spurt) until the activation of the gonads (menarche in girls, production of sperm in boys).

b) *Adolescence proper*. From this point until the termination of the pubertal process, manifest in a drastic deceleration of body growth, ossification of the epiphyses in *both sexes*, equilibrization of the menstrual cycle and fertility in *girls*, appearance of active sperm and change of voice in *boys*.

c) *Late, or post-adolescence*, from that point until the attainment of 'adult status', especially in respect to sex, work and legal responsibilities, taking into account, as already noted before, that this criterion is vaguely defined.

It will be noted that by virtue of this sub-division, post-adolescence becomes visible as a separate stage. However, it also turns out that among the phases of adolescence it is the most difficult to delineate because the other two substages have more or less objectively demonstrable physiological landmarks, which this substage does not.

It may, of course, be asked why should post-adolescence be isolated from the general context of adolescence and considered as a separate objective of research and problem area *sui generis* in educational and psychological practice? To answer this question, some historical aspects of adolescence in general, and its manifestation in the form of a 'post-adolescent phase' in particular, must be discussed.

Viewed from a historical perspective, it may be stated that adolescence as a separate stage in human life is a relatively recent phenomenon. In the pre-technological era, puberty occurred about two to three years later than today (Tanner, 1968) and pre-adolescent boys worked alongside their parents in agriculture and workshops. They did not experience any substantial change in their role and status throughout and after the pubertal period until they gradually took over their father's occupation. In a similar way, girls from childhood onwards worked as domestic aids and infant caretakers, and became housewives and mothers without a 'stressful search for identity', usually being married off to a partner whom they had had little say in choosing (Muchov, 1962). Also, before modern preventive medicine and antibiotics had succeeded in defeating premature death, the mortality rate for children, adolescents and women in childbirth was conspicuously high (McLaughlin, 1974; Wrigley, 1969). Consequently, the intensive investment in childcare and long-term formal education, which nowadays has become a routine, was rather hazardous and not the rule. Thus, there was much less room for deep parent-child attachment and all the 'adolescent' problems centered around High School and College, clashes of cultural and educational values, and 'pubertal revival of oedipal conflicts and separation anxieties'.

These circumstances changed with the advent of the industrial revolution. On the one hand, sophisticated machinery and better industrial organization restricted the demands for child labor, but, on the other hand, required manpower with high educational level and better developed motor and mental abilities. Gradually, compulsory elementary education was introduced in most Western countries during the second half of the nineteenth century, and an increasing number of children and youngsters found themselves in schools and institutions for elementary and higher education. Thus, the stage was set for the 'moratorium' and for all the psycho-social phenomena representing contemporary adolescence. It must not be forgotten that during that period, adolescents became 'visible' in another, rather negative context. Youngsters, were unable or unmotivated to find work and, later, all those who did not adjust to compulsory education for various reasons and dropped out, became wayward and loitered in the streets of the great, industrialized cities. This lead to the formation of street gangs and subcultures of juvenile delinquency. Keniston (1975) cites a nineteenth-century writer who defined this type of adolescent as 'a dangerous class'.

There is still another, more philosophical aspect of the relatively late emergence of adolescence as a phase *sui generis* of the human life-span. Until the second half of the eighteenth century and the French Revolution, childhood was generally viewed as a 'downwards extension' of adulthood. Children were believed to be born wicked and thus had to be trained to conform to adult norms and morals as soon as possible through harsh discipline. The fact that children were dressed as miniature adults symbolizes this attitude (Muchov, 1962). Obviously, such a style of education and early indoctrination with adult values and rules of behavior, together with the restricted mobility of the pre-technological society, left little leeway for change, transition and experimentation with new tasks and roles, in the sense of an adolescent 'moratorium'. It was Rousseau who in his book *Emile*, expressed for the first time the view that childhood is an autonomous phase of human life, meaningful in itself and worthy of being respected as a period of human growth in a permissive, supportive and encouraging environment. Treating childhood as a period of disciplinary conditioning in 'preparation for the hardships of life' and, as often happened in the nineteenth century, recruiting young people as cheap labor, cripples the potential for human development and existential expansion. It is easy to forget that this bold and revolutionary approach to childhood, which is the basis of modern general and special education, was conceived by Rousseau only 200 years ago.

Once childhood had been differentiated from adulthood, the transition or 'second birth' at adolescence emerged naturally (Hall, 1906; Rousseau, 1969). Viewed from a somewhat different angle, society must allow for permissive growth at childhood and for expansion and experimentation at the threshold of adulthood in order to create conditions for higher personal, emotional and mental development during the second and third decades of life. There is considerable consensus that these conditions were not created before the French Revolution and therefore adolescence in its present form was not a clearly visible phase of life until after the beginning of the nineteenth century (Keniston, 1975; Muchov, 1962). This somewhat 'philosophical' account of the relative recent acknowledgement of adolescence as a stage in it's own right, complements rather than contradicts the sociological interpretation presented earlier.

The historical process of differentiation between childhood, adolescence and adulthood gained momentum after the two World Wars in several respects. First, there is a 'secular trend' manifest in a gradual decrease of the age of puberty, the average age of menarche descending from 14 to 15 years at the beginning of the century to 12.6 today in most Western countries (Tanner, 1968). On the other hand, more and more time is required for education and professional development and, implicitly, the attainment of adulthood − at least in the sense of economic independence − is considerably delayed. This double shift in opposite directions at the beginning and the end of adolescence necessarily leads to its 'protraction'. In addition, a new era has begun variously labelled as 'post-technological', 'electronic', or 'cybernetic'. It is characterized first of all by the establishment of a tight network of world-wide communication systems, linking within fractions of seconds one pole with the other and turning the nations of the world into one indivisible neighborhood, where once far and distant events have become as relevant as if they happened next door. Another feature of this new period is the enormous overstimulation of the individual, produced by the mass media, the intensity of vocational and private life and the frequent and abundant travel, resulting in a much wider and more varied range of social contacts than ever experienced by pre-cybernetic societies. However, there is also the constant fear of annihilation by the atomic bomb, which looms as an invisible background behind the hectic life of the post-World War II generations. The impact of all these factors of environmental stress on the growing child and adolescent is evident. As formulated by Keniston (1975, p. 304):

> ... behind these measurable changes lie other trends less quantitative but even more important: a rate of social change so rapid that it threatens to make obsolete all institutions, values, methodologies and technologies within the lifetime of each generation; a technology that has created not only prosperity and longevity, but power to destroy the planet, whether through warfare or violation of nature's balance: a world of extraordinarily complex social organization, instantaneous communication and constant revolution. The 'new' young men and young women emerging today both reflect and react against these trends.

The ability to confront this reality of modern post-technological society at what is supposed to be 'an adult level of psychological maturity' seems to require more than successful 'role experimentation', 'crystallization of identity', 'primacy of genital drive organization', and so on, often assumed to be the main issues of adolescent development in current psychological theories. That is to say, 'post-technological adolescents' have first of all to adjust to the speed of contemporary historical events, producing drastic changes in value systems, economic structures, political constellations and cultural trends, within relatively short periods. They have to look forward to an overextended period of studies without the security that they will find a position in the distant future. If not preparing for an academic career they will have to fear competition of the constantly increasing availability of higher qualified personnel. They will face more dilemmas of how to solve the problems of sexual life given the greater amount of freedom, especially of the young woman.

Obviously, all these problems will have to be confronted at the later part of adolescence. This explains, why, as a natural result of the protraction and increasing complexity of the adolescent period, *late adolescence* or *post adolescence* has emerged as an additional section of the bridge between childhood and adulthood after the gap between the bridgeheads has widened and the load to be processed has increased.

Apart from these historical and psychosociological considerations outlined before, the treatment and investigation of post-adolescence as a separate stage seems to be justified for the following, predominantly pragmatic reasons:

1) Inspection of population statistics reveals a conspicuous rise on the rate of severe delinquency (robbery, rape, homicide) as well as attempted and fatal suicide in the age group of 15 upwards. There has been a general increase of these types of asocial and antisocial actions during the last two decades in many countries. (Chronique O.M.S., 1975; Davidson, 1976; Holinger, 1978). Although these phenomena refer only to a small, assumedly psychopathological fragment of the population, they nevertheless testify that this age period is a critical phase which needs to be taken into special consideration by educators and counsellors.

2) The already mentioned rapid pace of historical changes have direct and indirect effects on the structure and perspectives of vocational and academic careers, so that an increasing number of youngsters between ages 16 and 20 are in urgent need of vocational and educational counselling at a much higher level of sophistication than two or three decades ago.

3) In these age groups we witness a conspicuous drop-out from school and work, not only among the disadvantaged, but also in middle-class populations. This occurs often in spite of the fact that the teenager may be at the verge of completing High School or Junior College, that he has not failed in any academic subject and does not suffer from physical or psychological breakdown. This phenomenon will be discussed later in greater detail.

4) As already discussed in the introduction to this book, the development of *disadvantaged* youth at ages 15 to 20 urgently needs to be investigated. The general observations on this popula-

tion presented in current literature delineate certain important facts, such as:

a) precocious conformity with the externalized life style of the disadvantaged parents;
b) stagnation of mental development at the concrete stage of operations;
c) preference for a stereotypic imitation of adult roles instead of confrontation with new life tasks;
d) return to the disadvantaged community instead of existential expansion, etc. (Feuerstein, 1980; Frankenstein, 1968; Starr and Kahane, 1978). It seems, however, that in addition to these focal issues there is a host of unexplored questions related to the social-emotional and cognitive problems of disadvantaged youth in the post-technological era, overlooked or underestimated by current adolescent and post-adolescent research which has been focussing on middle-class or lower middle-class High School populations.

5) There is a tendency to raise the lower age threshold of the adult criminal law and penal code — which automatically places most post-adolescent delinquents in the category of juveniles — in need of custody, re-education and therapy. This creates a new category of 'post-adolescent delinquency', which hitherto had been treated as a group of adult delinquents and criminals. The importance of exploring ways and methods of rehabilitation for these populations needs no further explanation.

6) There is also growing concern for the rights and civil responsibilities of handicapped post-adolescents, which poses many problems rooted in the wide discrepancies between chronological age, and between mental, emotional and social levels of maturity in the various groups of abnormal, delayed, distorted and retarded development.

Having presented these theoretical and pragmatical considerations which seem to provide sufficient arguments justifying the treatment of post-adolescence as a separate stage, we shall now proceed to discuss the specific dynamics of this period, first in normal and then in culturally disadvantaged populations.

CHAPTER 2

Psychodynamics of Normal Post-Adolescence

Attempting to describe the pertinent aspects of post-adolescent psychodynamics in a systematic way, we shall try to deal with the following topics: Cognitive Growth, Ego Development, Close Interpersonal Relations, Adjustment to the Distant Social Environment (School, Work, Community), and Existential Expansion. As this description is based on empirical data, gathered predominantly from American and European middle-class populations, its universal validity is obviously limited. It does, however, cover a wide spectrum of High School, Vocational School and Junior College populations in contemporary, culturally developed and economically prosperous countries.

1. Cognitive Growth

Traditionally, an analysis of psychodynamics focusses on the non-intellective aspects of personality, often emphasizing the dependence of cognitive (perceptual and intellectual) functions on emotional, partly unconscious, processes. (Adler, 1964; Frankenstein, 1968; Freud, 1953; Jung, 1964; Horney, 1950; Sullivan, 1953). This approach seems to be appropriate when dealing with psychodynamics of *adolescence*, considered to be dominated by emotional turmoil and psychosocial conflict. On the other hand, to consider the dynamics of adolescents' *cognitive* processes as a starting point to explore their personality development appears to be justified for three main reasons:

1) By virtue of recent strides in behavior genetics (Gedda *et*

15

al., 1981; Kohen-Raz, 1981b; Matheny and Dolan, 1975; Scarr-Salapatek, 1976; Wilson, 1974b, 1981) important, genetically-rooted patterns of physical and psychological growth rhythms have been discovered, which can be clearly observed in objective measures of *cognitive* functions at adolescence, (Fischbein, 1981).

2) Several authors emphasize the interdependence of levels of intellectual functioning and overall personality development, namely morality (Kohlberg and Gilligan, 1971; Kohlberg and Kramer, 1969), self-image (Manaster, Saddler and Williamson, 1976), conformity (Salzstein, Diamond and Belenky, 1972), ego identity (Manaster, 1977, p. 115), ego development (Frankenstein, 1966), etc. Although evidence of such interdependence does not permit one to reach any conclusions as to cause-effect relationships, the rehabilitation of cognitive functions by adequate intervention methods has yielded positive effects on post-adolescent personality growth and psychosocial development (Feuerstein, 1980; Frankenstein, 1979).

3) Finally, in culturally disadvantaged post-adolescents (as will be discussed in detail later) it is their displayed *mental* inferiority which fatally determines their *social* status as pupils placed in the lowest tracks of the High School system, as well as their *self-image* which is shattered by their scholastic failure and its consequences (Perkal, 1980).

Essentially, the most important aspect of cognitive development at post-adolescence is the mastery of 'formal operations' (Ennis, 1978; Inhelder and Piaget 1959; Lunzer, 1965; Piaget, 1972), which is defined as follows:

a) The capacity to perform mental acts which refer to *statements* and *abstract concepts* not necessarily related to any concrete object or its representation.

b) To be able to examine relations between relations — i.e. 'second order' relations as defined by Ausubel (1966) — as to their compatibility. This essentially means the ability to decide whether a statement, which expresses the relation between one or more relations, is true or false.

c) The ability to conceive a group of second order relationships as a 'combinatorial system', or a 'set of subsets' exemplified by Piaget in the form of the 16 basic propositional logic formulas, created by the 15 possible combinations (plus an empty set) of true statements within a set of four elements, which themselves represent the four possible combinations of two statements and their negation (p and q, p and non-q, non p and q, non p and non-q) (Piaget, *op. cit.*).

d) The ability to combine two basic forms of reversibility: (i) Inversion (such as simple negation, affirmation and annulation, addition and subtraction, multiplication and division etc., or the fact that a double inversion results in the re-establishment of the status quo). (ii) Reciprocity, which means operations of relations, such as if A is to the left of B, then B is to the right of A (Piaget, 1972). While children, functioning at the level of concrete operational reasoning, understand these two types of reversibility only if they appear separately, the adolescent is able to combine them, thus understanding the interdependence between Identity, Negation, Reciprocity and Compensation. In other words, the adolescent, who has attained the level of formal operations, will know that an effect can be eliminated by its cancellation as well as by its compensation, viewing these two processes not as two separate phenomena but as alternatives.

4) Formal Reasoning is independent of content and context. Being the highest form of mental equilibrium, it transcends reality, and certainly the spatial and temporal limits of the human life-space and the human life-span. That is to say, by virtue of the application of formal (i.e. scientific) reasoning, people are able to predict astronomic events at a temporal and spatial distance of thousands of light' years, as well as to displace themselves to the moon.

In terms of psychological testing, this aspect of formal reasoning can be assessed by letting subjects solve syllogisms with empirically absurd premises, such as: 'If the air would be water, and all people breathe air, all people would breathe water.'

While formal reasoning, by definition, is independent of content, its efficient application within various contexts and academic subject matters, as well as in professional practice, seems to depend on experience and exposure to specific problem areas (Dulit, 1972; Karplus, 1981; Levine and Linn, 1977; Linn and Rice, 1979). In addition, there is a considerable difference between the chronological ages at which different persons, and even the same person, will attain the mastery of formal reasoning in different domains of mental activity (Beard, 1960; Dulit, 1972; Karplus, 1981; Peel, 1960). This has been noted by Piaget himself, who advances three hypotheses to explain these discrepancies (or 'décalages' in his own terminology). One hypothesis focusses on the different speed of mental maturation combined with diversities of environmental stress, which would account for slow (or entirely absent) advancement to the level of formal reasoning in low SES populations.

The second hypothesis attempts to explain, that certain behavior patterns and aptitudes (such as drawing, perception of space, field independency, motor skill, perceptual acuity and speed, verbal fluency, etc.) do not necessarily follow the same developmental patterns as *operative* mental structures, and that with advancing age, these functions develop more and more independently, possibly divergently.

Thus, individuals, talented and devoted to study physics, will implicitly activate higher operational thought to cope with the subject matter of their specialization, and perform better (and probably earlier) on tasks of formal reasoning. On the other hand, 'humanists' and 'artists' will develop functional areas such as perceptual differentiation, categorization, space and time orientation, and so on, not necessarily stimulating formal thought. Piaget tends to prefer a third hypothesis, which 'allows one to reconcile the concept of stages with the idea of progressively differentiating aptitudes'. Here he assumes that all normal subjects will attain the level of formal operations by post-adolescence (age 15 to 20).

However they reach this stage in different areas according to their aptitudes, professional specialization or different types of apprenticeships, the way in which these formal structures are used not being necessarily the same in all cases (Piaget, 1972).

The issues related to cognitive development which are most pertinent for the understanding of general post-adolescent psychodynamics are:

1) whether indeed (as assumed by Piaget) *all normal* post-adolescents will reach the stage of formal operations;

2) what is the impact of such mental progress on the overall

post-adolescent behavior;

3) which factors or circumstances prevent the attainment of this highest form of mental equilibrium at post-adolescence and

4) to what extent is such developmental failure irreversible.

TABLE 1

Percentage of subjects who functioned at the fully formal level

	Rings experiment	Liquids experiment
Average younger adolescent	0% (21)	10% (21)
Average older adolescent	35% (40)	17% (36)
Gifted older adolescent	57% (23)	62% (21)
Average adult	33% (12)	25% (12)

Numbers in brackets are N.

Adapted from Dulit (1972), p. 294.

As to the first question, the answer appears to be negative, as demonstrated by Dulit (1972). According to his data (Table 1), no more than about two-thirds of even 'gifted older adolescents' function at the fully formal level. Dulit concludes, that the development of formal reasoning, in contrast to the stage of concrete thought possessed by virtually every normal child, is but 'one of the main tracks' of intellectual growth and that only 'some modest proportion of the normal population would proceed down that royal road to full formal function'. (*op. cit.* p. 298). As Piaget's speculations of gradual attainment of formal reasoning, by 'décalages' in adolescents and young adults as a general and universal phenomenon, have never been supported by experimental research in representative samples, we must have regard for Dulit's results, unless contrary evidence is produced by cross-cultural and cross-social class investigations in adequately sampled populations. Some cross cultural and cross social status studies recently carried out by Karplus and his associates (Karplus, 1981), lend support to Dulit's findings and cast some doubt on Piaget's claim that formal reasoning is a universal achievement of normally intelligent adolescents and young adults. As reported by these investigators, even in top groups of gifted middle-class high school students in selective European school systems, only 75—90% master simple tasks of proportional (formal) reasoning, while in comparisons of lower-class populations from four countries, (US, Germany, UK and Italy), this percentage ranges from 0 to 41. (*op. cit.*).

An array of recent research provides answers to the second question. There is a clear linkage between the attainment of formal reasoning and 'post-conventional' levels of moral judgement i.e. 'the ability to define moral values and principles which have validity and application apart from the authority of the groups or persons holding these principles and apart from the individuals' own identification with these groups' (Kohlberg, 1969, 1976; Kohlberg and Gilligan, 1971; Tomlinson-Keasey and Keasey, 1974). However, as demonstrated by these investigations, formal thought is a necessary but not sufficient condition for higher, i.e. post-conventional, 'principled' levels of moral judgement. In addition, post-adolescents demonstrate typical 'regressions' to lower stages of moral judgement, in spite of maintaining the level of formal reasoning. These regressions appear to be 'retrogressions' or 'regressions in the service of the post-adolescent's ego', which attempts to cope with two problems:

1) To become free from guilt feeling related to moral standards imposed by the family of origin. In other words post-adolescents ostensibly proclaim to adhere to relativistic and egocentric standards of moral behavior in order to demonstrate that they are free from regrets which such conduct previously would have evoked in them as children.

2) The second problem is the wide gap between moral expectations and opinions, held in childhood and endorsed at mid-adolescence by formal logical reasoning, and between the actual immoral behavior of the social environment suddenly perceived by virtue of the post-adolescent's realistic observations (Kohlberg, 1969).

Other linkages, between cognitive and social development at post-adolescence are relationships between moral judgement and peer conformity, subjects with higher moral maturity being less conforming (Salzstein, Diamont and Belenky, 1972). The level of moral judgement has also been shown to be correlated with parental identification, in expected direction, i.e. closer identification to be found in subjects with higher morality (Weisbrot, 1970). Furthermore, Manaster *et al.* (1977) have demonstrated that subjects with higher mental levels are better able to differentiate the many facets of their self. Mid-abolescents as well as post-adolescents (ages 15, 16) who have mastered formal operations think about their ideal self in terms of imagined or real persons not belonging to their families of origins, while those still functioning at the level of concrete operations view their ideal self in terms of their parents, heroes, or glamorous adults. The same authors, possibly going to some extreme, assume that the 'identity crisis' and the 'moratorium' — two characteristic phenomena of middle-class adolescence according to Erikson's theory — are sequelae of the ability to reason on a formal level. That is to say, the teenager reformulates basic personal constructs about himself, hitherto conceived in concrete terms, in frames of reference of abstract and formal operational schemata related to his self-image *vis a vis* the universe. Such newly-gained insight leads to a cognitive disequilibrium which in turn creates the emotional and social tensions, characterizing mid- and post-adolescent conflicts (Elkind, 1968, 1969; Manaster *et al.*, 1977, p. 115 ff).

As to the third question, which factors should be considered to be responsible for inadequate (i.e. sub-formal) mental performance at post-adolescence, there are no clear cut answers. However, it is certainly an oversimplification to explain the failure to attain the level of formal reasoning in non-pathological populations as a result of 'cumulative effects' of early socio-cultural deprivation (Deutsch, 1967).

Instead, three aspects of the problem seem to warrant attention:

1) There is a diversity of post-adolescent types who for various reasons are underachievers or low performers on tests of formal reasoning (Frankenstein, 1970b).

2) Biological, cognitive, emotional and social determinants of lowered mental functioning at pre-adolescence and mid-adolescence are interdependent and it is highly questionable, whether social factors predominate (Kohen-Raz, 1971, 1977a).

3) The nature of cognitive immaturity, impeded intellectual functioning and patterns of mental retardation at post-adolescence are different from those observed at childhood and cannot be understood on the basis of traditional intelligence testing (Feuerstein, 1979).

The fourth question, as to the reversibility of cognitive disturbances and deficiencies at post-adolescence, positive, albeit not yet fully evaluated, results have been obtained by several projects which intend to rehabilitate the intellectual potential and performance in disadvantaged teenagers (see Part III).

Overviewing the general trends of mental development of post-adolescence, it must be admitted that even within the range of 'normal' populations there is wide variety of mental performance which is not reflected by the intelligence quotient. The assumption that the human mental growth curve flattens and asymptotically reaches its ceiling at post-adolescence cannot be supported in light of the conspicuous advances in moral judgement occurring after the age of 16 (Kohlberg, 1969), the relative late application of formal reasoning in non-familiar content areas (Beard, 1960; Dulit, 1972; Peel, 1960; Piaget, 1972) and the disadvantaged adolescent's responsiveness to enrichment programs stimulating higher mental activities, (Feuerstein, 1980; Frankenstein, 1979; Kohen-Raz, 1980).

Finally, it is evident that cognitive processes are intimately involved in non-intellective functions of post-adolescent psychodynamics, as will be further discussed in the subsequent sections.

2.   Ego Development

The development of ego autonomy and the crystallization of the various aspects of the self is an area of post-adolescent psychodynamics which has been considerably investigated. In this context, Erikson's theory on the attainment of 'identity' which is widely known and acknowledged, has recently been further supported by empirical investigations (Constantinople, 1969; Marcia, 1966).

Erikson links the process of 'identity achievement' with the possibility of being granted a 'moratorium', in that youth is permitted to experiment with patterns of identity roles, relationships and ego involvements without the need of long-term obligations (Erikson, 1963, 1968).

According to Erikson (1972) the attainment of identity is the precondition for the next stage, Intimacy *vs* Isolation, consisting in the establishment of relations of mutual trust, free from barriers, inhibitions, secrets and second thoughts.

In a similar vein, Sullivan (1953) considers the ability to create intimate relations as an important milestone of post-adolescent personality growth. By attaining such a level of emotional maturity, the post-adolescent is able to overcome the feelings of loneliness and isolation which threaten the mid-adolescent, generate anxiety and block creativity and reality control. Although Erikson, as already mentioned, views the crystallization of identity as a precondition to 'intimacy', it may be argued that the experience of intimacy is a precondition of true identity. Actually, the study by Constantinople (1969) demonstrates that in four cohorts of college students, scores on intimacy were systematically higher than scores on identity, as measured by a Q-sort technique devised by Wessman and Ricks (1966).

Viewed in the frame of reference of a different theoretical model, post-adolescent ego development can be described as the growing ability to differentiate and to experience three basic existential modes, defined by Binswanger (1942) as the Plural, the Dual and the Singular. Essentially, the Plural mode is an instrumental interaction between the ego and non-ego, treating human beings directly or indirectly 'as means to an end', without considering their value as persons, their individuality and their autonomy. Actually, this mode encompasses the entire network of strictly economical, administrative, political and professional relationships in human society, as well as all those closer relations characterized by overt or covert exploitation of individuals within small groups, triads and even dyads. Such exploitation may be mutual or else taking advantage of the weakness or inferiority of one or more members of the group. The 'externalized style of life' described by Frankenstein (1968) is essentially a way of interpersonal communication and ego-alter interaction dominated by the Plural mode of existence.

In striking contrast, the Dual mode is based on the ego's readiness and ability to interact with another person while being aware of all aspects and dimensions of his personality, and being sensitive to the variety of his idiosyncratic needs. Taking such a perspective the ego is ready to satisfy the demands of the partner irrespective of his own momentary needs and interests, creating a true 'give and take' relationship. Also, and perhaps most importantly, the ego, by sensing the totality of the alter's personality, understands the fluctuations and moods of his behavior and tolerates them, even if they go to some extremes. Obviously, if such an interaction is mutual, we witness a satisfactory and stable partnership, such as required in marriage. It can be easily seen that Binswanger's 'modus' is close to the concept of 'intimacy' in Erikson and Sullivan's theories. It is also similar to Buber's conceptualization of the 'dialogue' between 'I' and 'Thou' (Buber, 1958).

Finally, the Singular modus is the confrontation of the ego with the self, with inner problems and the own (personal and impersonal) unconscious. Frankenstein speaks of 'the inner non-ego'. (Frankenstein, 1966, p. 35).

It seems that defining ego development at post-adolescence as experimentation and differential experiences with the Dual, Singular and Plural modi of existence, covers what Erikson has described 'search for identity' and Sullivan the 'collision of lust, security and intimacy need'. On the background of these general trends, a variety of phenomena characterizing post-adolescent behavior can now be better understood.

The post-adolescent, in contrast to the mid-adolescent, realizes, that a friend or heterosexual partner may be 'difficult' and 'unbearable' for a time, but it will be still worthwhile to keep up the relationship and to await a positive change. Another sign of post-adolescent ego maturity is the awareness that moral obligations cannot be understood only in terms of the Plural mode, but must be validated in the context of the Dual mode as well. This may explain why formal reasoning is an insufficient determinant of the last (post-conventional) levels of moral judgment, as already discussed before (see p. 20) and that the other necessary determinant might be the experience of 'intimacy' and Dual modus of interpersonal interaction.

A well-known phenomenon of post-adolescence is the urge to travel. The habit of post-adolescents to hitch-hike to distant places is by no means due to the availability of modern transportation. Previous generations have witnessed the 'wanderjahre' (the lust for adventures), precocious joining of overseas armies, etc. This urge has been recently interpreted as an unconscious search for partnership, intimacy, i.e. the 'Dual modus' by projecting the need to overcome inner distances onto the external space, i.e. to long for a partner 'somewhere far away'.

On the other hand, the post-adolescent seeks loneliness not in the sense of Erikson's 'isolation' but as an experimentation with the Singular mode. This ability to 'critical self-evaluation' and 'realistic confrontation with one's own needs and shortcomings' — Erikson's identity dimensions of 'self-certainty', or 'anticipation of achievement' (Maier, 1969) — is very different from the early and mid-adolescents' monologue with their diaries, their fantasies, daydreams and unreal evaluations of needs, urges and weaknesses.

Post-adolescents gain inner and outer 'distance' to evaluate critically their own and others actions. They differentiate between means and ends, understand the meaning of freedom, dependence and slavery. They grasp the difference between truth, probability and assumptions and realize hierarchies of social priorities and individual needs. It seems that in these mental acts the intellectual capacity to master formal operations merges with the emotional maturity based on the differentiation between existential modes and the experience of intimate partnership.

In contrast to the mid-adolescent who judges circumstances, objects and persons in extremes — black or white, good or bad, wonderful or disgusting, etc. — the post-adolescent ego is able not only to differentiate and to evaluate *intermediate* ranges of values, but also to tolerate ambiguity, overlapping and ambivalent situations and to discover a 'third' aspect of a conflict between two opposite parties, as well as possible compromises.

Parallel to growing realistic insight, inner distance and objectivity, the post-adolescent is supposed to overcome his 'life in principles', a typical stage of transition at mid-adolescence. During this stage, the mid-adolescent uses (or misuses) his ability of formal reasoning in order to set up principles, which serve to substitute realistic relationships by abstract speculations, discussions, declarations and utopian fantasies (Frankenstein, 1966, p. 167). According to Frankenstein's theory the return to reality at post-adolescence is not accomplished by means of a continuous search for identity, as postulated by Erikson, but by virtue of passing a critical phase of a 'deadlock' and 'existential despair', i.e. the life in principles becomes unbearable, the way back to the world of childhood is irreversibly blocked and the path towards adulthood looks as though it is leading to an impass too dangerous to be approached. Although in most cases the deadlock is successfully overcome at post-adolescence, there may be pathological outcomes in the form of suicide and/or psychotic breakdown, phenomena whose increased incidence at post-adolescence is well documented (Frankenstein, 1966, p. 169; Holinger, 1978). Whatever the theoretical model used to interpret this development, we see again that cognitive processes (in this case the establishment of principles) influence personal-social adjustment and eventually interfere with it.

Before concluding this description of ego development at post-adolescence, an interesting observation made by Blos (1962) should be mentioned which unfortunately has not been confirmed by systematic research. Blos draws attention to a phenomenon, well known to the educator, that middle-class post-adolescents interrupt abruptly their High School studies in order to engage in activities which are remote from academic objectives. This 'crisis' may occur typically close to the termination of a scholastic year, or even close to graduation, and thus has highly impracticable consequences. The strange conduct cannot be accounted for by pathological etiology, nor be interpreted as a neurotic or psychotic breakdown. Still more puzzling, most of these post-adolescents return, after one or two years, to their academic or vocational career, provided that administrative restraints and meanwhile disrupted social and public relations have not thrown them off their path.

Blos, examining and analyzing these 'intermezzi' has reached the conclusion that, during these episodes, the post-adolescent 'works through' traumatic childhood experiences, by enacting them and reviving them, as if he could not accept adulthood without freeing himself from a traumatic past by such catharsis. Superficially, this regressive acting out is reminiscent of what Frankenstein calls 'passing the deadlock' and Erikson would call a special form of 'role experimentation'. Whatever the issue, there seems to be a critical period of ego-crisis at a transitional point between mid- and post-adolescence, deserving further systematic investigation.

The development of the post-adolescent's self-concept shows a trend similar to that found in ego-development. Generally, the attitude towards the self is more realistic, which is manifest in a greater discrepancy between real and ideal self scores in post-adolescents compared with pre- and mid-adolescents. This discrepancy is greater in pupils with higher IQ's who aspire to complete a more ambitious career, and thus realistically perceive a gap between their present status and their prospective one. The students with lower IQ feel themselves closer to their adult roles, their aspirations are lower and therefore their 'real and self scores' are somewhat more positive and closer to their ideals (Katz and Zigler, 1967; Manaster, Saddler and Williamson, 1976).

Cognitive development (as measured by IQ and tests of formal operations) is decisively related to the development of the 'ideal self', the latter being significantly and positively related to mental level. On the other hand, the relationship between socio-economic status and ideal self, after the additional control of sex and age, practically disappear (Manaster, Saddler and Williamson, *op. cit.*).

3. Close, Interpersonal Relations

Close, interpersonal relations refer essentially to relationships with parents, peers, the other sex and the 'close educator'.

These close relationships must be viewed as a dynamic entity, although traditionally they are analyzed in isolation. At each developmental phase, (including post-adolescence) these relationships are interdependent. There is a dynamic equilibrium between them, in the sense that the optimal interaction in one relationship is dependent on an optimal degree of involvement in other relationships and vice versa. Disruption of one type of relation will lead to the impairment, or eventually to pathological overcompensation in other interpersonal interactions.

Parents and Peers

The post-adolescent realistically re-appreciates his parents as adult partners after the mid-adolescent 'dead-lock', which leads to a rift with the parental figures as they had been experienced during childhood. This establishment of mature parent-post-adolescent relationships is intimately linked with the involvement of the peer group in the socialization process. A critical phase of this involvement occurs already at pre-adolescence.

The equal level of libidinal organization in the relationship between the pre-adolescent and his family and in that between the pre-adolescent and his peers, facilitates the transfer of the strong libidinal attachments to parents and siblings onto group leaders and peers ... Such a constellation of elements makes possible the polar interaction between the two social environments and their respective social climates ... The emotional relation to the peer group and its leader guarantees the ego's autonomy (in the sense of Hartman's theory) when faced with the danger of becoming overinvolved in conflicts with parental figures. On the other hand, the still vivid emotional ties with the parents guarantee the ego's autonomy when faced with the danger of becoming enslaved to the peer group and its leaders. Loss of ego-autonomy by overdependence on the peer group results in delinquency, overdependence on parents precluding involvement in peer group relations leads to school phobia (Kohen-Raz, 1971).

Similar dialectic patterns appear during mid-adolescence: the function of the unisexual pre-adolescent peer group is taken over by heterosexual cliques which associate into crowds. With the approach of post-adolescence, crowds and cliques gradually dissipate and disintegrate to give way to loosely associated groups of heterosexual couples (Dunphy, 1963). However, each of these stages is accompanied by a parallel development in the parent-adolescent relationship, which serves as an anchorage to preserve the ego's autonomy in view of its relative weakness and not yet accomplished integration, integrity and identity.

It must be stressed, that during no phase of normal development — possibly except the 'dead-lock' — relations to parents are severed, parental values ignored and their opinion and advice not respected. In fact, the mid- and post-adolescent pendulates subtly between conformity with parental and peer group values, taking the freedom to chose in which situation the values of which of the two reference groups should guide his behavior.

... the responses reflect the adolescent's perception of peers and parents as competent guides in different areas of judgement. The general social orientation of the adolescent is of a dual character ...

Adolescents, for example, perceive themselves to be more like their parents in respect to tastes in clothes, however, in regard to feelings about school, peer favored alternatives are found to be psychologically closer and more acceptable (Brittain, 1967, 1969).

As recently reported by Rutter (1976), one of the most salient concomitants, and possibly a determinant of anti-social and psychopathological behavior at adolescence, is 'alienation' from parents. It appears that 'persisting' or 'alienated' parent-adolescent relationships determinate to a large extent adolescent normal or pathological behavior respectively. It thus appears that it is vital for the adolescent to maintain a flexible, generally positive relationship with his family of origin. On the other hand, 'alienation', i.e. the interruption or loss of emotional involvement, or the prevalence of mutually hostile attitudes between parents and adolescents, leads to a grave disturbance in adolescent socialization, mainly because the concomitant constructive function of peers, cliques and heterosexual partners as positive 'poles' to guarantee the 'ego's autonomy', is impaired and often destroyed, and may turn into a negative, destructive factor. We then are faced with various patterns of 'turmoil', i.e. delinquency and psychopathological behavior, the peer group or gang functioning now as a catalyst to mental sickness and waywardness.

It is thus erroneous to assume that with increasing age the adolescent separates more and more from his parents and that post-adolescent ego autonomy is a result of 'emancipation' from parental ties. Actually, the normal post-adolescent having gained a high degree of ego autonomy will be closer to his parents (in the sense of a realistic, autonomous relationship) than he has been as a pre- or mid-adolescent, when he tried to fight for 'freedom' from parental control.

It must be added, that the notion that adolescents strive to 'get away' from home and family is to some extent a projection on the part of the parents, who have difficulties in confronting adolescents for several reasons. They feel that methods of authoritarian discipline once useful during childhood, have lost their effectiveness. On the other hand, they are not well-enough prepared to control the adolescents by representing a 'Referent, Expert or Legitimate Resource' (Smith, 1970) chiefly because the adolescent intrinsically evokes repressed, unconscious remnants of the parent's own adolescent conflicts. So it is them who (without being aware of it) try to 'escape' from the adolescent and involuntarily enlarge the 'generation gap'.

The clear educational consequence of this analysis of parent-adolescent dynamics is the fact that parents still play a vital role in the post-adolescent's socialization process, even if the latter looks as being 'grown up' and 'on his own'.

The Other Sex

The development of heterosexual relationships shows a dialectic pattern similar to that characterizing the parent-peer dialectics described before. Here the unisexual clique, triad or diad represents the bridgehead from which the mid-adolescent launches his advances and adventures to conquer the other sex. Again over-dependency or unisexual relationships appears to lead to homo-sexual fixations, while the lack of support on the part of the unisexual clique may lead either to complete withdrawal from contact with the other sex, or to shallow, promiscuous hetero-sexual relations. Some authors explain female adolescent delinquency as the result of insufficient identification with the female erotic role, which normally develops at pre-adolescence by virtue of a very delicate interaction between involvement in unisexual cliques and heterosexual coquettery (Blos, 1962; Kaufmann, Makkay and Zilbach, 1959; Kohen-Raz, 1971).

The wayward and delinquent adolescent, fixated to his uni-sexual peer group, is unable to establish emotionally satisfying and stable heterosexual relations. Typically he takes resort to collective sexual intercourse or rape, which is the deviant counter-part to the normal 'dialectic' process described above.

At post-adolescence the period of experimentation and dependency on the unisexual clique is supposed to terminate. Instead heterosexual couples, eventually associating in small groups, are formed. Although there is still some experimentation and change of partners, the major trend is to 'go steady'. Obviously this maturation of heterosexual relations is based on the crystallization of ego autonomy and identity, the ability to experience the 'dual existential modus'.

A central issue in post-adolescent sexual development is the occurrence of sexual intercourse. This subject which has always been in the centre of interest of investigators of post-adolescence is being investigated from several angles, namely, the statistical, the psychological, the criminological and the educational.

Various statistical surveys indicate that at post-adolescence sexual intercourse between teenagers decisively increases and that physical sexual contact (including intercourse) is more frequent nowadays than one or two decades ago, the increase being sharper for girls (Kantner and Zelnik, 1972; Sorenson, 1973; Vener, Steward and Hager, 1974). Still, the majority of post-adolescents (between 60 to 65 per cent) seem to abstain from full sexual relations. If we deduct from the percentage of sexually fully active young people those who 'go steady' with a partner whom they intend to marry and eventually succeed in marrying, as well as those who are marginally wayward and sexually delinquent, only a relatively small number of 'promiscuous couples' remains. Unfortunately it is difficult to obtain reliable data on the quality of sexual relationships, although the above-mentioned trend is evident, especially for females (Kantner and Zelnik, op. cit.).

Thus it may be stated that, by and large, post-adolescents in post-technological society, live up to the moral standards of Western culture, discouraging promiscuity and emphasizing integration of sex and love. As may be expected, this holds true to larger extent for girls. On the other hand, there is evidence that the 'double standard' — restricting the sexual freedom of women while granting it to men — is vanishing and the differences in incidence and degree of sexual engagement between the sexes tend to shrink albeit they still persist (Vener et al., op. cit.). In any case, the image of the contemporary post-adolescent as a sexual adventurer enjoying unrestricted freedom from conventional moral restrictions is an artifact, produced to a large extent by modern mass media (Bandura, 1964; Castarède, 1978).

From the *psychological* point of view, the post-adolescent is apparently at a stage of emotional maturity, which enables him to establish stable, heterosexual relationships leading to marriage and procreation. In this respect we witness a 'downwards shift' in the age of marriage and age of first birth (Musgrove, 1964). It may be asked whether marriage, as a definitive sign of attaining adult status, does not implicitly exclude a person from the category of post-adolescents. If not, a certain percentage of post-adolescents are married, although they have still to struggle with other life tasks before reaching full adulthood, that is economic independence, professional competency, and so on.

Another psychological aspect of the teenage sex problem is the differential *meaning* of pre-marital intercourse for the two sexes. While for the boy it essentially signifies an assertion of his manhood and a 'test' of sexual potency, the normal girl is far from needing to prove her femininity by losing her virginity. On the contrary, also in contemporary teenage society, virginity in the female is still highly appreciated. Furthermore, the post-adolescent girl, having reached a fair level of ego identity, wishes to integrate sex, love and motherhood, and will thus be reluctant to accept intercourse with a man whom she cannot perceive as a potential marriage partner. Finally the fear of pregnancy out of wedlock deters adolescent girls from intimate sex, in spite of the availability of the pill and other contraceptive measures. In this respect two remarks must be made:

1) The majority of unmarried adolescent girls having intercourse do not use contraceptive devices (Cogner, 1975).

2) The psychological, ethical, medical and educational aspects of administering the pill to adolescents is still a matter to be investigated.

It must be added that full sexual life represents for the girl a drastic transition from virginity to womanhood (Deutsch, 1945), which challenges her still fragile identity and ability to establish intimate relationships. If its context is positive, such as an avenue to a permanent relationship or marriage, it still means, at its best, termination of the 'moratorium', which might be precocious. Presumably, early and precocious sexual life of the girl, even within wedlock — as is still the case in primitive societies and in lower SES strata — deprives her of her post-adolescence and curtails her mental and emotional growth. However, at worst, precocious intercourse for the girl might fixate her at a stage of 'identity confusion' or 'foreclosure', and handicap her overall personality development.

As to the *criminological* aspect, the problem of sexual inter-course (as well as pregnancy out of wedlock) has different dimen-sions in 'delinquent' populations† the majority of which are dis-advantaged. In that case, the typically promiscuous sexual activity of the girl is a *symptom* expressing the wish of self-assertation, fears of loneliness and separation, as well as an infantile need for body contact, physical closeness and craving for love. In Erikson's terms, the wayward and delinquent post-adolescent girl is com-pensating her 'role diffusion and inability to attain ego identity' by 'as if' feminine acting out. In a similar vein, eventual impregna-tion is in most cases *not* accidental or due to lack of precaution, but unconsciously or semi-consciously an intended act on the part of the girl, who wishes to attain the status of *motherhood*, at least, having been deprived of all other prospects of becoming a respect-able adult. Another, unconscious motivation to become pregnant, may be the wish to replace a recently lost love object, such as a parent, a sister, or a boyfriend who betrayed her. Finally, the girl may attempt to act out her un-resolved oedipal conflicts by competing with her mother in 'child bearing'.

From the *educational point of view* the problem of adolescent sexual intercourse poses serious questions. Should sexual inter-course be officially banned and prohibited to the extent of expell-ing from school transgressors who are still at the age of legal minority, as indeed it is the practice in conservative and religious educational institutions in many countries? At the other extreme, we witness the opening of special classes for pregnant mid- and post-adolescent girls, which symbolizes official tolerance of adolescent pre-marital sex life. Obviously, educators may take the position of non-involvement, shutting their eyes and mind from everything which happens behind the scene, intervening only in the case of emergency. Or they may, at the other extreme again, become experts in sex education, providing information and giving advice about everything, including the use of contraceptive devices.

---

†Although this topic does not belong to this part of the book, which deals with psychodynamics of *normal* post-adolescence, we prefer to present it in this context for the sake of completing the overall picture of post-adolescent sexual problems.

Without being able to propose alternatives to these approaches, which admittedly are far from being satisfactory, we may still find that there is a considerable consensus on the following educational aspects of post-adolescent sex education:

1) An educational atmosphere of 'permissiveness' or 'non intervention' is intrinsically 'seducing' and exposes the girl, wishing to preserve her virginity to the threat of being labelled 'old fashioned', 'neurotic', 'inhibited' etc.

2) Most post-adolescents, when left on their own, prefer to adhere to the moral values of the Western culture, not approving sexual intercourse which is divorced from a steady relationship involving respect and love for the partner.

3) Modern mass media distorts and exaggerates the nature, value and meaning of sex, while the high school curriculum does not provide any means to counteract this detrimental influence.

4) Most educators are ill-prepared, misinformed and confused in the field of moral and sexual education.

5) Parents are under the pressure of mass media, and impact of semi-professional literature, as well as flooded by the plethora of research published in the domain of sex, *without* being given guidelines on how to implement this massive amount of information in concrete educational situations.

6) A sharp demarcation line should be drawn between the sex problems of the normal and abnormal post-adolescent, in both psychological and educational theory and practice, in order to avoid misleading interpretations and extrapolations.

'Close Educator'

The 'close educator' is a type of social agent who is not known under this label, but actually exists under various 'disguises'. All those involved in rehabilitation projects of disadvantaged post-adolescents have recognized this person's vital role, as will be explained later. The 'close educator' is definitly not a member of the family of origin, neither does he belong to the 'enlarged family' (although this might have been the case in pre-technological societies). On the other hand, the person is not necessarily a professional educator, but definitly possesses competency in an area of specialization, as well as 'life experience' in a practical domain. His (or her) most important qualification is the ability to *interpret* (eventually to exemplify) the *personal meaning* of social and physical events impinging on the adolescent. Ausubel (1968, p. 455) speaks of 'personal commitment'.

It has been repeatedly mentioned in this chapter that the adolescent is capable of higher levels of reasoning, but has great difficulty in applying this potent tool of the human mind to relevant 'life tasks and issues'. It is exactly this gap which the 'close educator' is capable of bridging. In this respect we witness the utter failure of the high school teacher who, at best, is a scientifically competent lecturer, but is not — except in rare cases — a 'close educator', i.e. is seldom seriously involved in any process of adolescent *education*, socialization and value trans-mission (Ausubel, 1968, p. 450). In other words, at high school, and junior college, post-adolescents are bombarded with a quantity of information on sciences and arts, eventually fed with 'a bulk' of organized knowledge, which however, they are unable to digest, because they are not given any interpretation making the material meaningful in the context of their personality growth towards identity, intimacy and integrity. Thus they will mechani-cally memorize, and eventually try to 'feed' the subject matter into their individual 'system of principles'. They may prepare for their exams but remain unprepared for their 'life tasks'. On the other hand, the 'clinical' or 'educational' psychologist or counsel-lor, who is called upon to deal with 'emergencies' causing academic breakdown has been trained to focus on emotional, intra-psychic and intra-familial conflicts and is far from being able or competent to take over the role of the 'close educator'. On the contrary, the psychologist, counsellor or psychiatrist is viewed by the adolescent as esoteric and much too uninvolved 'in real life' to represent a 'meaningful' adult.

'Close educators' have been successfully employed in various projects of post-adolescent rehabilitation. One is the *social worker* in street corner gang projects, who 'infiltrates' the groups, makes himself available to the gang members and by virtue of turning into a 'close educator' acts as a potent lever to break the vicious circle of waywardness, despair and delinquent acting out (Leissner,

1969).

Other experimental evidence is the involvement of educators who act as agents to 'mediate learning experience' in Feuerstein's project of 'Instrumental Enrichment' (Feuerstein, 1980). These educators are intensively trained to become sensitive to the cognitive dilemmas, misinterpretations and anxieties of the disadvantaged adolescent, to select and to interpret stimuli, constellations of objects and social situations so as to make them maximally meaningful to the culturally retarded youngster. Frankenstein used teachers and social workers for a similar purpose (Frankenstein, 1979). Finally, Kohen-Raz (1972) has demonstrated the impact of foremen in agriculture, arts and crafts on the rehabilitation of severely disturbed immigrant post-adolescents in a Kibbutz. These adults (members of the Kibbutz), not possessing any professional training in normal and special education, took over the role of 'close educators', and by virtue of their status in the Kibbutz and their sensitivity to emotional and educational needs of the adolescents, had an immense impact on the rehabilitation process of these youngsters, as strong, if not stronger than the influence of professional educators, psychologists and social workers involved in the project.

4. The Distant Social Environment

Essentially, the 'distant social environment' of the post-adolescent is work and school. As these topics have been exhaustively treated in current adolescent literature (Ausubel, 1968; Barker, 1960; Bidwell and Kasarda, 1975; Buxton, 1973; Havighurst, 1964; Levin, 1965; Manaster, 1977; Silberman, 1970), we shall limit ourselves to summarizing certain shortcomings of the present High School system, which seem most relevant from the point of view of post-adolescent psychodynamics:

1) The accent of the curriculum on intellectual training and transmission of knowledge, without *interpretation* of the subject matter, in a way which is personally meaningful to the adolescent (see above).

2) Most educators are 'distant' and not 'close' educators.

3) The educational system is strictly hierarchic and produces status differences even within schools of the same type (see Havighurst, 1964). Thus a hierarchy of *pupil status* is implicitely created, each school having its 'reputation' on a sliding scale of high via medium to low prestige. This leads to emotional tensions, in normal as well as disadvantaged students with destructive effects on the self-image and class atmosphere (Perkal, 1980).

4) Educational policy of 'integration' is a poor remedy for this general current of the High School system (Chen, Levi and Adler, 1978).

5) The system is fixed to traditional methods and curricula although a plethora of innovations is introduced by experimental projects. However, it is a far cry from the demonstration of ad hoc experimental effects to the implantation of an innovative method into the 'life space' of the teacher-pupil interaction, implemented by the teacher out of spontaneous identification and commitment, and accepted by the pupil out of genuine interest and intrinsic motivation to respond to the new technique.

6) The 'informal', 'extra-curricular' activities, experiences of peer relationship and living in a social climate remote from the family of origin, appears to have a no less important impact on the socialization process of the adolescent than the achievement-oriented official teaching program (Barker, 1960; Florida Study, 1964; Manaster, 1977).

5. Existential Expansion

In addition to the various 'Life Tasks' which the post-adolescent is supposed to confront (family, peers, school, work, etc.) it appears that there is an 'Existential Task' to be fulfilled, which can be defined as 'Existential Expansion'. This conceptualization of human existential growth at post-adolescence is based on two principles formulated by Fromm and Parsons respectively. Fromm speaks of the necessity to cut off the infantile ties to parents in order to gain true human freedom and to be able to lead a full human existence, a process which must be accomplished at adolescence (Fromm, 1950). Parsons (1955), on the other hand, attempts to explain the existential meaning of sexual *vs* vegetative reproduction as the true source of the incest taboo found in all human societies. In contrast to vegetative reproduction, consisting in an indefinite re-partitioning of the same 'hereditary substance', sexual reproduction basically means fusion of two 'hereditary substances' whose 'life experience' is essentially not identical. In other words, the copulation of two different cells as a precondition to the procreation of a new organism ensures 'existential enrichment' by exchange and integration of two different sources of life experience. In human procreation, according to Parsons, this principle of existential expansion is manifest not only in sexual reproduction, but in addition in an institutionalized prohibition to copulate with the 'same' or 'proximal' genotype. That is, by virtue of the incest taboo, humans are forced to expand their biological and mental heritage in that they search a heterosexual partner 'at a biological distance', whose life experience is necessarily different from their own. In Parsons' own words:

The incest taboo ensures that each child undergoing anew his socialization process receives his cultural heritage from more than one source. In such a situation there are many more possibilities of cultural variations, than under conditions which would not force families to mix because of the incest taboo (Parsons and Bales, 1955).

This interpretation of the incest taboo is fundamentally different from Freud's explanation of its roots in the struggle between the sons of the primordial father to take over his wives after having committed collective patricide (Freud, 1948).

From the point of view of post-adolescent psychodynamics, the search for a heterosexual partner at distance from the family of origin is thus only one component of the general striving for 'existential expansion', inherent to organismic life in general. The model of existential expansion offers complementary explanations and interpretations to an array of phenomena of post-adolescent behavior: The 'dead-lock', in Frankenstein's theory; middle-class post-World War II delinquency, stemming from the impossibility of changing and expanding the technological preprogrammed existence (Eisenstandt, 1958; Frankenstein, 1958); hippy and drug culture; the 'post-adolescent crisis' described by Blos (1962); the drive to travel (see above, p. 25); and last but not least, Kibbutz adolescents tend to seek their marriage partners outside their Kibbutz of origin, and certainly outside the peer group in which they have grown up (Talmon-Garber, 1964). Recently they also like to spend a part of their post-adolescent period outside the Kibbutz and prefer a career in the army or the foundation of a new Kibbutz to staying 'at home'.

CHAPTER 3

Psychodynamics of the Disadvantaged Post-Adolescent

Having outlined the various general aspects of post-adolescence we shall now proceed to described the specific problems of post-adolescence in the culturally disadvantaged.†

As already mentioned, systematic research in this area is relatively scarce, possibly for the following reasons:

1) The bulk of investigations on post-adolescents has been carried out on high school and college students, i.e. populations enrolled in formal education between the ages 16 to 22. As disadvantaged youth does not tend to stay in academic high schools and a considerable proportion of them drops out from vocational and apprentice schools (Kitsis, 1974, Starr and Kahane, 1978), they cannot be as conveniently investigated as the academically stable middle-class post-adolescents, who can be tested and inter-

---

†In order to avoid confusion it is important to repeat here the operational definition of 'culturally disadvantaged' pupils, currently used in Israel, which is as follows:

1) Parental education does not exceed eight years of elementary school and may be less (or even nil), especially in respect to the mother.

2) Parental occupation not higher than unskilled or semi-skilled worker. Mother is housewife, and if employed in outdoor work, the job is of low status, such as clean-up woman, domestic aid, etc.

3) Number of siblings more than three. Living conditions are crowded, three or more persons in one room, sometimes persons are sharing one bed.

4) The residential quarter is known as a 'slum' (euphemistically an 'inner city' or 'urban' area). Its inhabitants belong to a certain socio-economically and ethnically well-defined group, generally labelled in a pejorative way, which in the past (and often in the present) has been (or still is) discriminated against, because they are minorities and/or immigrants and/or of a different race, color, etc.

viewed in school settings.

2) Neo-psychoanalytical and psychodynamic theory (Sullivan, 1953; Erikson, 1968; Frankenstein, 1968) supposed that lower-class populations (and implicitly the disadvantaged) do not experience 'the moratorium' and are assumedly not confronted with crisis, conflict and 'dead locks'. Thus, there is no transitional phase of 'identity diffusion', tentative relationships and experimentation with fluctuating roles. Eventually a 'foreclosure' (Marcia, 1966) occurs, i.e. an acceptance of behavioral stereotypes which have been shaped already in childhood by the externalized environment and now are reinforced and fixated at post-adolescence. Consequently, according to neo-psychodynamic theory there is no specific 'post-adolescent' period in the strict sense.

3) Although there has been considerable concern for the disadvantaged delinquent and drug addict (Boyd, 1971; Eliram, 1979; Frankenstein, 1970b) these deviant populations do not represent disadvantaged youth at large and research in this area cannot be considered to be generally relevant.

A priori, it seems justified to reject the neo-analytical approach unless it can be substantiated by systematic research, which is not presently the case. We shall thus attempt to describe disadvantaged post-adolescence without preconceived theoretical formulations, using as an empirical basis recent studies carried out in Israel, which obviously may limit the general validity of our presentation.

In our description we shall proceed to analyze the same aspects, which had been subject to our discussion in the preceding chapter.

1. Cognitive Growth

Starting again with problems of *cognitive development*, data based on high school selection and screening procedures as well as on academic progress, success and graduation indicate that the 'disadvantaged' have great difficulty in mastering the manipulation of abstract concepts and formal reasoning. (Frankenstein, 1970a; Kohen-Raz, 1973). Such limitation of higher cognitive development obviously obstructs their admission to academic high school and even restricts their eligibility for higher vocational schools which have options for advanced levels of technical education (Halper, 1978, p. 327).

Still, it would be erroneous to treat disadvantaged post-adolescents as a homogenous group of 'mild mental retardation' and to attribute the cause to environmental neglect. Instead, it seems that we are dealing with a quite heterogenous population, in which at least five sub-groups may be differentiated:

1) A certain proportion of disadvantaged post-adolescents functions within 'normal level' of intelligence (Kitsis, 1974; Kohen-Raz, 1979). This 'normal potential' may be revealed by 'testing the limits' in the context of traditional intelligence testing. It may eventually require more sophisticated methods, such as those designed by Rey (1947, 1968, 1969) and later extensively applied by Feuerstein (1979). Implicitly, these adolescents are able to cope with problems requiring abstraction and formal reasoning, sometimes without, and sometimes after, the application of specific intervention methods. (Feuerstein, 1980; Frankenstein, 1979; Kohen-Raz, 1973, 1980; Smilansky, 1979).

2) On the other hand, the number of disadvantaged post-adolescents who function at the level of borderline or mild mental retardation is not negligible. Their potential for attaining normal intelligence is rather doubtful (Kohen-Raz, 1980). There seem to be constitutional, and eventually congenital factors impeding the cognitive growth of these groups and it is plausible that adverse environmental conditions during pregnancy may in part be responsible for their impeded mental development, which in some cases is accompanied by a conspicuous lag in physical growth (Willerman, 1972; see all Chapter 6, pp. 91–94).

3) Some disadvantaged post-adolescents suffer from specific learning disorders manifest in dyslexia, hyperactivity, and an inability to concentrate, causing in turn general mental and scholastic backwardness. Such individuals, had they grown up in a normal, stimulating social environment would have developed quite normally, perhaps with some minimal problems at the first grades. However, under conditions of socio-cultural deprivation, their overall mental performance deteriorates at early childhood and they are unable to cope with the regular elementary school

curriculum. The incidence of this type of problem is high among delinquents, and it may be asked to what extent the learning disability is a determinant (and not a concomitant) of juvenile delinquency among the disadvantaged (Lane, 1980; Rutter and Yule, 1973; Silberberg, 1971; Myklebust, 1978).

4) There is a certain incidence of psychopathological cases whose intelligence is impaired because of grave emotional disturbances, manifest in withdrawal from reality, outbursts of aggression, inability to concentrate, loss of primary habits, etc. This type is close to what may be described as a 'psychotic borderline' or 'deep personality disorder' (Kohen-Raz, 1980).

5) Finally, there are 'gifted' disadvantaged adolescents, who function on an above average intelligence level, in spite of stressful environmental conditions and lack of cultural stimulation at home (Smilansky and Nevo, 1979).

As type 1 and type 2 seem to represent the majority, the distribution of mental scores in a random sample of disadvantaged adolescents tends to be bimodal or rectangular (see Figure 1a,b). This essentially non-normal distribution of mental level in disadvantaged populations may easily be overlooked in educational research, and poses obvious methodological questions which must be taken into consideration in experimental design.

In culturally disadvantaged post-adolescents there is not only a considerable *inter*-individual variability in intellectual level, but there are also *intra*-individual discrepancies in mental functions.

For the sake of better understanding the typical impairments of cognitive functions in disadvantaged adolescents, a demarcation line should be drawn between 'abstraction ability' and the ability to perform formal operations.†

Abstraction refers to the ability to 'ab-stract', from a given constellation of stimuli, assembly of objects or social situations, specific cues. These cues, from the point of view of the subject, appear to be relevant in respect of a well-determined purpose. Subsequent to this act of selection, an act of labelling is performed, using the abstracted cues as denominators of a concept. I.e.

---

†In a similar vein Keating (1980) speaks of the possibility of separating the use of logic and the use of logic with abstract content, (p. 213, *op. cit.*).

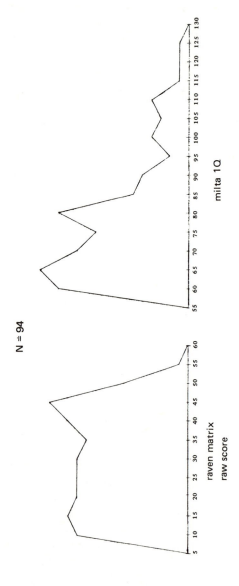

FIGURE 1a   Bimodal tendencies in distributions of mental scores of dis-advantaged adolescents (Kohen-Raz, 1979).

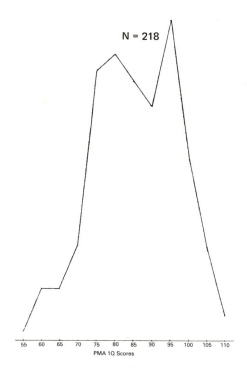

FIGURE 1b   Bimodal tendencies in distributions of mental scores of disadvantaged adolescents (Feuerstein, 1980, p. 337).

abstraction is not possible without a vocabulary of concepts made
available by an enriched and stimulating sociocultural environment. If the purpose of abstraction is the organization of stimuli
for the sake of egocentric convenience, the level of abstraction is
considered to be low, idiosyncratic and primitive. Such ways of
abstraction are characteristic of small children, who may call all
male persons 'daddy', all round objects 'ball', etc. Or taking
examples from performances of 6 year old children on the
Wechsler Similarities Test, the examinee says 'that a cat and a rat
are similar because they have tails', 'grapefruits and oranges
because they have juice', etc. On the other hand, if abstraction is
taking place for the purpose of creating a frame of reference for
scientific understanding and collaboration, clearly circumscribed

and universally accepted cues have to be selected as criteria of the concept, cues which are immune to bias by subjective interpretation and prejudice. In this case we speak of 'high level abstraction'. Obviously, the continuum from primitive to elaborate concept formation is roughly parallel to the widely accepted categorization of concepts as 'concrete' vs 'abstract', which in fact does not represent a clear dichotomy. Concepts such as 'family', 'love', 'hardware' and 'sea level' are difficult to label as either abstract or concrete. Abstraction is based on functions of *sensing, perceiving* and *input-processing.* Thus it is content bound and, in a large sense, content oriented. It is also vulnerable to changes in attitude, ego involvement and sociocultural atmosphere, which, as we shall see later, is crucial for the cognitive development of culturally disadvantaged adolescents (see p. 86).

Formal reasoning, on the other hand, as already described above (p. 16), is the ability to coordinate systematically sets of mental activities (i.e. complex internalized *actions*, in the sense of Piaget's theory), being aware of their *directionality* and *symmetry.* Thus formal reasoning is based on *output* processes and is relatively independent on content, i.e. perceptions, images and even abstract concepts. Formal reasoning may also involve reflection on the mental act itself, as is the case in propositional reasoning, or the manipulation of experimental problems involving palpable and concrete objects, as demonstrated by Inhelder and Piaget's classical experiments in physics and chemistry (Inhelder and Piaget, 1959).

This partly explains the varying levels of competency in applying formal reasoning to various situations and contexts. (Dulit, 1972; Karplus, 1981; Linn and Rice, 1979; Wason and Johnson-Laird, 1972). Piaget's terminology, juxtaposing concrete operations to formal reasoning has caused considerable confusion, which investigators such as Lunzer (1965) and Karplus (1981) have attempted to resolve and to clarify (see p. 70).

Returning to the problem of cognitive development in the culturally disadvantaged adolescent, it has been consistently reported that their *abstraction* ability is low and idiosyncratic in comparison to middle-class youngsters. This is plausible in the light of their externalized attitudes, cultural prejudices and egocentric interests and anxieties produced by socioeconomic stress.

Typically, they also lack a reservoir of an enriched vocabulary from which they would be able to draw appropriate concepts to label relevant aspects of the to-be-abstracted situations.

Here are some examples taken from Frankenstein (1970, p. 152):

1) Talking about rhythm, pupils said that 'rhythm is a type of dance.'

2) Being asked to define a man who behaves in a 'non-straight-forward manner' the pupils' reply was: 'this is a man with a hunch-back'.

3) Discussing the biblical story about Elkana and his two wives, Pnina, who had children and Hana who was childless, one pupil insisted that Pnina was the beloved wife because she had children. This opinion is obviously rooted in the traditional views of the oriental culture, in which this pupil had grown up, where child bearing is the criterion of appreciating women. This bluntly con-tradicts the biblical text, which provokes − intentionally − a higher 'non-conventional' level of moral judgement, in that Elkana loves Hana, the initially barren woman who later became the mother of Samuel, the prophet.

In similar vein, Frankenstein reports that disadvantaged High School students had difficulties in performing mathematical operations involving zero, zero being associated with being 'penniless', being left without any material means, i.e. evoking in the disadvantaged, who is fixated to the 'haveable', a kind of 'horror vacui'.

Although it seems probable that the egocentricity of the dis-advantaged rooted in his 'externalized style of life', is primary, and impaired abstraction secondary, the cause-effect linkage has not been convincingly demonstrated. The alternative hypothesis that lowered cognitive ability may lead to primitive conceptualization of life, prevent dissonance and efforts to change an unsatisfactory existential style may be plausible, but has not yet been examined.

As to difficulties in formal reasoning, they seem not be neces-sarily concomitant with impaired abstraction ability. In fact, as will be shown later, Feuerstein (1980) has demonstrated that disadvantaged adolescents may develop complex mental structures of formal reasoning, while remaining at relatively low levels of verbal abstraction. Unfortunately, to the best of our knowledge, there is no systematic research which focuses on the differential analysis of abstraction ability *vs* formal reasoning skills in disadvantaged post-adolescents. However, it seems, that verbal abstraction is the more vulnerable and also the more severely impaired higher mental function in the disadvantaged when compared to formal reasoning in non-verbal contexts. Possibly, this is due to the fact that the discrepancy between inferior verbal and superior performance skills, already found in intelligence tests of disadvantaged elementary school children, increases due to cumulative effects, which would intrinsically impede verbal abstraction. In this context, Kitsis demonstrated a conspicuously more severe retardation on verbal, as compared with non-verbal, intelligence tests in a sample of disadvantaged post-adolescents in Apprentice Schools, in comparison with a lower middle-class group of youngsters enrolled in Vocational and Industrial Schools (Kitsis, 1974).

It may be asked to what extent the five 'mental' types of disadvantaged adolescents, mentioned above, are differentially impaired (or intact) in the two domains of higher mental functioning (i.e. abstraction and formal reasoning), as well as in verbal *vs* non-verbal intelligence. In view of the persistent lack of systematic research, it is only possible to formulate our observations, which might serve as an hypothesis to be tested.

It appears that the first, 'normally intelligent' type is primarily handicapped in verbal abstraction, due to lack of environmental stimulation and a general improverishment of vocabulary. On the other hand, his ability to reason formally, although requiring re-educational efforts, can be easily mobilized (Feuerstein, 1979). The 'constitutionally retarded' seems to be impaired in both abstraction and operational skills, and resistant to intervention. It can be easily seen how a 'random' sample of disadvantaged adolescents will respond differentially to 'rehabilitation programs', when one of these two types is over-represented (Kohen-Raz, 1979). The third type — suffering from some kind of 'minimal brain damage' — thus has primary difficulties in visual perception, spatial orientation, temporal sequencing, etc., which, as already stated, can be overcome or compensated under normal conditions but definitely obstruct the development of higher forms of mental activity in the disadvantaged (Kohen-Raz, 1981a). The pathological type may have normal intellectual potential, in both abstract and operational functions, but very irregular disturbances, especially in concept formation. As to the gifted, it goes without saying, that their higher mental functions are intact, although difficulties in the application of formal reasoning in Humanities (grammar, literature, history) have been reported (Meisler, personal communication).

As far as we know, there are no replications of the already existing research on the relationship between formal reasoning, moral judgement, peer conformity, self-image, etc., on samples of disadvantaged populations (see p. 20). However, there is abundant anecdotical material gathered in the context of the various projects described in the second part of this book which shows that such relationships exist, although additional research efforts must be made to demonstrate these linkages statistically and systematically.

2. Ego Development

As already mentioned before, according to psychodynamically oriented theories, there is little evidence on 'identity crisis' and 'moratorium' in disadvantaged adolescents. It appears that these approaches are still under the impact of a classical essay written by Freud's disciple Bernfeld, who speaks of 'simple adolescence' in lower economic strata, in contrast to the 'protracted adolescence' in middle-class populations (Bernfeld, 1923). According to Bernfeld's model, the lower-class adolescent works and is economically self-supporting.

Sometimes he even supports his poverty-striken parents, which instrinsically symbolizes the liquidation of the oedipal conflict by taking over the paternal role. The lower-class boy, at the time Bernfeld wrote his essay, also indulges early in a full sexual life and there is little room for id-superego conflict and ego defense mechanisms characterizing the middle-class, 'protracted' adolescence.

However, this rather 'idyllic' picture of lower-class adolescence does not seem to correspond to post-technological reality.

First, the contemporary disadvantaged adolescent is passing a phase of 'moratorium' in either of two ways: many of them, especially the 'normally intelligent' are enrolled in a full-time Vocational High School program until the age of 18, which automatically places them in a social situation similar to that of their middle class, not disadvantaged age mates. The second possibility, and by no means a rare one, is dropping-out from school, partially or totally, or not attending school at all, or else passing an apprenticeship, which nowadays is hardly self-supporting. The apprentice is neither economically independent, nor replacing the father and more often than not in a 'marginal' social status of very low esteem, i.e. he has failed in his scholastic career eventually three times (a) he was not eligible for academic High School (b) was rejected from entering higher level Vocational Schools and (c) eventually dropped out from Apprentice School (Halper, 1978; Kitsis, 1974). Thus, he is passing a kind of moratorium, in a very negative, destructive sense in that in fact he is not committed to anybody and in that he is thrown into a marginal position, because nobody needs him. Actually, the disadvantaged post-adolescent drop-out is struggling for his identity not less than his middle-class counterpart, but has in addition to cope with an array of adverse circumstances:

1) The whole continuum of Erikson's pre-adolescent stages is weak and does not serve as a firm basis on which post-adolescent identity can be established. Especially if he had already encountered difficulty in identifying with his father at the oedipal stage, as the latter was either weak, tyrannic and psychologically (often also physically) absent from home. He had to struggle with the temptation to identify with his mother who naturally took over the role of the instrumental leader of the family.

2) As the feedback from career success or failure appears to be a decisive factor in post-adolescent ego-development (Bachman, O'Malley and Johnston, 1978), the disadvantaged drop-out drifts into a stage of 'identity diffusion', 'ego weakness' and 'disencouragement' in the Adlerian terminology (Dreikurs, 1950).

3) The marginally disadvantaged post-adolescent has great difficulty in experiencing 'intimacy' as well as in differentiating between Dual, Plural and Singular existential modi. He finds

himself fixated to the Pluralistic modus, i.e. to a more and more entrenched externalized style of life, not being able to gain inner distance either towards himself or towards an alter-ego. He thus becomes more and more an object of social exploitation and easily drifts into the hands of irresponsible gang leaders.

4) The disadvantaged drop-out, whatever his mental level, gains sufficient insight at post-adolescence, to become aware of his inferior status, even relative to his less marginal, well-adjusted disadvantaged peer who has succeeded in adjusting to Vocational or Apprentice Schools, not to speak of middle-class students.

He also understands very well the dim prospect that in the future he might be able to change or to ameliorate his social, educational and vocational inferiority (Kitsis, 1974).

5) In Israel, where military service is compulsory he may be exempted from the draft, which is a further blow to his prestige, and in addition a serious obstacle to his occupational career, as his exemption from active service is regarded as a testimony of mental and/or physical incompetency.

The Israel Defence Forces have recently established a special Rehabilitation Department for army rejectees, whose objective is to integrate them into the active service at a later date. Although the program appears to be successful, no systematic evaluations are yet available.

Between the disadvantaged marginal post-adolescent drop-out just described and the well-adjusted disadvantaged, sometimes lower middle-class student or apprentice in vocational schools there is a continuum of types of disadvantaged post-adolescents, who in descending order are: less intelligent, (especially in verbal intelligence); attend less demanding educational settings from regular vocational schools† to non-formal sporadic participation in one day per week courses, in specially established Apprentice Schools for the Severely Deprived; are less stable at work; are engaged in occupations demanding lower skills, and receive lower scores on a series of personality tests — even after intelligence, related to these personality variables, is rigorously controlled. Table 2 presents a list of variables, which have been shown to

†See also Table 3 on p. 59.

discriminate between extremely disadvantaged (including drop-outs) and less disadvantaged, marginal lower middle-class post-adolescents (Kitsis, 1974).

TABLE 2

Differences in scores on various personality tests between pupils in vocational schools (N = 139), special vocational courses (N = 263) and apprentice schools (N = 309)

Personality variable	F VALUES			Direction of difference		
	Intelligence not controlled	Verbal intelligence controlled	Verbal and non-verbal intelligence controlled	SCORES High	Med	Low
Rigidity	13.94***	9.00***	6.15**	[a]A	C	V
Concentration	17.67***	1.79	0.22	V	C	A
Anxiety	6.06**	1.41	0.88	A	C	V
Need achievement	24.85***	23.31***	3.92*	V	C	A
Extraversion	9.05***	8.98***	5.01**	A	C	V
Field dependency	26.28***	10.45***	2.22	A	C	V
Perseveration on task	67.35***	28.60***	22.11***	V	C	A
Active coping	12.51***	5.99**	3.92*	V	C	A

[a] A = Apprentices   C = Courses   V = Vocational schools
*   p = .05
**   p = .01
*** p = .001
Adapted from Kitsis (1974) p. 90. For details of personality tests and methods used in data analysis see original text p. 59.

Thus, in spite of the fact, that our knowledge about the post-adolescent's disadvantaged ego development is limited, the following points can be made:

1) In post-technological society, disadvantaged post-adolescents — from the point of view of their ego development again — do not represent a homogenous group, but a continuum, which on the upper end is represented by well-adjusted normally intelligent individuals, mostly enrolled in Vocational and Industrial Schools

and preparing for a trade career. These types probably pass through an adolescence similar to the middle-classes. On the other extreme, we find the post-adolescent drop-out of manifestly low intelligence, eventually working in temporary, unskilled jobs, who has lost his self-confidence and future time perspective and drifts into more and more marginal positions. There is a conspicuous lack of information about the trends and mobility within this continuum. But there are some encouraging signs that there is sporadic 'upwards' mobility in that disadvantaged post-adolescents leave an educational setting to enter a higher level one, which is actually not dropping out but a 'legal' change of pupil status (Kohen-Raz, 1979; Starr and Kahane, 1978). However, there is little doubt that we have to face a downwards trend of continuous school failure, ending up at the low extreme of the continuum described above.

2) The conceptualization of disadvantaged post-adolescence as a type of 'simple adolescence', characterized by absence of identity crisis, moratorium and role experimentation does not seem to be tenable in the light of the facts reported above. On the contrary, it is plausible that the disadvantaged post-adolescents, 'along the continuum' are passing critical phases of ego development, which are in urgent need of being systematically investigated.

3) There is no reason to consider the deteriorated state of ego 'exhaustion', which characterizes the disadvantaged post-adolescent drop-out as irreversible; there is growing experimental evidence that it is amenable to remediation and rehabilitation as will be described in Part III of this book.

3. Close Interpersonal Relations

In disadvantaged populations the basic proximal relationships with the 'significant others', parents, peers, partners of the other sex and the 'close educator' already show different developmental patterns throughout childhood and early adolescence, and consequently the dynamics of these relationships at post-adolescence are different from those found in middle-class youth. As to the parent-adolescent relations, the disadvantaged adolescent might suffer less from the 'revival of internalized parental conflict' and from 'separation anxieties', as, since childhood, his parental ties were less intensive and the oedipal involvement was attenuated.† On the other hand, he did not experience the dialectic interaction between parent and peer group which has been shown to be decisive for the growth of ego autonomy in middle-class youth. Instead, he gets involved in shallow and unstable peer-group relationships, inducing regressions which, in contrast to similar regressions observed in the middle-class peer group, are not regressions 'in the service of the ego' but regressions resulting in fixations to immature stages of psychosocial development, i.e. oral dependency on the group (as the family of origin fails to provide security), anal-sadistic primitive acting out (as higher levels of symbolic 'oedipal' communication are not fostered) and blind obedience to gang leaders, who are not − as in the middle-class group −. temporary alternatives to paternal authority but here become father substitutes. It can thus easily be seen, that the post-adolescent's positive identification with parents, based on a realistic perception of their virtues and vices, will develop less in the disadvantaged. The outcome tends to be either alienation and migration to other urban areas, eventual severing of family ties, or 'return to the family of origin' remaining more or less fixated to the parental externalized style of life (Frankenstein, 1968).

As to the *psychosexual development* of the disadvantaged post-adolescent, we shall focus on the 'drop-out boy', who represents the most urgent problem to the educator. As his masculine self-image has gravely suffered from continuous humiliations, frustrations and continuous experiences of intellectual and social failure, he will encounter great difficulties in establishing mature, 'intimate' and permanent sexual partnerships. In addition, his choice of partners is limited. Girls of higher SES strata seem to be beyond his reach, but also disadvantaged girls, as far as their families are more or less intact, will tend to look for the successful,

---

†Comparing middle-class and disadvantaged children at ages 10 to 12 Rahamim (1979) has found significant differences in social distance between the child and his both parents respectively, the disadvantaged perceiving themselves at greater distance.

trade or vocation-oriented types of the lower class boys as potential objects for 'steady' relationships. They may also aspire to seek contact with middle-class High School students. What is left to the disadvantaged drop-out post-adolescent male is the disadvantaged wayward, borderline delinquent girl, described before (p. 33) or those who are mentally retarded.

It must be emphasized that the chances of normal psychosexual development of the disadvantaged post-adolescent girl are in general much greater than those of the boy. Whatever her success at school, she has suffered less from humiliation, and, nowadays, she can easily find well-paid jobs of reasonable prestige, such as caretaker, babysitter, errand girl, cook, housemaid, teacher aid. Her self-image as a prospective mother and spouse is not affected by her eventually adverse scholastic experience, and she will generally be confident in her ability to establish a family life of her own. Data of a recent follow-up study indicate that there is a tendency to marry early (before the age of 20) in mentally borderline disadvantaged girls (Kohen-Raz, 1981a).

The role of the *close educator* in the rehabilitation process of disadvantaged post-adolescents has, in part, been sketched in the preceding section and will be described in detail in the context of presenting the various projects of rehabilitation in the second part of the book. It will be seen that most of these projects employ 'close educators', although in each case, they are differently labelled.

4. The Distant Social Environment

The problem of school and work adjustment of the disadvantaged post-adolescent represents one single issue, as the majority of the disadvantaged are generally in educational settings where work and academic studies are integrated, albeit to varying degrees. In order to understand these problems, which again are far from being thoroughly investigated, it is necessary to present a brief description of the present educational system for the disadvantaged mid- and post-adolescents in Israel.

As to the educational system for the mid-adolescent period, an important reform was carried out in 1968 which was explicitly aimed to foster the scholastic achievement, cultural emancipation and social integration of the disadvantaged pupil. The core principle of the reform was the establishment of regional large-scale integrative Junior High Schools,† for age groups 12 to 15, i.e. grades seven, eight, nine, which absorb the total population of the neighborhood within this age range, irrespective of socio-economic level, ethnic origin and scholastic achievement. The old system is based on an Elementary School Unit of eight years, which formerly covered the whole eight year span of compulsory education, meanwhile extended to 10 years. After the grade eight, pupils either left school altogether or continued their studies in various types of Academic or Vocational Schools, according to their abilities. (Some academic High Schools accepted specially gifted pupils after the fifth grade.) The reform, introduced in 1968, has been implemented gradually and today comprises about half of the pupil population within the respective age ranges.

In order to cope with the problem of the heterogenous mental and achievement level of the students, the Junior High School provides various tracks, and ultimately special classes, for the more seriously backward. Most of these Junior High Schools are linked with Senior High Schools with academic and vocational tracks, covering grades 10, 11 and 12. Thus in addition to the principle of integration, the reform attempted to create the basis for a continuous 12 years education, composed of three divisions: 1 to 6, 7 to 9 and 10 to 12, instead of the dichotomous split (1-8, 9-12). From the point of view of the education of the disadvantaged, it was assumed that the massive drop-out at the higher grades of the traditional Elementary School was, in part, due to the lack of motivation on the part of the disadvantaged adolescent to stay at school without any plausible outlook for further study, having in addition the feeling of belonging to a negatively selected group as the better pupils in some Elementary Schools left for High School at the sixth and seventh grade.

Another reason for introducing the reform was the low motivation of teachers to deal with the educational problems of the higher elementary school grades with increasing concentration of

---

†Smilansky (1979) designates these schools as 'Comprehensive Secondary Schools'.

lower level disadvantaged, and behaviorally problematic pupils. Last but not least, the Junior High School, requiring formal certification of higher qualification from its teachers, was supposed to raise the general level of educational personnel, confronting disadvantaged youth.

An evaluation after 10 years (Chen, Levi and Adler, 1978) revealed no significant gains in the scholastic achievements of the disadvantaged placed in the Junior High Schools as compared with those who continued to learn in the Elementary Schools, except possibly in mathematics. This finding would support the notion (p. 48) that higher mental functions linked with formal reasoning in non-verbal contexts (such as mathematics) are less impaired in the disadvantaged than verbal abstraction (required in other High School subjects). As to the class atmosphere, Junior High Schools split into two categories, those with an atmosphere characterized by general satisfaction, feeling of freedom, absence of discrimination, low anxiety and inner locus of control, against those with an atmosphere dominated by high anxiety, selectivity, lack of individual attention, external locus of control and accent on scholastic achievement. The higher concentration of disadvantaged is in the latter group of schools (*op. cit.*). Investigating class atmosphere in a more restricted sample, Perkal (1980) found a decisively worse self-image and a negative attitude towards school in the lower track of Junior High Schools, populated predominantly by disadvantaged pupils, in comparison with parallel classes in the traditional Elementary Schools with the same type of students.

Although these results do not demonstrate a substantial change in the intellectual, emotional and social development of the disadvantaged adolescent, which could be accounted for by the impact of the reform, it is argued by the evaluators that the reform should be nevertheless credited with the following achievements: the entire educational system has been influenced by its impetus; new curricula have been designed; the academic level of the teachers as well as their motivation and devotion to educate disadvantaged adolescents has been raised, and the basis for informal social interaction between disadvantaged and non-disadvantaged has been conspicuously widened. There are also definite signs that a higher percentage of disadvantaged pupils continue their studies at the 10th grade.

From the point of view of the 'marginal', 'drop-out prone', 'lower level' disadvantaged mid-adolescent, it does not seem that the reform has yet substantially contributed to solving their problems. Obviously, 10 years form a relatively short time span, and it must be admitted that only sporadic, systematic attempts have been made to provide specific curricula (such as increased trade work instead of academic instruction) for the lower tracks and special classes of the reformed Junior High School.

Turning now to the post-adolescent ages, the Israeli educational system offers a rather extended hierarchy of settings which will be briefly described (see Table 3). At the top we find the Academic High School, within itself subdivided into schools with varying 'prestige' and 'levels' (p. 37). The Vocational School, has two tracks; a general, with emphasis on theoretical trade subjects, and a practical, devoting more time to practical work. These two types of school are under the supervision of the Ministry of Education. The subsequent categories of schools supervised by the Ministry of Labour differ from the previous ones, in that the accent shifts decisively from study to work, i.e. in so-called *Industrial Schools* pupils spend a considerable amount of time at skilled, supervised work in a factory or enterprise located in the vicinity of the school, while a respectable part of the curriculum is devoted to trade theory, technology and technical drawing, besides basic academic subjects, such as language, mathematics, humanities and science.

The *Apprentice School*† differs from the Industrial School in that pupils work at different places, albeit in skilled jobs, and have only one day per week for theoretical and technological studies. Still, great efforts are made to relate job and 'theory', given one day per week with work experience. The *raison d'etre* of the Apprentice School is less a preconceived design of an educational setting than the law, which obliges apprentices up to the age of 18 to attend school one day per week (employers, in turn, being compelled to release them from work.††). Thus, a considerable

---

†Recently, the Ministry of Labour and Social Affairs has proposed to call these institutions 'Vocational Apprentice Centers', in order to emphasize the practical-pragmatic orientation of the pedagogical activities. Throughout this book the old designation 'Apprentice School' will be used.
††Israel Apprentice Act, 1953.

TABLE 3

The system of technological and vocational education in Israel

Type of school	Number of hours per week				Years
	Basic skills	General studies	Technological subjects	Work	
Vocational high school[a]	—	22	23	—[b]	3-4
Practical vocational high school[a]	—	18	27	—[b]	3-4
Industrial school	—	12	6-8	24-30[c]	3-4
Pre-army vocational courses	—	12	8-10	20-25	1
Intensified apprentice-ship[d]	—	10	10	24[e]	3-4
Skilled apprentice schools	2	2	3-4	35	3-4
Semiskilled apprentice schools	4	2	2	35	3-4
Kvotsot Avoda	10	4	4	26	1

[a]   Under supervision of Ministry of Education. Other schools on list supervised by Ministry of Labour.
[b]   Work experience provided by indoor workshops and is integrated in technological studies.
[c]   Work experience provided by indoor workshops as well as by outdoor work in adjacent industrial plants under close supervision.
[d]   3 days work and 3 days school per week.
[e]   Technological studies included in work experience
GENERAL NOTE: In light of the pressing and changing needs of the adolescent populations in the country, the system is in permanent change. The interested reader is referred to the respective Ministries (Education and Labour) for detailed and up dated information.

proportion of apprentices view the weekly school day as a necessary evil.

In spite of the already considerably lower mental level of pupils
and the reduced educational demands in the Apprentice School,
a not negligible residue of drop-outs and post-adolescents working
sporadically in unskilled jobs, remain outside school. For these
groups, the Ministry of Labour has later established special
Apprentice Schools, which might be designated as Semiskilled
Apprentice Schools'.† As may be imagined, the average achievement level and motivation to attend such schools, the one day
school attendance being again imposed by law, is still lower than
in the 'Regular' Apprentice Schools. Some of these Semiskilled
Apprentice Schools are linked with factories or shops, especially
with the Artisan Workshops of the Israeli Army, where women
soldiers who specialize in education are employed as teachers and
teacher aids. These schools are called 'Kvutzot Avoda' or 'Work
Groups'. Finally, there are centers for Wayward Youth, which
attempt to recruit post-adolescents loitering in the streets, providing them with temporary jobs. Some of them settle and adjust
and are then transferred to Semiskilled Apprenticeship Schools,
Work Groups, or even to Regular Apprentice Schools.

In spite of this highly flexible system and the extreme efforts
made to provide some educational framework even for the most
unstable and maladjusted, we still witness a massive drop-out rate
reaching 71% in the semiskilled Apprenticeship Schools and Work
Groups (Table 4). This high drop-out rate, even if attenuated
by a certain percentage of 'legitimate leavers', who eventually
prefer a higher level type of school, proves that for a considerable
proportion of disadvantaged post-adolescents no satisfactory

---

†The formal difference between Semiskilled and Regular (Skilled) Apprentice Schools consists in the fact that graduates from the latter receive
job certificates, whereas the former are provided only with a certificate
stating they have stayed in school for a certain period. However, apprentices
in the Semiskilled School are encouraged and guided to specialize in skilled
jobs and to enter Skilled Apprentice Centers (see Chapter 14). Recently, the
ministry intends to declare more semi-skilled jobs as skilled, which intrinsically qualifies apprentices and young adults to receive job certificates even at
later stages of their occupational carreer, eventually after completing their
army service.

solution to their educational and vocational career has been found.

To complete the picture we cite some findings on variables related to dropping out from Vocational and Apprentice Schools. The data are taken from Starr and Kahane (1978) and Kitsis (1974).†

As may be expected, factors related to drop-outs from Vocational and Apprentice Schools are not identical, although there is considerable overlap. Low scholastic achievement and grades, as well as reluctance to do homework, predict drop-out in both settings. Verbal intelligence has been shown to be unrelated, whereas non verbal intelligence is related to drop-out in Vocational Schools only, the less intelligent pupils leaving school significantly more frequently. This is not the case in Apprentice Schools, where mental level is essentially independent of the tendency to drop-out. This is also true for Semi-skilled Apprenticeship Schools (Kohen-Raz, 1979). Evidently, non-intellective variables seem to be decisive factors determining the disadvantaged post-adolescent's scholastic stability. The most important seem to be motivational. In both, Vocational and Apprentice Schools drop-outs are less ambitious, less persistent and declare openly not to wish to finish school. In Apprentice Schools only, drop-outs do not like certain school subjects, wish to learn a trade (and were deceived into believing they could do so), go to school because they must, and consider that it is not worth while studying beyond the age of 18. Teachers rated drop-outs in Apprentice Schools to have poor control over their affectivity, to be less clean, and more frequently unproperly dressed, less cooperative and less considerate. As may be expected they were more often sent out of the classroom. As assessed by objective personality tests, drop-outs in Apprentice Schools had lower achievement needs, tended to be more extremely either introverted or extroverted, as measured by Eysenck's Personality Inventory (Eysenck, 1963) and had a more restricted and less differentiated time perspective (Kitsis, *op. cit.*).

The overall impression from these data is far from encouraging. It must be added, that the educational personnel employed in the vocational school system is of a lower professional level than that employed in the Academic High Schools. General Vocational

---

†All cited differences and relations are significant at the .05 level at least.

TABLE 4

Percentage of drop-outs from the vocational
educational system in Israel

	Study		
	Starr and Kahane (1978)[a]	Kitsis (1974)[b]	Kohen-Raz (1979)[b]
Regular vocational school	33%		
Practical vocational school	34%	16%	
Industrial school	35%		
Apprentice school	56%	42%	
Semiskilled Apprenticeship School			71%

[a] 'Legitimate leavers', who left for other schools, completed school early or entered the army not included.
b 'Legitimate leavers' included.

Schools may be staffed with teachers, with high competence in technological subjects, however, as is the case in the Academic High School, they are 'distant educators'. As we step down the hierarchy of the vocational educational system, educators are less and less qualified so that, paradoxically, the 'marginals' and 'drop-outs' with the most severe educational and behavioral problems are left often with semi-professionals or persons who took the job of educator as a temporary solution before starting another career. In fact, there are some exceptions of excellent workers dedicated to these most problematic groups. Added to this, the engagement of women soldiers i.e., girls at aged 18 to 20, (most of them intending to become teachers after their discharge from the army) is a promising solution, providing that appropriate supervision and well-structured teaching material are available. It should also be noted, that among the foremen and employers 'close educators' may be found, who are most dedicated to the disadvantaged apprentice, and have often played a decisive role in keeping an unstable youngster on his job. However, these 'not visible' educators have not been taken into consideration by the educational system, and if they would join the team of teachers, counsellors and psychologists responsible for the education of the disadvantaged post-adolescents, great progress might be achieved in the process of rehabilitation.

5. Existential Expansion

The impediments to 'existential expansion' in the disadvantaged post-adolescent are multiple. Unless he has been able to terminate Vocational School or to receive a trade certificate (awarded by Apprentice Schools) he will be left without prospects for a reasonable occupational career amidst a highly competitive post-technological society. The relationship with a weak father, or absense of such a relationship, hampers the life tendency of expansion (Frankenstein, 1968). There are no challenges to surpass the parents, to create a new life-space, to induce change in the physical environment or to take initiative in social activities, typical signs of existential expansion in normal post-adolescence. For the severely disadvantaged, marriage is not an existential-cultural expansion, in the sense of Parsons' theory, but the perseverance of an externalized style of life, often with a mentally and emotionally inadequate partner. Attention should be drawn to the already mentioned tendency of disadvantaged post-adolescents returning to live with their nuclear family. This is an obvious testimony of lack of existential expansion, and a clear symptom that we are confronted with an 'unrealized adolescence' rather than with a 'simple' one, as some writers tend to assume.

On the other hand, the project of rehabilitation of behaviorally disturbed, disadvantaged post-adolescents in a Kibbutz (Kohen-Raz, 1972) demonstrated the effects of 'existential expansion' offered by the Kibbutz setting and its unique challenges.

Another example of giving culturally disadvantaged post-adolescents the opportunity of 'existential expansion' is Smilansky's program of Boarding School Fostering (p. 145).

PART II

Models of Normal and Abnormal Mental Development at Adolescence and Problems of the Curriculum

CHAPTER 4

Rey's Model of Practical Intelligence

André Rey, who has done monumental research in the domain of clinical developmental psychology at the University of Geneva, died prematurely in 1965. His writings, which have not been translated into English, are unknown to most educators and psychologists outside the francophone orbit. His model of intelligence, method of clinical examinations and rehabilitation system of impaired mental functions is highly relevant to the problems of disadvantaged adolescents and Rey himself, together with his former disciples, Richelle and Feuerstein, carried out pilot projects on culturally disadvantaged Jewish adolescents who had grown up in the Ghettos of North Africa and later immigrated to Israel. Subsequently, his methods were systematically and routinely applied in diagnostic and re-educational practice by the psychological services of the Youth Aliya (The Youth Immigration Department of the Jewish Agency), as well as further elaborated and disseminated by Feuerstein, who has recently summarized and published his experiences, based on Rey's theory and instrumentation (Feuerstein, 1979, 1980).

Rey's model of intelligence differs from the Piagetian in several respects which are not opposed, but rather complementary, to Piaget's theory of mental development. One is the emphasis on what may be called 'fundamental mechanisms' of intelligence, namely *automatisms* and 'basic performances'. Certain 'automatisms' are inherited. Contemporary research suggests that this is the case to a greater extent than had been thought during Rey's epoch.† Some of the automatisms change under the impact of

---

†Recent investigations on early oculomotor response patterns in newborns are a case in point (Karmel, 1974).

'telencephalisation', a well-known process of higher cortical centers taking over the control of subcortical reflex responses (for as example, the grasp reflex being replaced by voluntary grasp). However, most of 'automatisms' develop and are integrated within increasingly complex and differentiated response systems† which gradually are overlearned. The degree of overlearning of these responses, as well as the size and scope of the automatized response inventories, show great individual variations which, according to Rey, are important indicators of intellectual potential. Another 'fundamental mechanism' of intelligence is 'psychological tension' which is the ability to mobilize psychological energy in the form of 'mental effort' to solve a given problem. Impairment of this 'mechanism' hampers higher mental functions, as the individual is unable to remain alert throughout the execution of a mental task which, by the way, is typical of persons with cerebral dysfunctions.

The third 'fundamental mechanism' is what may be called the ability to expand and to organize the 'mental field' ('champ mental'). This means essentially the ability to perceive either simultaneously or in quick succession, several elements in a given situation, and to organize them by assigning to them relevance, dominance, salience, 'figure' vs 'ground' valence, etc. It can easily be seen, that in order to solve certain problems 'intelligently', the 'width' of the mental field must be expanded, as for example in a game of chess. However, in other situations, the rapidity of figure-ground reversal may be decisive, such as in the case of driving a car, recognizing the sudden relevance of a improperly observed obstacle camouflaged in the background.

Apart from these mechanisms, Rey speaks of *basic performances,* which consist in the voluntary mobilization and organization of the automatisms leading to the acquisition of new habits, which in turn enrich the inventory of the already existing automatisms. In these processes, attention and memory play a central role.

Finally, 'intelligence proper' intervenes on top of these systems, being characterized by the ability to establish flexible equilibria between internally crystallized structures and externally presented

---

†Staats (1970) has recently investigated these automatisms and early crystallizing response systems, designating them as 'basic behavioral repertoires.'

problem situations, by virtue of being able to view a given constellation of events from different points of view, and by virtue of coordinating two or more actions to induce adaptive changes ('assimilations') in this constellation. This description of intelligence roughly corresponds to the definition of concrete operations in Piaget's theory.

In Rey's own words:

Intelligence consists in the possibilities of coordinating the activities possessed by an individual. In this sense it is a resultant which is dependant on the number of such activities and their level of differentiation. The efficiency of intelligence changes qualitatively and quantitatively according to the different levels of mental development (Rey, 1947, p. 77).

Rey's description of intelligence is reminiscent of Frankenstein's 'ego mobility' as a critical factor in higher mental functions (see p. 86).

Visual-spatial abilities, an important factor of intelligence, is, according to Rey, somewhere 'in between' 'basic performances' and 'operations'. That is to say, certain responses related to orientation in space are certainly habits and voluntarily evoked 'automatisms', such as differentiation of directions, perception of top *vs* bottom, front *vs* back, and left *vs* right, etc. However, manipulations and imaginations of displacements, especially if they are multiple, as well as orientation in space involving changes of point of view, require mental activity on operational levels. This interaction between intellectual processes and perceptual mechanisms in spatial orientation has been extensively explored by Piaget (1961) in his comprehensive work on perceptual development.

This dichotomy of visual-spatial abilities (orientation *vs* imagination of displacements) roughly corresponds to results of factor analytical studies recently reviewed by Mc Gee (1979).

Images, as well as symbol systems and language, act as potent mediators and catalysts in these interactions between intellectual operations and basic mechanisms. These mediating functions determine what Rey calls the 'forms of Intelligence', which are essentially three: Practical-Intuitive, Visual-Imaginative and Verbal-Abstract. Although Rey's classification of 'forms of intelligence' appear to be similar the well known dichotomy of

Verbal and Performance intelligence tests, his notion of Practical Intelligence, is different from traditional conceptualizations of 'factors' 'components' and 'types' of intelligent behavior. We shall attempt to elaborate this point in some detail.

According to Rey's original formulation, 'practical intelligence is defined as an activity, which prior to or *independently of* the development of language leads to behaviors enabling the organism to cope with new parts or aspects of the physical environment' (Rey, 1935, p. 1, author's italics). However, as Rey continued and developed his research in this domain, more peculiar aspects of practical intelligence well beyond this general formula, were uncovered, which will be outlined below.

First, practical intelligence, although operating exclusively in practical and concrete situations has the same dimensions of development and complexity as other forms of intelligence i.e. this implies that practical intelligence can function variously on the 'sensory-motor', 'concrete operational' and 'formal operational level' and can be applied to very simple, as well as extremely complex, problems. Obviously, here we run into some semantic difficulties since 'formal' is generally conceived as an antonym for 'concrete', although Piaget himself has shown that 'formal operations' can be performed on concrete objects and situations

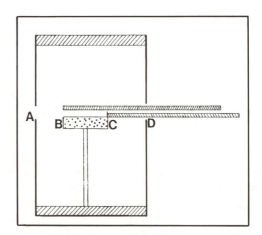

FIGURE 2   Task of practical intelligence at concrete operational level. (Adapted from Rey, 1947, p. 99.)

(Inhelder and Piaget, 1959). In similar vein it is conceivable that a problem requiring formal reasoning can be solved by practical intelligence in concrete context. The difficulty lies not in the clash of logically correct notions, but in the inappropriate labelling of psychological phenomena an issue we have already discussed before (p. 46).

If the Piagetian terms of 'concrete' and 'formal' operations were to be replaced by terms such as 'first order operations' and 'second order operations' such semantic complication and confusion could be avoided.†

We shall present some examples of levels of 'practical intelligence' in ascending order of difficulty, taking them from Rey's rich inventory of simple, but ingenious examination techniques. Examples of tasks of *practical intelligence at sensori-motor level* are problems of 'reaching Objects by Detour and Tools' which have actually been used in experiments with antropoids (Rey, 1935, p. 25). A test of astonishing simplicity, which Rey has designed in this domain, is the following: A piece of candy is suspended at about two meters above the floor in a room which is furnished with chairs and tables of varying height. In addition, sticks of different length are available. The child who is invited to fetch the candy is observed in his efforts to reach the object, which obviously is impossible without superimposing at least two pieces of furniture and using one of the sticks. Rey has demonstrated that most children are unable to succeed in this task under the age of four (Rey, 1935, p. 43).

---

†Recently, Karplus (1981) has proposed to contribute to the clarification of this issue by differentiating between *reasoning patterns* defined as 'identifiable and reproducible thought processes directed at a type of task' and examplified by mental acts such as classification, conservation, seriation, proportional reasoning etc, and between *application levels* of these reasoning patterns, ranging from 'concrete' to 'formal'. Examples of concrete level applications would be mental manipulations of real objects, directly observable properties and simple relationships. On the other hand, formal level applications would involve hypothesized or idealized objects with postulated properties, as well as logical, mathematical or other complex relationships, including assertions that are contrary to experience. Between these poles, Karplus leaves space for 'a gray area of intermediate applications which would not fall clearly into either of the two levels' (*op. cit.* pp. 288, 289).

The example shown in Figure 2 (Rey, 1947, p. 99) is a task involving the notion of reversibility and coordination of at least two actions, consequently it is *concrete operational.* The problem is as follows:

A ruler whose length is B-C is mounted on a stick which is placed in the center of a transparent cylinder with a diameter A-D. Through two holes on both 'sides' of the cylinder, located opposite the edges to the ruler, two thin metallic wires can be introduced, so as to pass smoothly above the top of the ruler. The subject is asked to measure exactly the length of the ruler, without of course having any access to the target except by manipulating the wires. While the 'abstractly' thinking person will probably introduce the two wires from each side to measure A-B and C-D, add the two distances and subtract this total from the diameter AD, the 'practically intelligent' individual will use the first wire, touch the edge D and let the second one slide on its top until it reaches the other edge B. B-C can now be obtained directly as being equal to the section between the edges of the upper and lower wires, which remain outside the cylinder. Although both ways of solving the problem nessitate concrete operational thought (because they involve the coordination of two actions) the 'practical' one is the more efficient, straightforward and rapid.

Another experiment in testing practical intelligence at the level of *'concrete operations'* is the following (See Figure 3). Two Blocks, A and B are mounted on a horizontal platform. They are fixed by a screw which, however, allows them to slide within the limits of the slot cut along their midline. The directions of free movement for each block are mutually opposite. Towards one of the smaller edges of the platform, a lever can be pivoted around its midpoint, which results in narrowing the gap between one of its ends and one of the blocks without touching the latter. In addition, the examinee is offered free blocks and sticks of various length, which can be placed in between the ends of the lever and the ends of the fixed sliding blocks, as indicated by letters i_1 and i_2 on Figure 3.

A piece of candy is put in front of block B and the child is asked to push the candy forwards. However, the candy, the fixed sliding blocks and the lever cannot be directly touched or manipulated, as the whole assembly is enclosed by a transparent cover,

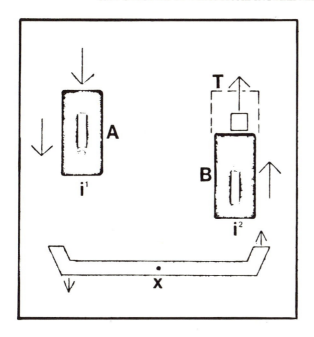

FIGURE 3   Test of practical intelligence at concrete operation level. Candy
T has to be pushed forwards by (a) inserting mobile blocks at i_1 and i_2
between sliding blocks A, B and lever X; and by (b) pushing block A in
direction of arrow. (Adapted from Rey, 1935, p. 161.)

leaving only the platform edge opposite the lever open to insert
the free sticks and blocks. It is evident that the task requires a
person not only to push the free blocks along the platform into
such positions where they may function as transmittors of force
between the sliding blocks and the lever, but also to imagine the
two mutually inverse movements of block A and B. Thus again,
concrete operational thought is involved. As clearly demonstrated
by Rey, this task is not tackled by children under the age of six,
which is the critical period of reversible thought (*op. cit.* p. 161).

At the level of *formal reasoning*, Rey proposes to invite the
examinee to 'invent' various machinery, such as 'a machine, to be
driven by a stream of running water, which should operate a lever
in rhythmical fashion, so that it might be used as an instrument to
cut'. Here chains of interaction, feed back and mutually exclusive

relations have to be imagined, as well as logically sufficient and necessary consequences of given premises (albeit of concrete character). Such mental strategies place the problem within the realm of formal operations.

As an additional example of a practical problem requiring formal reasoning (not taken from Rey) we cite the frequently encountered unpleasant situation of defects or blockages in water installations or electronic systems. Unless inbuilt automatic detection devices are provided, the system can be re-activated quickly only by deductive 'formal reasoning in practical context' in that the circuit of water or electricity is systematically closed and opened at critical points of linkage and branching. In such cases, chains of syllogisms are examined: Five water pipes, A,B,C,D, and X, each controlled by their respective taps, A', B', C', D' and X' are linked in such way, that A supplies water to B and B to X, while C and D, each supply water directly to X, which is a common outlet to the whole system. Suddenly, the water in X comes out muddy, because of a leakage somewhere in the system. We close tap A', the water is still muddy. Consequently, the leakage must be in either C or D. We close tap C'. The water continues to be muddy. Thus, the leakage must be in D. Obviously, one might proceed by trial and error, which is the typical practically unintelligent way to do so.

It will be noted, that verbal-abstract forms of reasoning† are not always an asset. The width of a mental field presented verbally, is narrow, as linguistic information has to be processed in *temporal sequences*. In certain situations when a rapid performance is vital, the 'practically' intelligent person being able to manipulate a wide mental field of visual-spatial concrete data presented simultaneously has a definite advantage.

---

† Rey himself, in his first systematic presentation of his model of practical intelligence (Rey, 1935), has made the following comment on this issue: 'Although it may be stated that there is a continuity between practical intelligence and rational (i.e. verbal and abstract) intelligence, in the sense that these two types of mental activity mutually support themselves in the organized synthesis of the human psychism, this does not imply that reason is a simple prolongation of sensori-motor action; actually, practical intelligence is *self sufficient* (italics ours), and in spite of the advantages which the individual might have (from verbal-abstract reasoning), there is no necessity whatsoever that he has to symbolize his actions.

In this context, attention should be drawn to a recent paper by Ferguson (1977) who attempts to demonstrate, that basic and revolutionary technical inventions and innovations have not necessarily been preconceived by theoretical and abstract reasoning, but by intuitive handling of practical tasks in practical situations. According to Ferguson, most shapes and structures of tools and machines are the result of visualization and haptic manipulation. Levers, wheels, transmissions, handles, screws, switchboxes, etc., were constructed by experimentation in close contact with concrete, real problems and not as the result of theoretical meditations.

As already mentioned, Rey's model complements more than it contradicts Piaget's theory, as well as other current conceptualizations of intelligence. However, some remarks are necessary on how to differentiate between practical intelligence and other forms of intelligent behavior which appear to have similar designations.

Practical intelligence is not *sensori-motor intelligence*, although both operate in concrete, immediate situations. There is a fundamental difference as to the amount of automatisms, width of mental field, memory and attention-span, as well as in the quantity and quality of coordinated reversible mental operations involved. It might be said that while all acts of sensori-motor intelligence are practical by definition, the amount of practical intelligence manifested by a child who functions at the level of sensori-motor intelligence is rather low and primitive.

Performance tests, or all kinds of 'non-verbal' tests are not necessarily tests of 'practical intelligence'. Tests such as Kohs Cubes, Raven Matrices, Digit Symbol, Puzzles, etc., do not involve 'practical situations'. Some of them put the accent on visual-spatial abilities and some measure what Rey has defined as automatisms (albeit of higher order) such as Digit Symbol, Object Assembly, Picture Completion, etc. In a similar vein, *psycho-technical tests* are not identical to Rey's tests of practical intelligence, although there is some overlap. The latter are more sophisticated and sensitive to developmental-retardation and pathological disturbance. They also have downward extensions which make them appropriate diagnostic tools for Kindergarten children.

Finally, there is a fundamental difference between practical intelligence and Jensen's *'Level I'* intelligence (Jensen, 1969). The latter consists essentially of functions, which Rey would define as 'mechanisms' or 'basic performances'. Practical tasks, involving concrete or formal operational thought, such as those exemplified above, would by definition, belong to Jensen's Level II. As the disadvantaged seem to master such items (Feuerstein, 1980; Kohen-Raz, 1980), Jensen's dichotomy, intended to elucidate the upper limits of mental performance in the disadvantaged, loses much of its rationale.

Rey's contribution to developmental-clinical psychology resides not only in his model of practical intelligence which is highly useful in general and special education, but also in his diagnostic techniques based on his theoretical conceptualization of intellectual functioning.

Mental testing, according to his approach, is not the assessment of a prescribed (supposedly 'new' and not previously learned) performance to be completed within a prescribed span of time, but a process of meticulous observation of the way, manner and pattern of responding to the test stimulus, irrespective of the 'score' to be earned. Thus, Rey pays great attention to the child's attitude towards the test situation, his preoccupations, anxieties, resistences, his ability to concentrate, to maintain mental tension as well as to keep alert. Most important is the detection of his error patterns and reactions to frustration. Again, whether and how a child 'warms up' to start to attack the test items is an important aspect of the test performance.

In accordance with his model of intelligence, Rey will not proceed to measure 'higher mental functions' before assessing various forms of 'automatisms', such as synkinetic and synergetic movements, reaction speed, phonetic dysfunctions, concentration, mobilization of physical energy, voluntary inhibition and hyper-fatiguability. Hereafter, the voluntary performances based on the already acquired automatisms are examined, namely memory and attention, as well as the width of the mental field.

Finally, 'higher order' operations (concrete and formal) are assessed, exploring which 'form of intelligence' (practical, ikonic or verbal) is dominant.

The contribution of Rey's model and method to an understanding of the structure and dynamics of mental functioning in culturally disadvantaged children and adolescents is impressive. Firstly, it has become evident that under conditions of environmental stress and deprivation, the basic skills (automatisms) and basic voluntary performances (attention and memory, mobilization of mental energy and width of mental field) are conspicuously impaired.

Secondly, if instead of being given problems of verbal abstraction, the disadvantaged young person is confronted with tasks requiring practical intelligence, even at higher operational levels, he performs astonishingly well and reveals his true 'intellectual potential'. Thirdly, as demonstrated by Feuerstein, (to be described in detail later) if the defective basic skills are adequately trained, the overall mental level of the disadvantaged can be conspicuously raised even if intervention is launched as late as the post-adolescent period.

We shall subsequently give some examples of Rey's tests and their rationale. For comprehensive presentations of Rey's theories and methods, the interested reader is referred to Rey's original works (Rey, 1935, 1947, 1968, 1969) as well as to Feuerstein's translations and applications of his instruments (Feuerstein, 1979, 1980).

Rey's tests of *automatisms* cover a wide range of modalities and functions. There is a variety of tasks involving 'visual closure', such as recognition and completion of incomplete drawings, reading passages of words or sentences with missing letters, etc. Other tests examine 'overlearned' arithmetic skills, such as counting, addition of small numbers, and simple multiplications. There are also tests involving visual scanning and tracing, and quick visual grouping of similar figures. Although Rey considers timing *per se* as one of the weak spots of general intelligence testing, his tests of automatisms are meticulously timed. The purpose of this procedure is to eliminate the eventual intervention of higher mental processes in tasks, supposed to measure 'overlearned' responses (Rey, 1969, Vol. 5).

At the level of *performances* Rey has designed ingenious tests to assess the memory of sequences of exact spatial positions. One of these tests consists in a display of 25 (5 x 5) squares placed before the subject. The experimenter touches seven of them in a predetermined sequence and the examinee, after a lapse of time has to repeat the sequence (see Figure 4). In similar vein, his test of 'plateaux', and 'fixation of sticks' (Rey, 1968, Vol. 3) requires the subject to remember the position of four out of nine sticks or round blocks placed on a wooden plate in a 3 x 3 square pattern, the subject being aware that five elements are fixated on the plate and four are loose. In the plateau test, four plates are presented in sequence, only one block per plate being loose, while its position varies from plate to plate. By turning the plate 180 degrees, or by reversing the sequence of presentation in the plateau test, the ability to invert a memorized pattern is examined. It can easily be seen, that these tests tap important antecedents or determinants of operational thought, namely the ability to 'visualize and to internalize' complex sequences and to invert them, i.e. attaining the notion of reversibility.

Tests of *visual-spatial abilities* are abundant in Rey's test collection (Rey, 1968, Vol. 2). We shall describe two of the most original among them. Organization of Dots requires the exact imagination of geometrical forms which have to be projected onto predesigned patterns of dots at various degrees of complexity (see Figure 5a). The more difficult items require the insertion of geometrical figures into increasingly complex and competing backgrounds (see Figure 5b). The test has been shown to correlate with non-verbal intelligence tests (Rey, 1968, Vol. 2), the Raven Matrix, as well as with other visual-spatial tests, but also with tests requiring verbalization of spatial relations (Rey, 1968, Vol. 2,

FIGURE 4   *Test of short time memory of visual-spatial sequence.* Examiner touches *empty* squares of 5 x 5 matrix in sequential order as indicated by digits. Examinee has to repeat sequence after lapse of 1 sec. (Rey, 1968/1969 Vol. 3 p. 20.)

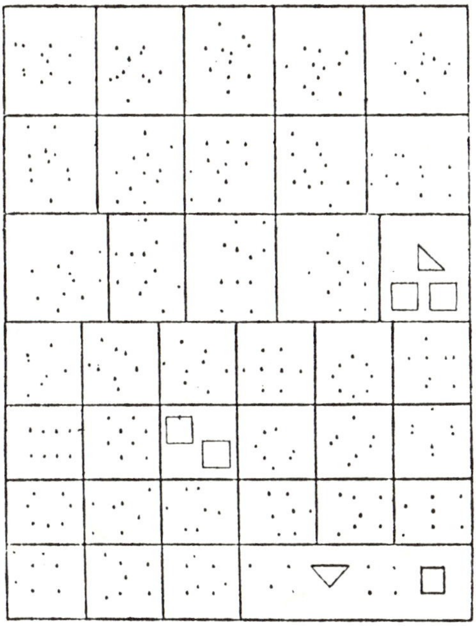

FIGURE 5a   Rey's test of organization of dots (Level I). Geometrical forms as outlined have to be inserted into dot patterns displayed in subsequent frames.

p. 80). Feuerstein who has effectively used this task as an instrument of diagnosis and rehabilitation has found that it is suitable to train, besides projection of visual relationship, non-intellective functions such as planning and restraint of impulsivity, visual transport and precision (Feuerstein, 1980, p. 128). Another of Rey's original tests of spatial imagination is to estimate he midpoints of curved and curled lines, such as shown on Figure 6.

Among tests of 'practical intelligence' proper we find tasks such as the disentanglement of a set of interlocked rings, fixed to a plate, but separable by virtue of a narrow gap cut into their circumference. The disentanglement by itself might be considered as a practical task at pre-operative level. However, by demanding examinees to re-establish the status quo of the locked set i.e. to reverse the action, the task will become concrete-operational.

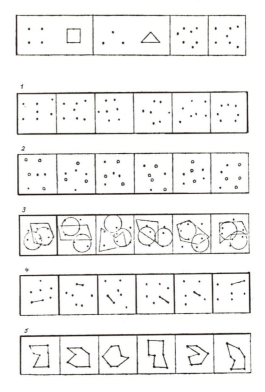

FIGURE 5b   Rey's test of organization of dots (Level II). Square and triangle presented at left upper edge to be inserted into increasingly complex and distracting patterns of points.

Rey has designed several exercises of practical intelligence at concrete operational levels on similar principles, consisting in the composition and de-composition of sets of blocks, varying in size, form, and color, some of them having 'cut-outs' to insert parts or to produce patterns of transparency.

It must be added, that Rey's tests are easy to administer. The equipment to be used has been deliberately chosen so as to be inexpensive, generally available and easy to manipulate (such as paper and pencil, wires, rulers, ordinary tools and simple boxes.) Instructions are brief and straightforward, often they can be

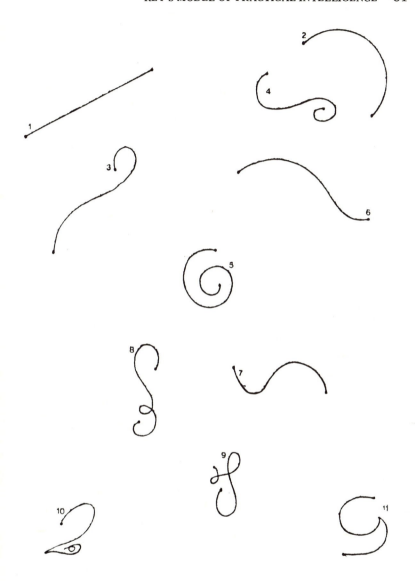

FIGURE 6   *Estimating locus of midpoints on curved and curled lines.* (Adapted from Rey, 1968/1969, Vol. 2, p. 37.)

replaced by exemplification and gesture, so that they are not only suitable for the disadvantaged, whose inferiority in verbal communication is notorious, but also for all types of 'non-verbal' exceptional children, such as the deaf, severely brain-damaged, profoundly retarded and aphasic.

In the light of this outline of Rey's theoretical and practical approaches to the problem of intelligence, it is evident that his model not only contributes essentially to an understanding of impairment of mental growth in disadvantaged and exceptional children, but also serves as an excellent frame of reference for designing programs for their rehabilitation, as will be described in detail in the third part of this book.

CHAPTER 5

Frankenstein's Psychodynamic Theory of Intelligence

Frankenstein's model of mental development is based on a psycho-dynamic conceptualization according to which intelligence is an integral function of the ego. Thus normal and abnormal mental development throughout adolescence cannot be understood without concomitantly exploring the whole complex of ego and psychosocial development.

First of all, it is clear, that intelligent behavior, in contrast to instinct, is flexible and necessitates an inner distance to the problem situation and that time must be left to evaluate alternatives and to chose between them.

This fundamental difference between instinct and intelligence has been well observed and defined by ethologists and psychologists (Eibl-Eibesfeldt, 1970; Guhl, 1956; Lorenz, 1970; Scarr Salapatek, 1976; Tinbergen, 1955) and is also discussed in great detail by Piaget (1971).

According to Frankenstein's theory, 'ego autonomy' is the basic condition of intelligent behavior, 'ego autonomy' being defined as the capacity of the ego of guarding its subject position as an object of a non ego, which is perceived and accepted as heteronomeous and independent, but on the other hand is ready to be changed and differentiated under the impact of the ego's intentionality, the ego in turn being aware of the fact that it is changed and differentiated by an actively and intentionally responding non ego in an ongoing process of interaction and reciprocation. It is the simultaneity and exchange of these subject-object positions which is the structural condition of normal development. (Frankenstein, 1966, p. 6; p. 34). Actually, this definition is close to the notion of 'overcoming egocentricity' in the sense of Piaget's theory (Piaget, 1956). It also fits the criteria of social maturity required to attain Kohlberg's 'post-conventional level' of moral judgement. However, the actual emphasis of Frankenstein's theory is on the linkage between the non-intellective, and unconscious spheres of the ego and what may be defined as the 'deep structure' of the intellect.

In order to elucidate this relationship, Frankenstein used a 'functional' definition of intelligence, based on Stoddard's comprehensive formula (Stoddard, 1951):

Intelligence is the ability to solve difficult and complex problems abstractly, economically, adaptively and originally under conditions that require concentration on a meaningful task as well as readiness and ability to resist illegitimate interferences of emotions with the cognitive process. (Frankenstein, 1968, p. 30.)

He then proceeds to analyze how the 'externalized' way of life of the disadvantaged pupil interferes with the normal development of each of these 'functions'. In order to understand this interference, the dynamics of 'externalization' will be briefly outlined: externalization means essentially an overdependence of the ego on the non-ego, preventing the integration and systematization of experience through interaction between the life principles of expansion and consolidation ('staticness'). Among various conditions, leading to an externalized patterning of the life space, growing up under conditions of extreme poverty and neglect, or of cultural deprivation, is the one relevant to our discussion. Such externalization as generated by economic stress and educational negligence is characterized by the following patterns of behavior: An overevaluation and over-estimation of the importance of whatever is 'haveable', i.e. material goods and advantages, depreciating everything which has no immediate consumer value. The 'haveable' must also be immediately available so that any activity linked with delayed gratification is not reinforced. The externalized disadvantaged individual sticks to the known, that which is close, familiar or predictable from narrow concrete cause-effect chains. He is not attracted by the new, the challenging, the improbable, in striking contrast to the normal child and adolescent who are thrilled by novelty, seek adventure and are driven by curiosity. As externalization 'weakens or even eliminates the ego's regulative and integrative power', the ego is not perceived as actively participating in the process of deciding and determining external events. Things just 'happen', nothing is caused by personal neglect or irresponsible behavior, there is just 'bad luck'. Thus, there is no intrinsic motivation to cope actively with the physical personal and social environment. Instead the 'externalized' individual has the experience of being 'driven' and 'carried along' by an apparently omnipotent power of external factors such as the 'ruling class', the establishment (and whatever symbolizes it — the police, public authority, the school, etc.). Eventually, he revolts against these public institutions. In the domain of higher mental processes externalization hinders the perception of different and eventually contradictory aspects of the same situation, and in similar vein ambivalent and ambiguous stimuli are not tolerated.

Consequently the coexistence of contradictions is rejected. Again, natural alterations between continuity and change in social processes and relations are not understood, i.e. no change in continuity and no continuity after change can be perceived. For all these reasons, complex situations and problems will be either avoided, circumvented or treated as simple and one-tracked. The errors, which will be committed by such behavior, may be fatal in the context of modern, mechanized and electronically controlled life, such as the faulty administration of a medicine to a baby by a disadvantaged mother or asking a disadvantaged youth to supervise an electronic emergency system. Implicitly, the externalized person is unaware of long range effects and consequences, his future perspective is restricted and in consequence no responsible tasks can be delegated to him.

How does the externalized style of life affect the development of intelligence at post-adolescence? We shall focus first on two functions which in normal development reach crucial levels of proficiency at post-adolescence, i.e. the ability to form abstract concepts and to perform formal operations (see Chapter 2).

As already discussed (p. 43), these two functions should not be confused. Abstraction is predominantly an input function, closely linked to perceptual processes and under the influence of organismic needs and emotional states. On the other hand, operations, whatever their level, are internalized manipulations of planned actions, thus primarily involving output systems. We shall deal first with abstraction.

Frankenstein's definitions of abstraction 'a form of ego mobility', 'the ability to use tools of information differentially' emphasize that this function frees the human stimulus-response system from dependence on 'fixed valences' inherent in objects or situations by virtue of inherited mechanisms, early conditioning or entrenched habits.

It is evident how externalization inhibits abstraction ability and higher concept formation. Abstraction requires discrimination between 'objectively' relevant and irrelevant cues. However, the disadvantaged considers as most relevant whatever is 'haveable', 'immediately consumable' and 'extrinsically rewarding'. Abstraction, meaning 'detachment', is incompatible with the tendency of the externalized person to stick to the known and familiar. The end product of abstraction is the formation of a concept, the latter being *defined* by criteria, yielded by the former. A concept, especially a high order concept, is a mutually agreed, permanently valid formula designating a certain array of events, assembly of objects or groups of phenomena. Concepts thus have considerable functional resemblance to laws, and although not all abstract concepts have the form of laws, certainly no law can be formulated without abstract concepts. However, the externalized individual actually prefers chance, hazard, happy-go-lucky approaches to the appreciation of laws, not to speak of his reluctance to obey them. He thus sees not only little purpose and meaning in concept formation, but unconsciously abhors the lawfulness and mental obligation associated with higher order conceptualization. Finally, accepting higher order concepts involves a change of attitudes towards events and objects which hitherto have been perceived and conceived from a different angle. This again runs much against the externalized way of life, fixated to staticness and routine within a closed system of 'concrete' values. Although Frankenstein focussed on the effects of externalization on abstraction, and does not deal explicitly with issues of formal reasoning under conditions of externalized behavior, it is evident that formal reasoning requires a higher degree of 'ego mobility' than concept formation. That is to say it is clear that 'thinking about thinking', i.e. second order operations, are incompatible with externalized patterns of reasoning which focus on the haveable, concrete, static and single-tracked. Furthermore, formal reasoning requires the evaluation of a problematic situation from at least two, but often three and more, independent aspects.

Finally, formal reasoning may lead to conclusions which are dissonant with experience or may be based on absurd premises. It must, however, be added that within the realm of formal reasoning there is a wide range of difficulties, not to speak of the additional dimensions of formal thought as recently outlined by Ennis (1978) and Karplus (1981). Thus, certain dimensions of formal reasoning such as content, might not be as diametrically opposed to externalized cognitive styles as has been outlined above, and thus offer points of anchorage for remedial teaching.

As to other aspects of higher mental functions, impeded by externalization, Frankenstein emphasizes the importance of internalization of values, as an important prerequisite to the development of complex symbol systems, especially elaborated language and differentiated vocabulary. Obviously, moral judgement, even at its 'conventional levels' is based on internalization 'of significant and meaningful others', a process which in turn is based on identification with positive parental figures.

The absence of motivation to 'plan ahead' and the reluctance to establish a meaningful future perspective is another crucial obstacle to higher intellectual activity in the disadvantaged. An additional factor deterring the disadvantaged from engaging in more differentiated mental operations is their fear of responsibility. Playing the ignorant and stupid has a definite advantage in the pretence of not being responsible for the consequences of aimless drifting, malicious negligence or uncontrolled acting out. To gain insight means to augment suffering and to take on more responsibility.

In similar vein, activation of the intellect is based on curiosity, as well as on the courage to seek the unknown. It is assumed that the oedipal stage is a critical phase in the development, or impediment, of this drive to explore. Classical psychoanalysis interprets these dynamics as the domination of the endeavor to 'penetrate' (a 'phallic' function) as well as to uncover the secrets of sexual relations between the parents. There are well-known 'oedipal' fairy tales, letting the hero face death or castration for lifting a hidden secret or treasure. Erikson speaks of 'initiative' *vs* 'despair'.

Frankenstein emphasizes that the importance of identification with the father at this critical stage, symbolizes (and enacts) the principle of 'expansion' and confrontation with the new, distant and unknown. The disadvantaged boy whose oedipal identifications are weak, not to speak of the fact that many disadvantaged families are physically or psychologically fatherless, has great trouble in mobilizing his 'curiosity' drive and in overcoming the fear of novelty and change. These essentially oedipally rooted impediments of intellectual functioning in the disadvantaged are reinforced throughout adolescence by continuing school failure and the feeling of being unable to compete with gifted age mates.

Finally, there is another source of mental malfunctioning under conditions of externalized socialization which is rooted in the confrontation of the ego with the personal and 'collective' unconscious in the sense of Jung's theory (Jung, 1964, 1974). According to the Jungian model the unconscious, especially the collective unconscious is not only a locus of suppressed conflicts, forbidden drives and destructive instincts, but also the source of productive fantasy and creative thought. Frankenstein applying this model to education, considers the interaction of the ego with the 'internal sphere' of the non-ego (i.e. the 'pro-social' unconscious) as vital for normal intellectual and emotional development.

The externalized, disadvantaged child is no less alienated from his inner sources of productive unconscious content than he is from meaningful social agents in the sphere of his 'external' non-ego. The result is an impoverished fantasy, a restricted inventory of symbols and an impaired ability of sublimation. The inability of disadvantaged children to engage in symbolic play, to draw pictures expressing dreams etc., is a clear documentation of this defective function. The sequelae of this impoverished 'inner life' of the disadvantaged at post-adolescence are evident. We are faced with youngsters, who have lost interest in creative arts, who are unable to interpret proverbs, metaphors and parables and who are shut off from the world of fantasy, fiction and day-dreaming which surrounds the normal adolescent and which serves as an important reservoir of mental energy and a source of ego strength.

This 'weak spot' in the dynamics of the disadvantaged post-adolescent deserves special attention on the part of the special educator, as it opens a convenient avenue to fruitful intervention as we shall describe later (Chapter 10).

Frankenstein's contribution to the understanding of the psychodynamics of cultural mental retardation can be summed up as follows.

Intellectual retardation of the disadvantaged adolescent is not the simple result of insufficient stimulation at preschool age and inadequate schooling at pre-adolescence, nor a 'cumulative deficit' due to socio-cultural neglect. It is caused by a deep disturbance of the ego/non-ego interaction, resulting in an externalized style of life with multiple components, each of them impairing in a specific way the various functions of intelligence, namely:

1) Abstraction cannot develop due to the fixation on immediately gratifying, 'haveable' valences of situations and objects.

2) The prerequisites of formal reasoning (the ability to perceive multiple aspects of problems and situations as well as the motivation to consider thought *per se* as an objective of mental activity) are absent under conditions of externalization.

3) The externalized individual abhors responsibility and is basically not motivated to know more in order not to be obliged to think more and to obey laws of behavior imposed by abstract conceptualization. He also lacks motivation to explore and to search novelty.

4) The inner world of the disadvantaged is impoverished because of a deficient interaction between his ego and the 'inner sphere' of the non-ego (i.e. the personal and collective unconscious). Therefore he is not creative, and deprived of inner resources to support his mental acts by productive fantasy.

CHAPTER 6

Psychobiological Aspects of Mental Development at Adolescence

The exploration of psychobiological aspects of mental development at adolescence necessarily focusses on maturational processes which, however, are important from the educational point of view as they may shed light on hidden potentials, as well as on 'late chances' of mental growth during the second decade of life.

To a certain extent investigations in this domain counterbalance the widely accepted belief, that the weight of maturational and physiological factors in human development decreases gradually from infancy to late childhood in favor of the growing impact of the social environment.

These investigations also implicitly lead to a re-evaluation of one of the central issues of rehabilitation policy, namely the reversibility of various types of mental retardation. This means essentially

1) Adolescence should not be considered the terminal of mental growth, but rather a late, albeit critical, phase of unfolding potentials in various functional areas of cognition.

2) More attention should be paid to the timing of intervention programs, taking into consideration variations in 'late stages of mental maturation' in individuals as well as in groups. Although the information available nowadays on linkages between physiological and mental maturation at adolescence is not sufficient to be operative in the context of educational innovation, nevertheless, it seems worthwhile to report some findings in this domain, gathered during the last two decades.

Generally, there are four areas of research, which seem to be pertinent to the problem:

1) Comparison of physical and mental development in normal and disadvantaged adolescents.

2) Exploration of correlations between physiological and mental development at various phases of pubertal growth.

3) Investigations of the possibility of a mental growth spurt, parallel or concomitant with the well-known pre-adolescent *physical* growth spurt.

4) Twin studies on physical and mental development at adolescence.

We shall elaborate on these points in greater detail.

1. Comparison of Physical and Mental Development in Normal and Disadvantaged Adolescents

Comparing four populations of adolescents, namely higher middle-class, lower middle-class, 'regular' diadvantaged and 'retarded' disadvantaged subjects at ages 12, 13 and 14, consistent (not always significant) differences in height and weight were found between the disadvantaged and the combined middle-class subjects, as well as between the retarded and non-retarded disadvantaged (Kohen-Raz, 1977b). The retarded disadvantaged were operationally defined as all the pupils of a larger sample of disadvantaged, who had at least once repeated class. As might be expected, they were also significantly retarded on verbal and non-verbal mental tests in relation to the rest of the disadvantaged of the same chronological age (see Tables 5 and 6). It must be added that the retarded disadvantaged did not differ from the regular disadvantaged population in ethnic background, parental occupation, or father's education. They did tend to have mothers with lower education level, some of whom had not completed elementary school. In any case, these data indicate that 'regular' and retarded disadvantaged adolescents are retarded not only in mental development but also in physical growth. No follow-up data are yet available, so it remains an open question whether they will reach the height and weight of the non-disadvantaged as adults.

The great discrepancy in weight and height between the middle

TABLE 5

Comparison of mental achievement and physical growth in middle-class and disadvantaged adolescents, boys[a]
(Kohen-Raz, 1977b)

Age group	12			13			14		
Socioeconomic group	A	B	C	A	B	C	A	B	C
N (range)	73–85	83–89	—	62–67	77–82	23–26	54–73	51–53	24–26
Numerical analogies	18.3	14.6**	—	20.1	19.7	12.9***	23.2	22.7	12.8***
Verbal analogies I	15.3	9.9***	—	18.2	12.6***	7.1***	20.1	14.6***	8.9***
Raven	31.8	22.5***	—	33.5	27.5***	19.2***	35.5	31.4**	24.6**
Height (m)	145.9	142.3	—	151.0	148.4	146.5(*)	159.8	155.6	153.7(**)
Weight (kg)	38.3	35.1	—	45.0	39.8	36.0(***)	49.9	45.5	43.3(***)

[a]Level of significance of t test relative to adjacent left column. Asterisks in brackets indicate significance level relative to column A of same age. Tabulated data are mean scores.
A = Middle-class, upper and lower level combined.
B = Disadvantaged regular pupils.
C = Disadvantaged retarded pupils.
*$p = .05$.
**$p = .01$.
***$p = .001$.

TABLE 6

Comparison of mental achievement and physical growth in middle-class and disadvantaged adolescents, girls[a]
(Kohen-Raz, 1977b)

Age group	12			13			14		
Socioeconomic group	A	B	C	A	B	C	A	B	C
N (range)	85-92	104-111	—	71-75	75-85	14-15	61-73	51-57	18-20
Numerical analogies	15.8	13.7	—	18.1	17.3	9.4***	22.0	23.0	14.7***
Verbal analogies I	14.4	10.3***	—	17.7	12.2***	9.0*	19.1	15.3***	9.7***
Raven	29.6	22.4***	—	35.1	26.0***	18.9**	37.7	32.4***	24.7***
Height (m)	145.1	145.0	—	157.3	150.0***	146.7(***)	156.7	154.4	149.2**
Weight (kg)	38.6	37.2	—	44.0	42.5	39.4(*)	49.9	46.7	40.2**

[a]Level of significance of t test relative to adjacent left column. Asterisks in brackets indicate significance level relative to column A of same age.
A = Middle-class, upper and lower level combined.
B = Disadvantaged regular pupils.
C = Disadvantaged retarded pupils.
*$p = .05$.
**$p = .01$.
***$p = .001$.

class and retarded disadvantaged (approximating mean differences of 10 kg and 10 cm) cannot be attributed to food deprivation under adverse socioeconomic conditions. To the best of our knowledge, undernourishment in Israel is largely prevented by health and welfare services. Thus, it must be assumed that genetic and biological factors are involved in the retarded disadvantaged adolescent's intellectual and physical retardation. Socioeconomic stress may have seriously impeded biological growth in very early, possibly prenatal phases of development, which would accord with recent theories of the biosocial etiology of cultural deprivation (Willerman, 1972).

2. Correlations Between Physiological and Mental Development at Various Phases of Pubertal Growth

Substantial evidence of a general relationship between physical and mental precocity, was corroborated in two large-scale British studies (Douglas and Ross, 1964; Nisbet and Illsley, 1963). The findings unanimously indicate that boys and girls with earlier puberty are mentally precocious not only at adolescence but also in late childhood. Nevertheless, there is some controversy about the continuity of this mental superiority during postadolescence. Douglas and Ross demonstrated significantly higher cognitive test scores continuing among such boys and girls as old as 15, but Nisbet's data present contrary evidence.

An attempt to examine the general relationship between physiological and mental maturation was made in three studies (designated I, II, and III). All three studies were carried out in Israel between 1967 and 1972.

The samples used in the investigations were selected from preadolescents and adolescents of both sexes enrolled in the four upper grades (five, six, seven, and eight) of elementary school, their mean ages at the beginning of the scholastic year being 11, 12, 13, and 14 years. The samples were recruited from the upper middle and lower middle classes in studies I and II and from lower class, culturally disadvantaged homes in study III.

The results of these studies were as follows: (For details of the samples, and as well as the criteria and instruments used to assist physiological and mental development, see Kohen-Raz, 1977b).

Relationship Between Height and Mental Achievement in Girls

Among the premenarcheal upper middle-class girls of study I, height correlated with Raven matrices, verbal concept formation, and verbal analogies in the sixth and seventh grades but *not* in the eighth. In study II, among middle class subjects, height correlated positively with deductive reasoning and sentence completion at the sixth grade level, with no test whatsoever at the seventh, and negatively with numerical analogies, concept formation, and Raven matrices at the eighth. (All correlations cited were significant at the .05 level.)

Comparison of matched pairs of the same population demonstrated significantly higher (p=.05) mental scores among taller girls on the Raven matrices and sentence completion tests at the fifth grade level, on the Raven, verbal analogies, II and GSA† tests at the sixth, marginal superiority (p =.1) on the Raven and GSA tests at the seventh and no relationship (with a tendency to insignificant inversion) at the eighth.

A similar pattern appears in the sample of disadvantaged girls (study III). After an isolated significant positive correlation between height and the Raven test at the seventh grade level, significant inverted relationships show up the eighth.

These results indicate that a relationship between height and mental achievement typically appears in grades five, six, and seven (when the majority of girls are still in their preadolescent growth spurt) and vanishes or inverts at grade eight (when 90% have passed it). Although the disappearance of this relationship could be caused by the restriction of range resulting from the physical growth deceleration around and after menarche, this would not account for the inversions, as will be discussed later.

Correlation Between Menarcheal Age and Mental Scores ‡

In the upper middle-class sample of the first study, menarcheal

---

†The GSA (Guttman–Schlesinger Analytical Test) (Guttman and Schlesinger, 1966, 1967) is an instrument similar to the Raven matrices. However, the patterns used are much more complex and distractors (characterized by variation in directionality) have been carefully and systematically constructed.
‡The positive relationship between pubertal maturation and mental achievement is supposed to show significantly *negative* correlation between menarcheal age and mental scores.

age was found to correlate negatively and significantly (p=.05) with the Raven test (p=-.65, N = 13) and marginally significantly (p= .1) with verbal analogies (p=-.44, N = 12) in the combined group of sixth and seventh graders. No relationship was found at the eighth grade. In the lower middle-class groups of the first study, menarcheal age and mental scores were unrelated.

In the sample of study II, both upper and lower middle-class subjects showed similar relationships between menarcheal age and mental achievements during the sixth and seventh grades but discrepant patterns during the eighth grade. Therefore data on all middle-class sixth and seventh graders are combined in Table 7 but they are presented separately for eighth graders. It can be seen that pronounced relationships between physiological and mental maturation appear in the sixth grade group that are entirely absent in the seventh. Although *lower* middle-class eighth graders show correlations in the expected directions between menarcheal age and numerical analogies, GSA, and vocabulary, zero correlations and even a tendency to inverted relationships (in verbal analogies and deductive reasoning) appear in the *upper* middle-class sample (Table 7).

The pattern of relationships between menarcheal age and mental achievement among disadvantaged girls is similar to that found in the middle-class samples. At the sixth grade level (age 12), correlations are significantly negative, indicating a positive relationship between physiological and mental maturation. At the seventh grade level, the relationship vanishes, and at the eighth (age 14) it tends to invert.

The subgroups of retarded girls show a somewhat different pattern. The positive relationship between physiological and mental development that disappears among the older upper middle-class and regular disadvantaged girls persists at age 14. This pattern is similar to that of the lower middle class subjects.

Relationships Between Physiological Maturation and Mental Achievement in Boys

In boys, height and stage of pubic hair growth were used as criteria of physiological maturation.

TABLE 7

Relationship between menarcheal age and mental development[a] (Kohen-Raz, 1977b)

Grade-age	Socioeconomic group	N	Nonverbal			Verbal				
			Numerical analogies	Raven	GSAT	Verbal analogies I	Verbal analogies II	Deductive reasoning	Vocabulary	Sentence completion
6 (12)	Middle-class	43	−30†	−33*		−48*	−41*	−43*	−27†	−28*
	Disadvantaged	48–52				−28*	−32*	−24†	−25	−39*
	Retarded	—								
7 (13)	Middle-class	63								
	Disadvantaged	70–78	+27	+22						
	Retarded	10–12						−23	+33	
8 (14)	Upper middle-class	34				+49*		+37*		
	Lower middle-class	24	−24		−40*				−39*	
	Disadvantaged	30–36	+33*			+35†				
	Retarded	13–14	−44†	−30		−29	−28	−44†	−38	−31

[a]Data are Spearman rank correlation coefficients.
†p = .1.
*p = .05.

TABLE 8

Relationship between height and mental scores, boys[a] (Kohen-Raz, 1977b)

Grade-age	Socioeconomic group	N	Nonverbal			Verbal				
			Numerical analogies	Raven	GSAT	Verbal analogies I	Verbal analogies II	Deductive reasoning	Vocabulary	Sentence completion
6 (12)	Upper middle-class	41								
	Lower middle-class	50			+31*			+31*	+32*	
	Disadvantaged	81–86				+22*				
7 (13)	Upper middle-class	32	+38*						+34†	
	Lower middle-class	44								
	Disadvantaged	71–73	+26*	+23*		+28*	+34*		+53†	+35*
	Retarded	18–21	+30			+20	+26*			+39
8 (14)	Upper middle-class	36	+38*			+35*	+38*		+44*	
	Lower middle-class	38								
	Disadvantaged	15–23	+34	+34		+25		+46*		
	Retarded	21–26	+34†	+41*		+48*	+24	+35		

[a]Data are Spearman rank correlation coefficients.
†p = .1.
*p = .05.

Correlation techniques showed a significant relationship between height and numerical analogies, verbal analogies, and vocabulary among the upper middle-class eighth graders (Table 8). In contrast, in the lower middle-class sample, height correlated significantly with verbal analogies (r = .34), deductive reasoning (r = .28), and vocabulary (r = .30) at the fifth grade level (data not tabulated), and with deductive reasoning, vocabulary, concept formation, and GSAT (also significantly) at the sixth (i.e., during the prepubertal period), but no relationship appeared at the near pubertal and pubertal phases of the seventh and eighth grades (Table 8).

In the samples of regular and retarded disadvantaged boys, height and mental scores correlated consistently at the seventh and eighth grade levels (Table 8). The overall impression obtained from Table 8 is that there is a definite relationship between physical and mental growth which is most pronounced during the pubertal physical growth spurt (ages 13 and 14) in three of the four groups investigated.

When growth of the pubic hair was used as a criterion of pubertal maturation, in pairs drawn from the middle-class sample matched for chronological age, mental differences reflected earlier or later maturation. They are more pronounced in the upper middle-class group and definitely larger on two nonverbal tests, numerical analogies and GSA (p = .02). A significant difference on the verbal analogies test appears only in the upper middle-class population (Table 9).

In both disadvantaged groups (study III) the relationship between the pubic hair growth and mental tests was assessed by correlational technique. As can be seen from Table 10, the results confirm the assumption that physiological and mental development are interrelated. There are pronounced relations to nonverbal tests (and to verbal analogies) similar to those found in the middle-class sample.

Explorations of the Possibility of an Adolescent Mental Growth Spurt

The hypothesis that the well-known phase of prepubertal physical growth acceleration might be paralleled by mental growth spurt has attracted many investigators (Abernethy, 1936; Anastasi, 1958;

TABLE 9

Relationship between growth of pubic hair and mental development, boys[a] (Kohen-Raz, 1977b)

Grade	Socioeconomic	N	Non-verbal				Verbal				
			Numerical analogies	Raven	GSAT	Verbal analogies I	Verbal analogies II	Deductive reasoning	Vocabulary	Sentence completion
7 and 8	Upper and lower middle-class	35-39	3.8*	2.1	3.3*	1.2	-0.5	0.1	0.6	0.5
7 and 8	Upper middle-class	20-24	5.1**	3.2	6.6**	2.7	1.1	0.5	1.9	1.3†

[a]Partners with earlier and later pubic hair growth, matched for chronological age. Tabulated data are differences of scores between earlier and later maturing matched partners.

†$p = .1.$
*$p = .05.$
**$p = .01.$

TABLE 10

Relationship between growth of pubic hair and mental development, boys[a] (Kohen-Raz, 1977b)

Grade-age	Socioeconomic group	N	Non-verbal			Verbal				
			Numerical analogies	Raven	GSAT	Verbal analogies I	Verbal analogies II	Deductive reasoning	Vocabulary	Sentence completion
6 (12)	Disadvantaged	71–79	+27*	+29**						
	Retarded	—								
7 (13)	Disadvantaged	71–73				+20				
	Retarded	19–21	+52*	+48*		+46*	+32	+22	+56*	+41
8 (14)	Disadvantaged	13	+55*	+35		+61*	+27	+40		+40
	Retarded	18–23	+50*	+50*		+20		+23	−25	−22

[a]Data are Spearman rank correlation coefficients.
*p = .05.
**p = .01.

Kuhlen, 1952; Ljung 1965; Tanner, 1962). However, exhaustive overviews of the pertinent literature by Ljung (1965, pp. 7-15) and by Tanner (1962, p. 208) lead to the conclusion, that the occurence of a pubertal mental growth spurt is rather doubtful. It must be added that the objective measurement of mental growth accelerations posed methodological problems chiefly because increments in mental achievements over short periods cannot be reliably measured and compared. One possibility, which was used by Ljung (1965) and Epstein (1974) is to calculate correlations of mental age with chronological age as measured in months within age cohorts. Abrupt decrease of these correlations could be interpreted as a sign of increased variability of mental age produced by different mental growth rates. Ljung (1965) found such decreases occuring in both sexes at the period of their pubertal physical growth acceleration and considered these findings as an indirect evidence of pubertal mental growth spurts. Epstein (1974), basing his results on extensive surveys and data re-analysis of numerous studies in the field of neurophysiology, anatomy and educational and developmental psychology, concluded that mental growth spurts occur in regular biennial intervals, two of them at pre-adolescence and post-adolescence respectively, (ages 10 to 12 and 14 to 16), mid-adolescence, being, according to Epstein, a phase of mental growth stagnation. Kohen-Raz (1977b), also basing his findings on cross sectional fluctuations of correlations, found that in girls, positive relations between physiological maturation (as measured by menarcheal age and height) are pronounced during the pre-menarcheal period (which is known to be the period of the female pubertal growth spurt). They disappear with the advent of the menarche and tend to invert during the post-menarcheal period (see above, Table 7). This might be explained by the possibility that girls with delayed menarche remain longer in the prepubertal accelerated mental growth phase and subsequently surpass their earlier menstruating age mates who initially (i.e. during their own prepubertal mental growth period), had been mentally superior to the late maturers, at a time when the latter had not yet started their pubertal growth (see Figure 7). However, while these cross-sectional data seemed to support the hypothesis that a pubertal mental growth spurt exists, longitudinal data failed to do so. Also, there was no convincing evidence that training of formal reasoning would be more effective during assumed phases of mental growth spurts (Kohen-Raz, 1973).

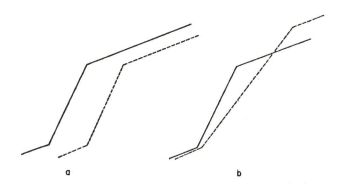

a   b

FIGURE 7   Comparison of two types of late maturing subjects (– – –) compared to an early maturing (———) matched partner assuming the occurence of a mental growth spurt

Summing up these findings, it must be admitted that the existence of a pubertal mental growth spurt has not been unequivocally demonstrated. However, in view of the sporadic evidence, further research employing more sophisticated methodology should be recommended.

Twin Studies

Twin studies have yielded the following results:

1) Mental growth during infancy and the preschool period is not linear, but passes typical phases of acceleration and deceleration (Wilson, 1972, 1974, 1975, 1981).

Similar phase patterns have not yet been observed during adolescence, primarily because the longitudinal twin data on which the early childhood findings are based, have not yet been fully elaborated. (Wilson, personal communication).

2) Physical pubertal growth rhythm and patterns are genetically determined.

3) Mental development at adolescence is affected by both, genetic and environmental factors, the environmental effect being manifest in verbal and mathematical skills, trained and fostered by school and home, while weak or absent in the case of inductive reasoning, not explicitly taught in class (Fischbein, 1981).

Overviewing the information on psychobiological aspects of mental growth at adolescence, it is evident that this area of educational and developmental research is still at a stage of pilot investigations. However, in view of the great strides made by modern biology and behavioral genetics, (for recent overviews see Gedda *et al.*, 1981), education cannot ignore the possible contribution of these disciplines to the understanding of adolescent problems, and therefore due consideration should be given to future investigations in the domain of psychobiological correlates of adolescent mental development.

CHAPTER 7

The Role of Context in Mental Development

Although 'context' and 'content' may have similar roles in cognitive processes, 'context' — in contrast to 'content' — refers not only to the salient dimensions of a given stimulus, but also to 'background' factors which decisively affect the stimulus value in a given situation. In fact, the saliency and 'content valence' of a stimulus will vary under the impact of what has been defined by sensoritonic theory as 'extraneous' stimulation, i.e. situationally proximal stimuli which change the pattern of perceptual responses evoked by the salient 'object' stimulus (Wapner and Werner, 1957). Examples are; the impact of body tilt upon the perception of the vertical, (*op. cit.*), the effect of color on the maintenance of body balance (Halpern, 1963), the increase of 'movement response' to ink blots produced by immobilization of the body, etc. (Goldman and Herman, 1961).

The role of context in semantics and communication needs no further explanation, neither does its importance in higher symbol processing such as reading and metaphorical language.

From the point of view of problems of mental development of culturally disadvantaged adolescents, it is important to compare the traditional 'structural approach' with the recent 'contextual model'. This need arises because it seems that in educational theory and practice — under the impact of Piaget's theory — attention has been focussed on *structural* aspects of the pupil's intellectual inventory. This bias might not have any peculiar effect on teaching practice and curriculum design in normal education. However, in the domain of the education of the disadvantaged it is prone to lead to misinterpretations and distortions of educational programs and processes.

A priori, it might be stated that it would be strange indeed, if contextual variables, whose importance in perceptual and linguistic communication has been convincingly demonstrated, should be irrelevant in higher mental functions. Although psychologists and educators, strictly adhering to Piaget's theory, assume that mental growth proceeds essentially with the emergence of qualitatively different structures, becoming more and more similar to adult-like schemes represented by models of logic, Piaget himself has never ignored the role of context in cognitive growth. Generally, he has used the term 'décalage' to explain, why, even after attaining a certain 'higher stage' of reasoning, a child would persist to function on a lower level when confronted with tasks of different content, or in different context.

As already discussed (p. 18) he has also been aware of the fact, that there is a considerable variability in the degree of mastery of formal reasoning in different content areas, attained at different chronological ages by different persons. There is also evidence, that the 'mental structures' at the formal level may mature and become 'functional' only in certain parts of the general population (Dulit, 1972; Keating, 1980), and even then individuals within such subpopulations will efficiently apply it only in selected contexts (Wason and Johnson-Laird, 1972).

Within the framework of the Piagetian model, the most famous example of décalages is Elkind's study which demonstrates that when children between the ages five to 11 were confronted with the conversation problem of mass, weight and volume of two pieces of clay, only the majority of the *nine*-year-olds were able to solve the weight problem, and not until the age of 11 years was volume conservation mastered, although the conservation of mass was attained at the age of seven, i.e. the age at which the mental structures at the level of 'concrete operations' are supposed to crystallize (Elkind, 1961). In a similar vein, Ennis (1980) has demonstrated that conditional-logic principles could be mastered by about 50% of children at ages six to eight who were asked to reason about some physical objects in front of them (i.e. in concrete context). This would indicate that there are 'décalages' 'downwards' in the domain of formal reasoning, which certainly conflicts with Piaget's view, who sets the threshold of structural maturation required to master such operations at ages 11 and 12. On the other hand, Ennis remarks that most college students and intelligent adults will have difficulty in handling propositional logic if presented in the format of logistic formulae used by Piaget to explain 'the structure' of formal reasoning in adolescent thought. We remind the reader again that the paradigmatic tasks of 'formal reasoning' given by Piaget and Inhelder to their adolescent subjects, are embedded in concrete situations of experiments in elementary physics (Inhelder and Piaget, 1959).

Returning to the problem of décalages in the domain of 'concrete' operations, Odom (1978) has shown, that the crucial variable determining the level of mastery of two-way visual spatial matrices, considered to be a reliable test of competency in concrete operations, is the salience of the stimulus dimension (color, form, direction). This finding, according to Odom's views, proves the dependency of mental operations on developmental changes in *perceptual ability*. From the point of view of the 'context-structure' controversy, Odom's results support the contextual approach, as the saliency of the perceived stimulus values is determined by contextual variables, which may be 'extraneous', i.e. proximal stimuli, 'introceptive', such as moods or affective states, preferred styles of stimulus organisation, etc. Obviously, general modes of ego/non-ego interaction, such as that manifested in 'externalisation' (Frankenstein, 1968) intrinsically determine stimulus saliency, and thus, by extrapolation of Odom's model, the range and direction of 'décalages'.

Odom presents an interesting example of a task of 'conservation of mass' not mastered by 85% of above-average intelligent adults (college students) who according to Piaget should have firmly established structures of concrete operational reasoning. The task is as follows:

Imagine that I have two cans. One has red beads in it, and it is called the red-bead can. The other has blue beads in it and is called the blue-bead can. There are the same number of red beads in the red-bead can as there are blue beads in the blue-bead can. Let me repeat that. There are the same number of red beads in the red-bead can as there are blue beads in the blue-bead can. Now imagine that I dip a cup into the red-bead can and take out five beads. I pour them into the blue-bead can. Then I mix up all the beads in the blue-bead can. I then dip the cup into the blue-bead can and take out five beads and pour them into the red-bead can. Will the number of red beads in the red bead-can and the number of blue beads in the blue-bead can be same or different? *Correct answer*: The same. (Odom, 1978, p. 121.)

Odom explains that the failure of adults is due to the experimentally induced saliency of the act of 'mixing the beads', which in the case of the sophisticated college student seems to put the problem into the context of 'probability theory'. As can be seen by some reflection, such context is entirely irrelevant. When presenting the problem in algebraic form (see Table 11) it is immediately evident that it is a task of 'conservation of mass' which has nothing to do with calculation of probability. It may be assumed that if Odom would have permitted his subjects to solve the problem mathematically (and not verbally) it would have remained in its 'familiar' context and not have posed any difficulty.

TABLE 11

Algebraic representation of Odom's problem of beans and cans

	Red can	Blue can
Before transfer	Rn	Bn
After transfer	$Rn - Rx$	$Bn + Rx$
After return of beans from blue to red can	$Rn - Rx + Rp + Bq =$ $= R(n-x+p) + Bq =$ $= R(n - q) + Bq$	$Bn + Rx - Rp - Bq =$ $= B(n - q) + R(x - p) =$ $= B(n - q) + Rq$

n = number of beans in each can before transfer
x = number of red beans transferred from red to blue can
p, q = unknown proportion of red and blue beans transferred back to red can, given that $p + q = x$
R = red beans, B = blue beans

Actually, Odom has demonstrated that eight-year-old children, unfamiliar with the problem of probability, stick to the concrete context of transferring and returning a constant number of beads, and 'paradoxically' 95% gave correct answers and justifications (*op. cit.*).

The decisive role of content and context in higher forms of human reasoning has been convincingly demonstrated by a series of ingenious studies carried out by Wason, Johnson-Laird, and Evans. (Claxton, 1980; Evans and Wason, 1976; Wason, 1969;

Wason and Evans, 1975; Wason and Johnson-Laird, 1972). It has been shown that adults of above average intelligence, such as college students and university professors, commit systematic logical errors when confronted with negative statements lacking context and almost obsessively go on to verify generalizations and resist falsifying them, because these statements appear to represent an idiosyncratic context of rules which they are reluctant to abandon. Furthermore, there is an array of experimental evidence which shows that implicit terms of logical premises, which are not explicitly mentioned in the formulated context of a given problem, are simply ignored, or considered as irrelevant when eventually perceived. In a similar vein, inversions are treated as if they were embedded in the context of a one-to-one relationship, and are consequently considered to be perfectly symmetrical with the original statement (Wason and Johnson-Laird, 1972).

A striking example of failure to reason at a formal level in unfamiliar contexts is the confrontation of highly intelligent persons with Wason and Johnson-Laird's 'Four Card Problem'. Subjects are shown four cards, displaying a vowel (E), a consonant (K), an even number (4) and an uneven number (7) respectively. They are given the following instructions:

'You know that each of these cards has a letter on one of its sides and a number on the other side and you are presented with the following rule which refers only to the four cards: 'If a card has a vowel on one side, then it has an even number on the other side? Your task is to name those cards, and only those cards, which need to be turned over in order to determine whether the rule is true or false.' (Figure 8.)

Essentially, the rule, expressed in formal logic is, 'If p then q' (p = E, q = 4; non-p = K, non-q = 7). In order to prove its truth it is sufficient to *verify* 'if p then q' and to *falsify* 'if non-q then p', i.e. to turn over E and 7. However, the vast majority of Subjects (about 80%) is tempted only to *verify* 'if p then q' and to go on and to verify 'if q then p', i.e. proposing to turn over E and 4. The critical act of *falsifying* 'if non-q then p', i.e., stating the necessicity to turn over 7, is performed only by 5% of subjects given the task (Wason and Johnson-Laird, *op. cit.* pp. 182). However, if the same problem is presented in a highly familiar context (Johnson-Laird, Legrenzi and Legrenzi, 1972), in that p is the back of a sealed envelope, *non-p* the back of an unsealed envelope, *q* is the front of an envelope with a stamp valid for a sealed letter (say, 15 pence) and *non-q* the front of an envelope with a stamp valid only for an unsealed letter (say, 12 pence), the problem becomes trivial. That is to say, the subject is asked which envelopes have to be turned over in order to make sure that the post office has not been cheated (by putting only 12 pence on a sealed letter). It is obvious that the subject will turn over only the back of the sealed envelope (*p*) to check whether it bears a 15 pence stamp and the front of the envelope bearing 12 pence i.e. *non-q*, to see whether it is unsealed. About 88% of subjects performed correctly on this task (Wason and Johnson-Laird, *op. cit.* p. 192. See Figure 8).

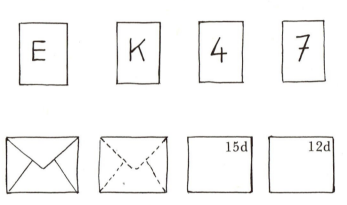

FIGURE 8   *Problem of simple implication in non-familiar and familiar context.* Card game with *ad hoc* invented rules *vs* envelopes stamped as letters and printed matter respectively. (Adapted from Wason and Johnson-Laird, 1972.)

The role of context in the acquisition of higher forms of reasoning has also been recognized by scientists engaged directly in curriculum design and teaching materials for adolescents, especially in the field of science teaching.

As a case in point, Levine and Linn (1977), after considerable experience and pilot experimentation in this area, have reached the following conclusions:

Programs which aim to teach scientific reasoning will be most successful, if they emphasize *recognizing and organizing relevant information*, (italics ours) rather than if they simply emphasize a particular strategy such as 'make all other things equal' to control variables (*op. cit.* p. 380).

The authors further state that 'familiarity dimensions interact with the format of the question' (*op. cit.* p. 381).

In the light of these findings, educators should be wary of following a strictly 'structural approach', which states that pupils, normal or disadvantaged, can be classified according to the level of operational structures manifest in their mental performances. As there is little doubt that the general curriculum to which disadvantaged pupils are exposed is embedded in a context unfamiliar to them, no conclusions should be drawn as to the development of their mental structures, which, as the above mentioned research demonstrates, cannot crystallize in a vacuum of irrelevant values and in the absence of salient stimuli.

On the other hand, as shown by the various rehabilitation projects described in the third part of this book — especially the Curriculum of Contextual Learning Units — even the low level, marginally disadvantaged post-adolescents are able to perform tasks on formal operational level when these are put into proper familiar contexts.

After having outlined the psychodynamics of culturally disadvantaged adolescents against the background of the various models of mental development relevant to the psycho-educational problems of these populations, we shall now proceed to overview some recent programs for their rehabilitation. However, before describing the programs, which essentially attempt to implement curricular innovations based on the theoretical framework presented in the preceding chapters, it seems important to review critically some principles of the *traditional curriculum* which evidently has failed to meet the educational needs of disadvantaged populations, before and during the adolescent period.

CHAPTER 8

The Traditional Curriculum as a Source of School Failure of Disadvantaged Adolescents

General discussions on the scholastic failure of the disadvantaged tend to blame various factors linked with disturbances in their early personality development, such as insufficient exposure to patterned stimulation of infancy (Marans and Lourie, 1967), inadequate maternal care (Wortis, *et al.*, 1963), insufficient opportunity to elaborate a system of verbal and non-verbal symbols (Bernstein, 1975; Cazden, 1967; Edwards, 1978), absence and/or incompetence of the father (Kriesberg, 1970), an externalized style of socialization (Frankenstein, 1968), an anomy of social control (Clinard, 1964), and so on.

However, as we shall attempt to demonstrate that there are additional crucial determinants of school failure of the disadvantaged which are primarily rooted in the rationale and structure of the general curriculum and which are independent of the educational problems already accumulated during the pre-school period, but which evidently aggravate them most severely.

First of all, current teaching programs take it for granted that a part of the schooling process takes place outside the classroom, i.e. the pupil is assumed to do 'home work' which he is supposed to carry out in an educationally supportive and encouraging home environment. This, however, implies, to much greater extent than is visible, the involvement of the parent or, stated more explicitly, the active participation of the parent in the educational and instructional process initiated at school. This may take the form of direct assistance in the preparation of lessons, but also in a more indirect but perhaps more effective way, in the form of a stream of educationally highly relevant information, which flows from parent to child in everyday life, be it routinely responding to the child's questions about events, places, news, accidents, cultural facts and acts, be it glances at the professional activities of father and mother, be it the opportunity to read journals, books and pamphlets available at home. It must be added that the middle-class parent is alert to learning disabilities in his offspring and ready, at the slightest signs of imminent school failure to hire a personal tutor to prevent deterioration of the learning situation. This parental participation in the schooling of the child, taken tacitly into account by the general curriculum, is very restricted and eventually non-existent in the disadvantaged family.

Another covert prerequisite of the general curriculum is the assumption that the pupil is intrinsically motivated to acquire knowledge, to investigate the unknown and to seek novelty and change. Psychologists have designated these dynamics as Explorative Drive (Berlyne, 1960; Montgomery, 1954), Functional Pleasure (Funktionslust) (Bühler, 1947), Initiative (Erikson), Intrinsic Motivation (Hunt, 1963), Life Tendency of Expansion (Frankenstein, 1959). There is evidence that in the disadvantaged child these drive dynamics have been depressed and hampered in early childhood by environmental stress and educational neglect, and also by minimal CNS dysfunctions due to complications of child bearing under socio-economic stress (Willerman, 1972).

Thus, while a learning process initiated by the teacher will be reinforced by the curiosity and exploratory activity of the normal child during and after school hours, there will be no such initiative on the part of the disadvantaged pupil for self-propelled learning, outside the classroom.

Besides ignoring the fact that the disadvantaged parent is 'psychologically absent' from school (Frankenstein, 1963) and that the disadvantaged pupil is handicapped in his exploratory drives, the curriculum has some additional shortcomings from the point of view of the educational needs of disadvantaged populations.

One is the predominance of symbolic modes of communication between teacher and pupil manifest chiefly in verbal methods of instruction. It is well known that the disadvantaged child has been conditioned to prefer concrete, immediate, material means of interaction with his social and physical environment. Symbols are not appreciated and preferred as an optimal way to convey information to human beings. Thus, the disadvantaged preschool child does not use symbolic dramatic role play (as does his normal age-mate) to reduce emotional tensions and to work through intra-familial conflicts (Smilansky, 1968). Instead, he choses rude acting out or withdrawal from social contact. As a result of such an 'externalized' style of social life, language development is impaired, which is not only manifest in an impoverished vocabulary and deficient concept formation, but also in a defective deep structure, as subject/object relationships and ego/non-ego differentiation have not been sufficiently experienced (Frankenstein, 1966).

Consequently, there is a wide discrepancy between the differentiated patterns of linguistic communication, prescribed by the curriculum and the 'restricted code' (Bernstein, 1960) which the disadvantaged pupil uses to interact with his social environment.

Another aspect of the regular curriculum which is problematic for the disadvantaged is the fact that the acquisition of literacy and basic arithmetic are the core objectives at the lower grades, while at the medium levels we find a heavy emphasis on abstract conceptualization of subject matter. In other words, already at the medium grades the normal curriculum envisages the formation of a highly literate, widely informed and intellectually bright citizen, who should be optimally eligible for a high school, or college career. Obviously, we are faced with a dissonance between the 'distant' objectives of the curriculum and the learning potential of the disadvantaged, who already struggling to keep abreast of their normal peers in the mastery of basic scholastic skills, are unable to develop abstract attitudes at higher grades and have only dim prospects of graduating from High School or College at post-adolescence (Halper, 1978).

A somewhat less salient but not infrequent difficulty of disadvantaged pupils in coping with the regular curriculum is rooted in their weaknesses of spatial perception, spatial orientation and imagination of spatial displacements. These functions are not only related to arithmetic and mathematic skills (Rourke, 1978) but also seem to facilitate symbolization and formal reasoning (Feuerstein, 1980; McGee, 1979). (Logical inclusions, exclusions and syllogisms are often illustrated and represented in the form of spatial relationships; also, many abstract concepts are actually derived from visualization of spatial relations, such as *progress, superior, overcoming, breakthrough, proximal, promotion, humiliation,* etc.) Deficit in these functions may not be crucial until the fourth or fifth grade, when greater emphasis is placed on the study of mathematical problems and equations, geometry, physics, etc., which require the understanding and manipulation of spatial relationships.

Another basic function, impaired in the disadvantaged, is the perception of *temporal sequences*, which has been also investigated under the heading of 'auditory perception' (Deutsch, 1972).† However, it should be stressed, that in addition to difficulties in discrimination and recall of rhythmical patterns, melodies and intonations, learning disabled subjects (among whom the disadvantaged are strongly represented) may suffer from maturational or constitutional deficiencies in the perception of *visually* presented temporal sequences such as pictures or letters in slow motion, or fixed figures on a mobile background (Frank and Levinson, 1976). As the general curriculum presupposes that all these functions which have been shown to be linked with reading ability, are intact in an average expected pupil population, the disadvantaged will be unable to cope and will quickly experience failure in basic school subjects.

It is nowadays assumed that these difficulties in spatial and temporal pattern perception may be partly due to pre- or perinatal risk factors, related to circumstances of socio-economic stress. Hence their relative frequency in disadvantaged populations (Kohen-Raz, Russel and Ornoy, 1975; Slovin-Ela and Kohen-Raz, 1978; Willerman, 1972).

Finally, we mention certain basic, universally valid principles of curriculum construction which, theoretically, should be taken into consideration but in practice are often neglected. These are:

1) The principle of systematic recapitulation of learning material.

---

†In this context, investigations on the relation between perception of temporal sequences and speech and language functions should be mentioned (Fay, 1966; Poeck and Huber, 1977).

2) Consistency in the use of modes, models and methods of instruction, as well as in the ways of organization, presentation and elaboration of subject matter.

3) Continuity of systematic and well graded, cumulative information.

These principles are often violated by natural circumstances such as turnover of educators, employment of substitute teachers, ill-introduced innovations in the teaching program, and mobility of the pupil's family. While the normal pupil is well able to cope with circumstantial adversities of schooling, the disadvantaged child is easily thrown off balance by such events, and will have great difficulty in adjusting to inconsistencies in the teaching program.

Obviously, all these areas of incongruence between the objectives, methods and practices of the regular curriculum and the educational needs and capacities of the disadvantaged have a cumulative negative effect, and at the threshold of adolescence we witness a crisis leading finally to a massive drop-out (Halper, 1978, p. 294). This 'drop-out' may be physical and factual, but in most cases it is 'psychological' in that the disadvantaged pupil continues to 'decorate' the classroom by his physical presence, but mentally and emotionally he is absent from class. Not only does he not profit from the teaching program, but he regresses and deteriorates, gathering negative emotional experiences of humiliation, frustration, rejection and boredom. The outcome of this process is the disadvantaged post-adolescent who has become unmanageable, socially, emotionally and intellectually, and lacks motivation to work, to learn and to study, being hostile to any form of formal education and instruction.

Thus any curriculum which is supposed to meet the educational needs of disadvantaged post-adolescent drop-outs, must carefully take into consideration the sources of failure of the normal curriculum described above and attempt to disentangle the vicious circle created by accumulations of cognitive deficits, impoverished language and communication, lowered self-esteem and deteriorated motivation to study and to acquire basic skills and knowledge vital to social and vocational survival in the post-technological society.†

---

†It might be argued that the economic structure of our society offers

First, it is necessary to deal with the most recent effects of the self-defeating feedback loop, namely the negative associations and connotations linked with traditional school, teacher and teaching methods. This may be achieved by presenting materials in an innovative and attractive fashion, emphasizing individual needs and individual pace of progress, and avoiding as far as possible the 'frontal method', which 'confronts' an undifferentiated group of low motivated, passively participating pupils with a domineering, 'distant' and detached teacher figure. *Second*, the dormant curiosity and exploratory drives must be awakened by presenting stimulating and provocative teaching materials, closely linked with the context of the disadvantaged adolescent's everyday life and basic existential problems. In a similar vein pupils should be optimally encouraged to take initiative in the learning process, in that *they* are asked to invent exercises, to participate in peer teaching and evaluate the work of their classmates. *Third*, language and communication, again in close context with life situations, should be considered as the core curriculum, *without* necessarily putting emphasis on reading and spelling at the beginning stages of the program.

Fourth, exercises in space and time perception, as well as in the retention of visual-spatial and auditory-temporal sequences must be considered essential components of the revised curriculum. *Fifth*, higher forms of thought (including formal reasoning) should be taught in appropriate contexts, notwithstanding the prejudices created by extremely 'structural' approaches which consider the

---

sufficient vacancies for unskilled labour, which require neither intellectual skill nor elaborate literacy, but some reasonable level of 'social intelligence and adaptability'. Consequently, the most straightforward way to rehabilitate lower strata of disadvantaged post-adolescents might be to 'throw them' into the labour market, providing them with guidance and supervision which would improve their social skills, without worrying any more about their scholarization. Such an approach seems not to be justified. Without the correctional emotional experience to be able to cope with scholastic subjects and whatever this means intellectually, socially and vocationally — the self-image of the disadvantaged will remain impaired and breed emotional tensions and conflicts. Besides that fact, the unskilled, poorly educated worker is the first to fired and become unemployed, whenever there are changes in the tide of economic affluence. Some direct evidence in this matter has been corroborated in the context of a recent follow up study (Kohen-Raz, 1981a).

disadvantaged as *a priori* incapable of abstract and scientific attitudes. *Sixth*, the traditional teacher and tutor figure must be replaced by the 'close educator' (see above, Chapter 2, p. 34) who alone is capable of tackling the deeply rooted, primary learning deficits, created by inadequate socialization and schooling, especially the ill effects of the lack of parental participation in the process of formal education which may have hampered the pupils' spontaneous efforts and endeavours to acquire knowledge and to interpret reality.

Finally, attempts must be made to restore the 'symbolic attitude' towards the physical and social environment, by overcoming the 'externalized' cognitive style and 'materialistic' approach towards life. Here extra-curricular activities and concentration of educational, social-work-type and therapeutic intervention might be necessary.

In the subsequent chapters we shall describe some recently developed programs, which attempt to implement these principles of curricular revision and to cope with the difficult task of reestablishing the motivation and ability of the disadvantaged to profit from formal education.

PART III

Current Projects of Rehabilitation of Disadvantaged Post-Adolescents in Israel

CHAPTER 9

Feuerstein's Program of Instrumental Enrichment

Feuerstein's program of Instrumental Enrichment, originally designed for culturally disadvantaged immigrant adolescents has been expanded and introduced into the general Israeli Educational Junior and Senior High School system, including Vocational and Industrial Schools (see above p. 58). It also serves as an anciliary method of remedial teaching in Special Classes for learning disabilities and the educable mentally retarded. Pilot studies have also been carried out on more severe cases of trainable retardates, brain damaged and autistic children.

In addition to its routine use in regular and special schools (comprising about 1300 classes in 1979), Instrumental Enrichment is also offered to individual cases at Day Centers, and Guidance Clinics, the Headquarters of the program being the Hadassah-Wizo Canada Research Institute in Jerusalem (Feuerstein, 1979, 1980).†

The rationale of Feuerstein's program is based on two assumptions:

1) The *cognitive* retardation of culturally disadvantaged adolescents must be viewed as the core of their general emotional social and personal maladjustment (an approach, which, as already discussed before, p. 16, differs from classical psychoanalytical and neo-psychodynamic models, emphasizing the primacy of emotional disorder in adolescent turmoil.) Therefore, rehabilita-

---

†A large scale project, applying Feuerstein's method to populations of educable mentally retarded, learning disabled and emotionally disturbed adolescents is currently in progress in the U.S. and Canada (Arbitman–Smith, Haywood and Bransford, in press).

tion of intellectual performance is the key to the re-education of socio-culturally deprived youth.

2) Modifiability of cognitive functions and plasticity of ego development is still high throughout adolescence, and traditional models postulating gradual stagnation of mental growth during the second decade of life are inappropriate theoretically, as well as pragmatically.

Consequently, there is no reason not to invest efforts in re-educational programs for the more advanced age groups, not to speak of the fact, that a high percentage of disadvantaged adolescents profit from the teaching programs offered by the official educational system only marginally, or not at all (see above, 60-63).

Hence, Feuerstein challenges the validity of routine mental tests, an attitude already taken by Rey (1947) and recently shared by numerous psychologists and educators (Cronbach, 1975; Ferron, 1965; Hunt, 1975; Sundberg, 1977). The short-comings of traditional intelligence tests are evident. They have been originally constructed with the explicit aim of predicting scholastic achievement and have more or less remained so, being routinely revalidated against such achievement. If used with disadvantaged populations, they actually 'sample' representative segments of their scholastic failure, which, as has been unequivocally shown, is in most cases not the result of inadequate intellectual potential. Besides they are saturated with items based on vocabulary, verbal skills and general knowledge acquired in an average expectable culturally enriched environment, thus penalizing the disadvantaged who is notoriously deprived in this respect. Performance at measured and prescribed speed is one of the criteria of scoring for most items. Last but not least, the testing situation per se is associated for many disadvantaged with reminiscences of failure and humiliation in the classroom.

To overcome this fundamental obstacle on the way to breaking the vicious circle of scholastic failure — low IQ, labelling, disrupted teacher-pupil interaction — Feuerstein has started his rehabilitation program with the introduction of an assessment device assumed to be adequate for measuring the true mental ability of the disadvantaged. He thus constructed his Learning Potential

Assessment Device, which is based in part on an information theory model, in part on Rey's model of intelligence (see Chapter 4), i.e. Feuerstein maintains that a differential analysis of 'input, elaboration and output' phases in cognitive processes is vital to uncovering the weak spots of deficient intellectual performance, especially in the disadvantaged. Second, as originally postulated by Rey (see p. 76), deficiences in automatisms, basic performances, width of mental field, attention, sequential memory, spatial organization, etc., must be diagnosed first, before proceeding to examine higher mental operations and verbal abstractions. Third, again a principle established by Rey (1947), the 'how' and not the 'what' in test performance must be meticulously observed, i.e. the tester-testee situation, instead of being some kind of a stop-watched interrogation of the pupil by a menacing examiner is transformed into a socratic dialogue in an atmosphere of tolerance and empathy, free from time pressure. Under such conditions, the minute details of a whole gammut of psychosomatic, motor, perceptual, intellectual and emotional, verbal as well as non-verbal responses can be observed and registered, the wealth of material gathered in such a way, supplying the true image of the examinee's mental potential. The functions, which the Learning Potential Assessment Device is supposed to measure, are according to Feuerstein (1980, pp. 73, 74) the following.

Within the 'input phase': patterns of perception (stable, organized vs. diffuse, sweeping); exploratory behavior (planned, calm and systematic vs unplanned, impulsive and chaotic); spatial organization and spatial systems of reference; temporal orientation; conservation of size, i.e. shape and quantity constances across variations in certain domains of the perceived object; precision and accuracy in data gathering; capacity of considering two (eventually overlapping) sources of information simultaneously.

Within the 'elaboration phase': adequacy for experiencing the existence of an actual problem and ability to define it; ability to select relevant cues in a problem situation; spontaneous comparative behavior over varying fields of needs; width of the mental field; summative behavior; ability to project virtual relationships; need for logical evidence, as an interactional modality with one's objectal and social environment; interiorization of behavior; planning and execution of inferential-hypothetic thinking and implementation of strategies for hypothesis testing; degree of reality testing and scope of verbal inventory adequate to elaborate vital cognitive categories.

Within the 'output phase': egocentric *vs* socially acceptable communication; the amount of flow and flexibility of general communication (verbal and non-verbal); the degree of impaired verbal communication; precision of communication; adequacy of visual transport; presence of factors, which disturb communication, such as affective outbursts, blockages, anxieties.

It can be seen, that most of these variables belong to the category of Rey's 'automatisms' and 'basic performances'. Thus, in accordance with Rey's methodology, the more elaborative, higher mental functions, i.e. operations on concrete and formal level, are assessed only *after* these *prerequisites* of intellectual functioning have been properly diagnosed. As is convincingly demonstrated by Feuerstein, the core deficits of mental malfunctioning of the disadvantaged adolescents are rooted in these basic functions, meticulously assessed by the Learning Potential Assessment Device.

From the point of view of instrumentation, Feuerstein uses original and modified forms of Rey's tests (Organization of Dots, Memory for Positional Sequences, Plateaux) as well as adaptations of the Raven Matrices and the Grace Arthur Inventory. For details of the rationale, structure and application of the LPAD the interested reader is referred to the original publication (Feuerstein, 1979).

Once having diagnosed the deficient pattern and organization of mental functioning in disadvantaged adolescents, the way was paved to design appropriate rehabilitation methods, turning the rationale of assessment into a rationale of re-education and training, again a principle originally conceived by André Rey (1947).

However, in the context of planning the rehabilitation program, Feuerstein came across another important factor in the etiology of the intellectual-social-personal maladjustment of the disadvantaged pupil, namely the *'proximal social environment'* represented by a 'close', 'proximal' social agent, 'a close educator' in our terminology (see Chapter 2, p. 34). Feuerstein, speaking of 'mediated learning experience' emphasizes, that the child cannot learn to interact adequately with his social and physical environment unless the stimuli, impinging on him are 'mediated', 'interpreted' 'selected' 'tuned' and 'scheduled' by a close social agent, which of course in normal development, are the parents, especially the mother in early infancy. (These processes have been experimentally investigated by Ainsworth and Bell, 1974; Cherry and Eaton, 1977; Gewirtz and Baer, 1958; Tulkin, 1972, and others).

In culturally disadvantaged populations, this mediating function of the proximal social environment is restricted for two main reasons. One is socio-economic stress which reduces the amount of leisure time parents have available to interact with their offspring; talking to them, pointing to salient aspects of the immediate environment and putting relevant aspects of objects and situations into focus. In addition, emotional tensions, frustrations, covert and overt aggressions, conspicuously interfere with the social role of the 'mediator' which requires inner distance, effective control, the overcoming of egocentricity and insight. On the top of these adverse circumstances we encounter the second potent factor disturbing the mediating process. As culturally disadvantaged populations generally represent minorities within a dominant culture, they perceive specific advantage in adapting to the dominant culture at the expense of their culture of origin to the extent of trying to surpress it and to relinquish it. In Feuerstein's formulation:

Through this process, transmission of the past is obstructed . . . In many cases, integration is by no means complete and successful, with consequent accompanying effects of alienation from both cultures, that vary in severity. The obstruction of cultural transmission can become a harsh and even cruel condition for parents to bear as they feel compelled to reject their past to gain acceptance . . .

Such internal tensions, repressions and symptoms of alienation must necessarily have their repercussions on the mother–child relationship.

By rejecting one's own worth as a person, the mother limits her relationship with her child to the fulfillment of his biological needs. Inclination to provide the child with anything beyond his immediate requirements is diminished, if not eliminated. Many such parents openly declare that they are ignorant, illiterate and unskilled people and have nothing to give their children . . . Clearly, such an attitude will have a considerable impact on the self image, identification, socialization and moral cognitive development of the child. (Feuerstein, *op. cit.* p. 39).

   To counteract this socio-pathological process, Feuerstein has delegated to the teachers, assigned to implement the rehabilitation program, special roles as 'mediators' and 'close educators', in addition to being required to master the instruments, rationale and didactics of the method. Firstly, this essentially consists in training the teacher to understand typical mental deficiencies, error patterns, emotional responses, frustrations and defence mechanisms of the pupil. Secondly, the teacher has to accept these problematic reactions with due empathy and respect, so as to be able to create an atmosphere in which pupils can be guided to gain insight by themselves, to understand why they erred, refused to look into themselves, disliked correcting their own mistakes, overlooked pertinent aspects of the task, etc. The teacher is also supposed to induce a process of gradual improvement of the pupil's self-image as well as to set into motion a new feedback circle of success, confidence, curiosity and readiness to encounter the new, unexpected', eventually 'painful' but 'challenging and promising'. Obviously, such 'sensitivity training' is laborious, but it seems to be the essential component in Feuerstein's method of preparing his experimenters, and possibly the central agent of the program.
   The intervention method itself, called Instrumental Enrichment, is presented in form of paper and pencil exercises, which are divided into 'instruments', each focussing on a particular cognitive function. Instruments are graded in difficulty, tasks becoming progressively more complex in their presentation. The exercises are evaluated by the teachers, as well as by the students themselves, and the material can be used for peer teaching. Pupils are also invited to invent exercises by themselves.
   The method as presented in routine use consists of a total of 12 instruments which are divided into two sub-groups, those that are accessible to even illiterate individuals and those that require a relatively proficient level of literacy and verbal comprehension.
   Although certain instruments must be taught first as a pre-

requisite to teach certain other ones, the order of administration can be adapted to the needs of the class.

We shall briefly outline the instruments and their rationale.

1) *Organization of Dots* originally designed by Rey (1953) (this instrument has been described before, see p. 78). This is a 'multipurpose' task, which, as already shown by Rey is related to many functions (Rey, 1968, vol. 2). Feuerstein uses it to train projection of virtual relationships, conservation of constancy, visual transport, precision and accuracy, summative behavior, planning and restraint of impulsivity, discrimination and segregation of proximate elements (Feuerstein, *op. cit.* p. 128 ff). It is generally given at the beginning of the intervention program, because it appears simple, straightforward, and instructions are minimal. On the other hand it is challenging and, as experience has shown, highly motivating. It surely covers a wide spectrum of automatisms, as well as basic performances in the sense of Rey's theory. It sharpens attention and widens the mental field, the more complex items may even require operational thought, as a constant form must be perceived against an increasingly complex and distracting background, in close vicinity to strongly competing stimuli.

2) *Orientation of Space* is an instrument which requires essentially the discrimination of directions; first relative to one's own body and, at more advanced levels, in relation to an external, objective frame of reference, such as a compass. The basic function of spatial orientation in non-verbal as well as in verbal intelligence is well known and needs no further explanation. The peculiarity of Feuerstein's format, based on Piagetian experimental designs, is in the linkage it creates, between spatial orientation and training of logical relationships, intrinsically training reversibility, additivity and transitivity. It thus seems that besides basic skills, operational, and eventually formal thought is stimulated.

3) *Comparisons* are a well-known type of exercise, found in many variations in intelligence and perceptual tests. Essentially, the subject is required to discover tiny, often hidden details which discriminate between two adjacently presented forms of pictures. However, Feuerstein has extended the scope of this instrument, originally used to assess 'perceptual automatisms', in order to train

visual-spatial classifications and categorizations, by virtue of giving instructions to formulate the criteria of comparison and by prescribing the categories to be used as criteria of discrimination.

4) *Categorization* based on the preceding instrument is an exercise in abstraction of visually presented objects or pictures. Criteria of categorization vary from elementary ones such as color, size, direction, to complex dimensions, such as characteristics of animal species, and aspects of social activities. This instrument should provide a convenient bridge to pass from visual-spatial to verbal abstraction, but as well be discussed later, the transfer to verbal intelligence, supposed to be stimulated by such tasks, appears to be weak.

5) *Analytic Perception.* This instrument includes tasks requiring articulation of a given field, detach a detail from its context, or in inverse direction, compose a whole from its components. Essentially these are exercises which train field independency, based on the principle of the well known tests of mosaics and embedded figures.

6) *Family Relations.* These teaching units define family relationships, starting with simple ones and ending with highly complex, multi-dimensional 'family trees'. The rationale of these tasks is the training of operational thought in the context of an assumedly 'familiar' situation, although the complex items are surely highly unfamiliar as well as improbable in everyday life. The format of these tasks gives ample opportunity to elucidate and to manipulate reversible and reciprocal relationships, as well as their combinations. These are thus tasks covering a wide range of concrete and formal operations at various degrees of difficulty.

7) *Temporal Relations* is a rather pragmatic series of exercises used to train time orientation in everyday situations. Simple and complex temporal relationships are presented, and pupils are asked for solutions, explanations and comments. At some point, two temporal sequences have to be compared as to their inter-dependence, and the notion of casuality is evoked.

8) *Numerical Progressions.* These are well-known exercises to extrapolate or to interpolate numerical progressions, which may be one-dimensional, two-dimensional, involve identical, inverted or different types of arithmetic operations, etc. As different relationships (eventually in divergent directions) must be conceived simul-

taneously, and rules must be found by induction, these exercises, besides being a good training ground for basic arithmetic skills, are closely linked to processes of formal reasoning in numerical contexts.

9) *Instructions* are described by Feuerstein as 'one of the few instruments in which verbal factors play an important and central position'. This straightforward and efficient instrument is intended to train the understanding of verbal instructions related to the manipulations of visual-spatial elements. An example: 'Draw a square and inside it a circle. Draw a line connecting the mid point of the baseline of the square with the centre of the circle'. Exercises on such principles were originally designed by Rey (1967, Vol. 1). It is evident, that besides the verbal function, visual-spatial imagination and orientation is strongly involved in these tasks.

10) *Illustrations* consist in the presentation of humorous, in part absurd, short picture series intended 'to produce in the learner an awareness of the existence of a problem, leading to the disruption of equilibrium and a search for a solution'. The value of this instrument is its highly motivating effect and proximity to 'real life situations', an element which generally is not given high priority in Feuerstein's program. As reported by the author, this instrument evokes vivid discussions and associations with the pupils' own experiences.

11) *Representative Stencil Design* is an adaptation of Arthur's Stencil Design (1930), used as a training device.

The learner must construct mentally, *not* through motor manipulation, a design that is identical to that in a colored standard. Colored stencils, some of which are solid and some of which are cut out, are printed on a poster and the student recreates the given design by referring to the stencils that must be used and specifying the order in which they must be mentally superimposed on each other. (Feuerstein, *op. cit.* p. 238.)

If, instead of stencils, solid three-dimensional objects were to be used, such as in Rey's block constructions (see p. 80) this would be an excellent exercise in 'practical intelligence', with a wide range of difficulty, from sensori-motor up to formal operational level. Feuerstein, by using abstract forms, puts the emphasis on internalized manipulation of complex visual-spatial relationships, requiring in addition, varying degrees of memorizing sequences of spatial positions. Thus, without using the potential of its downwards extension, this instrument becomes necessarily one of the most difficult tasks of the program.

12) *Syllogisms and Transitive Relations* are classical exercises in formal thought and manipulation of sets, and need no further explanations.

The structure and format of the items is clear and attractive. Some of them are presented figuratively, using circles to symbolize sets, and some are based on the classification of geometrical forms.

This set of 12 instruments, as already stated is routinely used in the context of a two year curriculum, three to four lessons per week and does not include some other instruments such as Absurdities, Analogies, Convergent and Divergent Thinking, Language and Symbolic Comprehension, Maps, Auditory and Haptic Discrimination (Feuerstein, *op. cit*, p. 126). The whole set is purposefully 'biased', so as to be optimally 'content free'. That is to say, according to Feuerstein's approach, the main objective of his method is to train higher mental *structures*, assuming that once a structure is established it will not only assimilate contents but also will increasingly accumulate and organize knowledge, intrinsically inducing a process of self-propelling mental growth. This process should be manifest not only in a significant superiority of 'experimental' over 'control' groups at the end of the intervention period, but in an *increasing* discrepancy in mental level between the two, throughout the *post-experimental period*; this in part has been demonstrated by Feuerstein's two years follow up (Feuerstein, *op. cit.* p. 371 ff; Feuerstein *et al.* 1979). However, the author takes the somewhat extreme position, that exposing the learner to *content saturated material* will interfere with the acquisition of structures. 'It is when cognitive processes become *detached* from · specific tasks, that cognitive structure develops' (italics ours) (*op. cit.* p. 11). This interference is assumedly more pronounced in the disadvantaged, as their style of life is 'externalized', i.e. 'stimulus bound' and thus their mental activity is easily distracted, if not absorbed by the 'given', 'immediate', and 'haveable' (Frankenstein, 1968).

Inspection of the Instrumental Enrichment Program will reveal another 'purposeful' bias, which is the over-emphasis on instruments intended to train visual-spatial relations and formal reasoning, or in other words higher mental activities (including formal reasoning) in the context of visual-spatial relations. Tasks which stimulate verbal intelligence, verbal abstraction, language development, etc., are conspicuously under-represented. (Instructions, Illustrations, and Syllogisms stimulate verbal functions but even here, visual-spatial organization is involved in many items.)

It is thus not surprising that systematic evaluation and follow up reveals experimental effects which are predominantly manifest in tests of visual-spatial representations. 'F'-ratios of experimental differences on the PMA subtests (Thurstone's Primary Mental Ability Test, Thurstone, 1962) in descending order are as follows: Spatial Relations (22.02), Numbers (15.34), Addition (4.32), Figure Grouping (3.79), Vocabulary, Pictures, Word Grouping, Perceptual Speed (NS). The five other tests, on which conspicuous experimental effects have been obtained were: Terman Non-Verbal Intelligence (*viz. op. cit.* p. 355), the D-48 Test (Gough and Domino, 1963) the latter being based on complex spatial relations, i.e. analogies and progression in relationships among dominoes; the Embedded Figures (Witkin, 1950); the Postures tests, a non-timed group test of spatial orientation (Finch, 1957); and the Human Figure Drawing. All these, except the last one, explicitly measure higher mental functions operating in visual-spatial contexts (*op. cit.* pp. 358 ff).

Experimental effects on scholastic achievement scores are limited to Bible and *Geometry*.

Impressive long range effects have been obtained on the General Army Intelligence Screening Test, the 'Dapar'. However, this test consists essentially of two equally represented parts, a modified form of the Raven Matrix, i.e. a test of visual-spatial analogies, and an Otis-like verbal Intelligence Test. Unfortunately no separate results on these two parts have been reported by the authors, but in the light of the absence of long term effects on the Hebrew Language Development Test (*op. cit.* p. 375) we must suspect, that the experimental effects on the 'Dapar' are produced by the Raven component, unless disproved by differential data analysis.

Feuerstein is conscious of the function specific effects of his experimental program, which is in consonance with his preconceived design to eliminate content and de-emphasize stimulation of verbal intelligence. As formulated by himself:

The present lack of emphasis on linguistic functions is reflected in the data obtained from the experimental groups throughout the four years period, for which data are presently available. The experimental program did not produce a significant . . . experimental difference . . . on the PMA verbal factor, and experimental subjects were significantly lower than the controls on the army test of language development. This is contrasted with the superior performance of the experimentals in virtually all of the intellect-related areas emphasized in the Instrumental Enrichment Program [i.e. formal reasoning in visual-spatial context.] This differential-efficiency of the program indicates that modifiability in Instrumental Enrichment, even though it is generalized over a variety of cognitive functions, is confronted with a specific resistance in the area of verbal functioning that may need to be treated as a *content* (author's italics) of cognitive behavior and therefore given specialized and focussed training in order to be modified. (*op. cit.* p. 394).

Research on such lines is under way, and hopefully positive results may be expected.

Meanwhile it is evident, that language development (including verbal abstraction) and formal reasoning are two distinct higher mental functions, the former being the more severely impaired in disadvantaged populations. Another point which should not be lost sight of is the effect of the Instrumental Enrichment on over-all adjustment as manifest in Classroom Participation (*op. cit.* p. 364). This supports the rationale of rehabilitation programs for the disadvantaged adolescents (and possibly also a basic hypothesis on adolescent personality development) namely that cognitive functions are primary determinants of adolescent emotional and social development, independent of, or in addition to, defence mechanisms, ego conflicts and peer group pressures. Consequently, stimulation of cognitive functions is the *via regia* to re-educate disadvantaged mid- and post-adolescents. Also, it should not be forgotten that Feuerstein's method is not so much focussed on the 'what', i.e. the format and design of the Instruments, which are to a large extent sophisticated modifications of devices already used before as psychodiagnostic tools, but on the 'how' i.e. his technique for stimulating the adolescent's insight, to analyze his errors, attitudes and prejudices and to correct his overall percep-tion of the physical and social environment. Here, the central role of the 'close educator' or 'modificator' must again be emphasized, which might be the true crucial determinant of the overall im-pressive success of the Instrumental Enrichment program.

CHAPTER 10

Frankenstein's Model of Rehabilitative Teaching

Frankenstein's model of Rehabilitative Teaching is based, on the one hand, on his psychodynamic theory of intelligence, described before (Chapter 5, p. 83) and, on the other hand, on extensive empirical evidence gathered by the application of his methods and didactics in numerous Elementary, Junior and Senior High Schools as well as in Vocational Training Centres with predominantly disadvantaged populations throughout the country (Frankenstein, 1979). The rationale of his system is the assumption that the majority of disadvantaged pupils suffer from 'secondary retardation', caused by a configuration of adverse environmental stress and pressure leading to a specific distortion of ego development, defined as externalization under conditions of socio-cultural deprivation (see p. 84). The important point in Frankenstein's *educational* approach to 'secondary mental retardation' is his belief, that it is largely and eventually totally reversible at all developmental stages, including post-adolescence. In contrast, he considers primary mental retardation, caused by genetic, and constitutional (i.e. pre-, peri- and post-natal) factors, as well as by CNS damage, as essentially irreversible, mainly because in such cases mental structures are irreparably impaired, while remaining generally intact in the secondarily retarded. He admits, that in practice it is difficult to draw a sharp demarcation line between these two types of retarded populations, and even in a 'homogenous class' of secondarily retarded, some primarily retarded will infiltrate. From a pedagogical point of view this must be taken into account and should in principle not be an obstacle to applying the specific re-educational methods, which Frankenstein has designed. Of course, most if not all classes for the disadvantaged will have a mixture not only of primarily retarded, but also of

133

normally intelligent, as well as of emotionally disturbed cases, a problem with which each teacher working in this field will have to cope irrespective of his pedagogical approach.

While being aware of the heterogenous composition of disadvantaged classes, Frankenstein views pupils with *secondary retardation* as the target population of his method, which seems justified as in any random sample of disadvantaged the latter will be the majority. He summarizes the characteristics of this type of intellectual inadequacy as follows (*op. cit.* p. 18):

1) *Insufficient differentiation* between essential and accidental properties of given objects or situations.

2) A tendency to *identify similarity with identity* and dissimilarity with 'otherness'.

3) *An incapacity to differentiate ambivalent and ambiguous aspects* of a problem and intermediate values of events and facts i.e. everything is absolute, either black or white, good or evil. Dichotomization is thus the preferred mode for organizing the universe of stimuli. This lack of differentiation leads in turn to the 'illusion of knowing absolute truth and value', generally by accepting and immitating stereotypes of the culturally different reference group of origin.

4) *Weakness of responsibility,* i.e. the incapacity to understand the function of man as a subject, actively shaping his environment, as distinct from the physical object, which moves and changes within a network of cause-effect relationships at various degrees of predictability, and as different from the vegetative and animal world, governed by laws of biological growth and by mechanisms of instincts, respectively. In a similar vein, the differences between intended and hazardous acts or events cannot be appreciated and evaluated. As an indirect consequence, the secondarily retarded child does not feel responsible for his acts of thinking and learning, and thus manifests an overdependence on authority in general, and teacher's authority in particular. This dependence, however, does not mean acceptance of the value system represented by such authority, but essentially an ad hoc conformity with externally perceived opinions. Another consequence of weak responsibility is the general reluctance to recognize objective rules and laws (implicitly evoked by higher mental processes) because they imply

commitment, abandonment of cherished beliefs, undermining of entrenched value systems and incompatibility with egocentric attitudes.

5) *Inability to separate* emotional and *cognitive processes,* a phenomenon defined by Frankenstein as 'contamination'. This means essentially, that the disadvantaged 'secondarily retarded' pupil often reacts to apparently 'neutral' contents of learning with irrelevant associations, rooted in his personal experience or emotional involvement in the problem, represented by the concept or topic to be learned. This affective interference with the learning process can take various forms. Besides being manifest in distortions and misinterpretations the pupil can block, i.e. be unable to respond, he may loose interest in the material altogether, or may respond with outbursts of rage, verbal aggression and general disruptive behavior.

6) *Concretistic thinking,* which means a preference for thinking in terms of examples instead of concepts, for clinging to the immediately available stimulus or its close, concrete association, instead of making an effort (or to have the courage) for abandoning the immediately 'given' (albeit secure), for the possible flexible and potentially 'rewarding' which obviously is only probable. Concretistic thinking necessarily restricts future time perspective and involves fixation to the present, eventually to the past.

7) Finally, secondary retardation is characterized by *'the difficulty to understand symbols,* analogies, metaphors, personifications and similar forms of indirect expression of meaning' (*op. cit.* p. 26). This weakness is a direct result of the disadvantaged's deeply entrenched belief, that only what is real and palpable is true. Any divergence from describing reality in concrete matter-of-fact style and format is typically considered by secondarily retarded pupils 'as a lie'.†

Overviewing the 'clinical picture' of the 'secondary retardation syndrome' it can be seen that Frankenstein adheres consistently to his basic approach (outlined in Chapter 5) that ego and intellect cannot be divorced and must be treated as one entity in psycho-

---

†Frankenstein reports one pupil criticizing poets for 'not writing like reporters in the newspapers.' (*op. cit.* p. 171).

logical theory as well as in educational practice. However, it must also be emphasized that the inadequacy of the ego in the externalized style of life under conditions of socio-cultural deprivation, to cope with flexible stimulus continua, ambiguous situations, commitments to laws, affective pressures, events of low probability, secondary symbol systems, etc., intrinsically inhibits the development of language, which is manifest in an impoverished vocabulary, deficient abstraction ability and concept formation, poorly elaborated syntax, difficulty in grasping implied meaning, lack of precision in decoding and encoding verbal communication, etc. In other words, Frankenstein uncovers the psychodynamic sources of the *notorious retardation in verbal intelligence* which has been unanimously established by all authors dealing with socio-culturally deprived populations. As verbal intelligence is the precondition of all academic studies at Junior and Senior High School level, the failure of disadvantaged adolescents and post-adolescents to cope with the curriculum of these institutions must be viewed as the direct consequence of this intellectual handicap.

Frankenstein thus sees in the fostering of differentiation, abstraction, concept formation, affective decontamination, understanding of metaphorical meaning, etc., through the medium of *linguistic communication* in the regular classroom, the *via regia* to rehabilitate the cognitive deficiency and implicitly to create an internalized style of life in disadvantaged adolescents. He proposes to delay the stimulation of 'formal reasoning' to the later phases of the rehabilitation process, i.e. at post-adolescence, unless it develops spontaneously under the impact of developing mental differentiation involving detachment from concrete content. He thus recommends postponing science teaching (closely linked to formal thought) to the last years of secondary school and 'to use the abstractive abilities developed in the meantime with the help of primarily humanistic subject matter to learn scientific thinking' (*op. cit.* p. 81).

Frankenstein attacks the cognitive sequelae of externalization described above by engaging the teacher as central agent of the rehabilitation process, mobilizing his personality, i.e. his knowledge, intuition, empathy, abstraction ability and of course his skill for employing a clear but sometimes elaborate language in order to develop the deficient mental skills of the disadvantaged 'secondly retarded' pupil by means of what may be defined as a 'classroom dialogue'. Frankenstein purposefully avoids the use of pre-designed material, in the form of questionnaires, paper and pencil exercises, audio-visual aids, all types of concretizations, etc. He considers such technical aids at best irrelevant, but eventually also distracting and disturbing the process of internalization. He de-emphasizes the importance of executing the lesson plan, although it is obligatory to prepare it. Instead, three principles of rehabilitative teaching must be rigorously observed:

1) *'Noninductiveness'* is a technique which has been shown to be necessary in order to avoid 'the danger inherent in the method of the inductive teaching' (widely used and recommended in general education) when applied to secondarily retarded pupils, in that it may lead to 'a non-selective question-and-answer game that takes the place of a genuine and well organized class discussion'.

Instead, non-inductive teaching implies that:

The teacher must know how to pose his questions as *meaningfully* and as *intentionally* possible (italics ours), when to interrupt the flow of associative answers and when they are irrelevant to the subject under discussion and to his intentions. He must know it by *giving* the correct answer, *formulating* the law or principle as exactly as possible.

At a second phase, he will try to activate the retarded pupil's initiative by asking questions such as:

Why was my answer formulated as it was? What would have been wrong with it, had I formulated it differently? Why was the answer suggested by me more exact than some suggested by you? Which data and phenomena are covered by the suggested law or principle etc. (*op. cit.* p. 33).

That is to say, the principle of non-inductiveness provides a firm framework (without creating a rigid structure) which stimulates the pupil to respond in a pre-designed direction planned by the teacher, and gives him a feeling of security, that he is led by a competent, knowledgeable interpreter who neither pretends to be all knowing, nor pretends to be ignorant, both of which are equally frustrating to the pupil.

2) The second principle is *branching* which actually means first of all, an openness of the teacher to 'branch off' in an initially non-planned direction, following an association, comment, re-

pressed wish or uncontrolled outburst on the part of a single or several pupils, evoked by the presented teaching material. That is to say, the teacher, after careful reflection and with due foresight, focusses on another problem or topic, which he feels the pupils push hard to clarify. On the other hand, the purpose of branching off is also to put a certain concept or topic into a different context, in order to clarify an erroneous attitude, or explain its additional, different or, for the pupil, new connotation when used in the frame of reference of a different discipline, different situation or a different purpose. This is especially true for concepts, which have been used traditionally in a certain concrete or symbolic sense, and then taken over by modern technology to serve as a scientific concept. A case in point is 'channel' in its original sense, as compared with its meaning in information theory.

3) The third principle is *Neutralizing Affective Reactions*, which means essentially that the teacher is ready to accept an affective reaction on the part of the pupil, that interferes with his thinking, and hereafter attempts, to calm his irritation by providing an appropriate association, eventually by 'branching off' to another, less emotionally loaded theme. It must be emphasized that the teacher is not supposed to provide an *interpretation* of the personal meaning of the 'explosive' topic, in the sense of a psycho-therapeutic intervention. (This is eventually the task of the social worker, as will be discussed later.) Neutralizing thus remains strictly on the level of conscious intellectual information processing with clearly defined educational-cultural goals.

To exemplify the three principles of rehabilitative teaching, we shall cite a series of biology lessons on the topic of 'blood circulation', given at the tenth grade of a senior High School (age 16), as reported by Frankenstein (*op. cit.* p. 203). The topic was presented *non-inductively*, by explaining in a directive and planned way the dynamics of the physiology of blood circulation. However very soon, emotionally laden questions poured in. Some of them were related to the 'quantity of blood' and the 'amount of blood which can be lost without dying'. Others related directly to death, the use of blood plasms in emergency situations, etc. Another array of questions was associated with anthropological-cultural issues, such as 'blood-relationship' and 'blood feud'. The biology teacher was aware that without branching off into medicine (calling upon the school physician to explain the various causes of dying, loss of blood being only one among many and not the most probable) and into anthropology (by transferring the discussion about blood feud and blood relationships to the history teacher), he will be unable to proceed to teach the 'science' aspects of the topic. Obviously, the branching off technique is here inextricably interwoven with neutralizing the 'affects'.

It can be seen that the teacher-pupil dialogue guided by teacher's insight into the *dynamics* of his pupil's associations, while always *remaining within the frame of reference of the subject matter and the curriculum*, is the core of Frankenstein's method. It also is evident why textbooks and exercises are of little relevance as the crucial determinant of the program's success remains the teacher's initiative, wisdom and flexibility. The most important *technique* of the method, which is inherent in all the three principles described before, is confrontation and comparison in order to find *differences, nuances, points of similarity* and *divergences*, not in the *external form* of the stimulus (such as required by tests of comparing details of two very similar pictures) but between the deeper meaning and refined connotations of *situations or constellations of events*.

In order to focus on the 'depth structure' of the various acts of differentiation, Frankenstein recommends abstaining from 'concretisations', 'illustrations' and all kinds of game-like activities as well as programmed teaching. This approach puts his method in striking contrast to widely used programs of 'remediation' and 'compensatory education' based on such techniques.

However, counteracting the vicious circle of externalization and cognitive stagnation by means of the 'teacher centered' rehabilitative teaching method is not enough. It is evident that the source of the externalized style of life is the inadequate interaction between the child and his parents, starting in infancy and continuing through childhood and adolescence with variations in intensity, scope and patterning. At adolescence, as discussed before, the relationship with parents passes critical phases of temporary alienation and reconciliation, leading finally to the recognition of the parent as an adult partner (see p. 29)

Under conditions of externalization the relationship between adolescent and parent becomes a source of tension and conflict in a sense which is essentially different from the middle-class pattern. Instead of 'revolting', the disadvantaged adolescent, now being intellectually able to evaluate the parent, will be 'ashamed' of him — an attitude which in Frankenstein's opinion jeopardizes his thinking and learning process, as it produces an inner tension between viewing his parent as 'primitive' and incompatible with his growing internalized value system, but also as part of his past which he cannot delete. There is yet another aspect of the parent-adolescent relationship, i.e. the attitude of the parents towards the adolescent's striving for higher education, and emancipation. Especially in the case of disadvantaged girls, parents might overtly or covertly discourage her from a professional career, not to speak of the fact that they need her as domestic aid, which in fact interferes with her studies.

Rehabilitation of the parent-adolescent relationship is thus one of the reasons why Frankenstein has introduced into his program the *social worker*, especially trained for the purpose of such intervention. It is him who complements the teacher, as he takes over the responsibility for the alleviation of tensions produced by the intellectual interpretations of social relationships in the classroom, in that he deals directly with the real social conflicts within the triangle, parent-teacher-adolescent. In addition, the social worker attempts to approach the inner, personal problems of pupil and parent, which might have been evoked by the rehabilitative curriculum but from the point of view of the teacher's function had to remain within the context of the teaching process. In line with this role division, it will be the social worker who also will be in charge of sex education, vocational counselling and preparation for final examinations as well as admission procedures for Higher Education. He will also work through periods of crisis precipitated by examination failure. Another assignment of the social worker is to assist the teacher in coping with his (her) individual problems, which naturally arise in the tension and conflict laden atmosphere generated by the intensive teacher-pupil interaction. The social worker will also help the teacher to plan those phases of the rehabilitation process which require cooperation and coordination between more than one teacher, as exemplified above in the case of teaching the lessons on blood circulation.

Finally, it is the task of the social worker to deal with the more deviant psychopathological cases, which show up in each classroom for the disadvantaged, namely psychotic borderline cases (see p. 43) and severe behavior disorders.

The integration of special education and social work centered around the depth dynamics of the cognitive processes in disadvantaged adolescents is without doubt an original and most valuable contribution to the understanding of the rehabilitation process of these age groups. It seems to consist in the employment of an efficient combination of 'close educator' and 'family therapist' which surely is worthwhile trying out in other settings.

Frankenstein's method seems to complement, to some extent, that of Feuerstein, although except for the central role of the 'close educator', the rationales of the two models are quite different. It appears that Frankenstein deals with the more critical component of the culturally disadvantaged post-adolescent's mental retardation, namely the impairment of ego functions under conditions of externalization, which primarily affect language development and verbal intelligence. Unfortunately, Frankenstein has never attempted to evaluate his experimental effects statistically, so that the impact of his techniques on measured verbal intelligence could be compared to Feuerstein's negative findings.

Still, Frankenstein's method has yielded impressive results in a systematically evaluated study carried out at the Hebrew University Secondary School, which is briefly described below. (See Frankenstein, 1979.)

The aim of the study was to explore the possibility of raising the mental abilities of disadvantaged adolescents to the level of academic High School graduates, given the fact, that the majority of the disadvantaged enrolled in academic High Schools tend to drop out before graduating, and among those who stay until the end of their studies, a considerable percentage fail to pass the matriculation examinations.

The experiment was carried out twice in close succession (1966, 1967). Each time a group of 60 disadvantaged adolescents was selected out of a three to four times larger sample of elementary school graduates considered by their principals as eligible for academic High School studies. The criteria of selection were the following: intelligence level within normal range excluding subjects with IQ under 83 as well as above 107; border-line retarded *as well as 'gifted'* were thus not included. The Excluded also were pathological cases, pupils from broken homes, and those whose parents were either totally uninterested in the future of their children as well as those whose parents were overambitious to have their youngsters graduate from academic High School. Background conditions were typical for disadvantaged populations i.e. 88% of the families lived in bad and overcrowded homes, 85% had three or more children, 97% of the mothers and 62% of the fathers had only eight years of education or less, 64% of the families suffered from economic stress. Each selected group of 60 adolescents was randomly divided into two subgroups consisting of 30 experimentals and 30 controls. Experimentals enrolled in the Hebrew University Secondary School, one of the 'high prestige' Senior High Schools in Jerusalem, and were exposed for four consecutive years (grades 9-12) to the Rehabilitative Teaching Program described before; Controls entered other academic High Schools without being involved in any intervention or enrichment program. Results were as follows: In the first experiment 29 out of 30 experimentals stayed until the end of the 12th grade and took the matriculation examinations, as against 10 out of 30 in the control group (p = .001). In the second experiment, 24 out of 30 experimentals completed their High School studies, the exact proportion of controls who reached the 12th grade being unknown, but estimated to be not larger than in the first control group. In the first experiment, 20 out of 29 experimentals passed completely, and eight out the 29 passed partially the matriculation examination, all the 28 out of the 29 being eligible for University studies, as against seven out of 10 controls (difference not significant). In the second experiment, 10 experimentals graduated fully, and 11 partially, (i.e. 21 out of 24 were eligible for University career), the proportion of graduating controls of the second study again not being exactly reported, but known to be smaller than in the first experiment (*op. cit.* and Frankenstein, personal communication).

It has to be pointed out, that, according to the original design, experimentals were taught in separate classes, i.e. in a non-integrated setting. However, they participated in various extra-curricular and artistic activities of the High School together with the regular students.

Although after the second year of the experiment they were given the option to continue their studies in 'integrated' classes, they preferred to remain segregated.

Controls, on the other hand, were all absorbed individually or in small groups in the regular classes of the various academic High Schools in which they had been enrolled; they were so to speak formally 'intergrated'.

Thus, the experiment might as well be considered to have tested the hypothesis, that putting disadvantaged High School students into a normal class — a situation which Frankenstein prefers to define as 'pluralistic' and not 'integrative' — is less effective than segregation supported by an appropriate rehabilitation program. Frankenstein summarizes his overall experiences in respect to the integration-segregation issue as follows:

Homogeneous classes proved to be more suitable than heterogeneous classes for preparing secondarily retarded pupils to continue their studies in mixed groups, at the high school or the university levels. The seeming success of so-called integrational classes (if it was achieved) could be observed more clearly in the lower than in the higher grades, in technical more than in academic high schools, in rural more than urban areas.

To the extent that changes took place in the cognitive and the social behavior of the underprivileged children within mixed groups, they were accompanied in almost every case by a feeling of inferiority, which, in turn, seemed to be responsible for frequently emerging and undesirable strong tendencies to imitate the 'privileged'. Such tendencies are a negative indication of seeming success only. They are observed more frequently in younger than in older age groups, and they coexist with opposite feelings, feelings of being discriminated against, of resentment (*op. cit.* p. 86).

Obviously, it would be worthwhile to replicate Frankenstein's experiment using a 2 x 2 analysis of variance design which would test separately effects of segregation and effects of intervention, as well as their interaction.

It would also be of interest to measure experimental effects on verbal intelligence, moral judgement, self-image, achievement need, parent-pupil and pupil-parent evaluation.

Meanwhile Frankenstein's method appears to be effective, given that suitable personnel, i.e. educators and social workers, are available, professional guidance ensured and the target population within the range of normal or lower range of normal intelligence.

However, there is no doubt that the method can be extended downwards, and be adapted to groups of lower mental levels among the disadvantaged, although systematic research in this direction has not yet been carried out.

CHAPTER 11

Smilansky's Boarding School Fostering Program

This rehabilitation program of selective groups of 'gifted' pupils initiated by Smilansky in 1961, is hitherto the best systematically evaluated study on the rehabilitation of disadvantaged post-adolescents in Israel. Findings are based on a country-wide, representative sample, on reliable criteria and on adequate control groups, and include follow up data after 10 years. The study has been recently published in detail (Smilansky and Nevo, 1979), so that we shall highlight only its most important and original aspects.

The impetus for the design and implementation of this program was the fact that at the time of its planning only 8.6% of disadvantaged elementary school eighth graders were eligible for academic high school (as determined by the Eighth Grade Screening Examinations)† while their representation in the total school population was over 50%. Out of these, only 37% reached the 12th grade (63% dropping out) and only 27.5% passed high school matriculation examinations, i.e. the percentage of high school graduates among the disadvantaged was about 2.2%. This was in contrast with 39% of normal youth being accepted in academic high schools, out of whom 55% graduated, their percentage of graduation being then ten times higher (22.5%) (Smilansky, 1966).

The target population, as already stated, were 'gifted' disadvantaged adolescents who were operationally defined as disadvantaged pupils scoring above the 30 percentile of the Eighth

---

†The 'Eighth Grade Screening Examination' was a procedure, routinely in use in Israel throughout the years 1955–1972 with the purpose of determining the eligibility for academic high school studies among the total population of Eighth Graders, i.e. the total population of elementary school graduates at that time (Ortar, 1960).

Grade Screening Examinations, which was the cut-off point of eligibility for academic High School.†

The rationale of the program was as follows:

1) The low scholastic achievements and high percentage of failure at academic high school should not be regarded as indicative of limited potential ability.

2) Although due importance should be given to directed fostering from early childhood, it is not too late to induce change at later ages.

3) Adolescence (i.e. ages 14–18 which is actually post-adolescence) is a particularly suitable time for fostering resocialization activities because it is a period of crisis; its directed intensification and exploitation may offer the prospect of meaningful change.

4) In order to 'intensify the crisis' the fostering program recommended that the adolescents should be brought to a new environment apart from their home communities and placed in selective, socially heterogeneous learning groups, i.e. in boarding schools, where they would be co-educated with normal, local middle-class high school students, who would attend the same classes on a day-school basis.

Such an arrangement, 'presenting the disadvantaged with intellectual challenges in schools with high academic requirements, placing them with adolescents of middle-class origin and supporting them to assume the role of gifted and non disadvantaged, is a directed experiment in the use of 'crisis' as positive learning experience'.

It is evident that the crucial point of the program is the separation of the post-adolescent from his disadvantaged home, an idea

---

†After the program had been run in, a more complex and efficient screening procedure was introduced, consisting essentially of a battery of three tests, namely the MILTA Verbal Intelligence Test (Ortar and Murieli, 1965), The Minnesota Formboard and a Standard Achievement Test in Arithmetics. In addition, candidates for the program were screened by personal interviews, excluding essentially cases of psychopathology (but not families on welfare), as well as subjects whose relatively well to do socio-economic status would make them not eligible for a scholarship under conditions defined as socio-cultural disadvantage (Marbach and Zahavi, 1980).

which raised strong objections among administrators including headmasters of schools, as well as among psychologists. The main contentions were three:

1) the removal of the more gifted children from certain disadvantaged communities would lead to a decline in standards of local secondary schools.

2) the fear that separation from the family and home environment would have a destructive psychological effect and cut the children off their families.

3) the high costs involved in the maintenance of boarding institutions.

The four counter-arguments were the following:

1) During adolescence such separation might have a favorable effect in strengthening personal autonomy and shape better relations with parents, provided that the separation is based on positive, mutually agreed goals (in this context we refer to the developmental patterns of healthy parent-adolescent relationships, described in Chapter 2, p. 28).

2) The boarding home is designed to promote success and is thus likely to have a beneficial impact on the home community through increased motivation for peers and younger siblings.

3) Post-adolescence is essentially an age period which gradually leads to a life distant from the family of origin, be it for studies, army service, travel, etc (see Chapter 2, p. 37 'the life task of extential expansion').

4) Finally, the argument that boarding school placement might evoke in these age groups 'separation anxiety' is irrelevant, as this phenomenon is typical for much younger ages, i.e. infancy and early childhood. It must also be noted, that the adolescents were in no way 'separated' from their parents in the strict sense, neither psychologically, nor geographically. They went home for long weekends every three weeks, as well as during vacations. On the other hand, parents visited regularily, and social workers and educators kept close contact with the family. It must be added, that geographical distances in Israel are small, and even far points can be reached within two to three hours of bus travel.

The second important aspect of this project is the co-education of 'the gifted' disadvantaged and normal middle-class high school students, at school as well as during various extra-curricular activities. Boarding school life, on the other hand, was essentially 'segregated'. Sociometric evaluation revealed that there was a considerable correlation between sociometric status at school (determined by the 'mixed population' class) and at the boarding school (determined by the ethnic reference group) indicating that the boarding (disadvantaged) students did not lose status while sharing a class with students of higher socioeconomic background. On the other hand, there was a clear tendency in both the disadvantaged and the middle-class groups to prefer in-group social relationships, a tendency which persisted although it became weaker towards the final grade.

After about 18 cohorts have been exposed to the program since its inception in 1961, it can be stated by now that this type of integration did not produce tension, hostility between the groups, resentment of feelings of inferiority or frustration. On the contrary, in view of the impressive impact of the project on scholastic achievements (which will be reported later) it must be asked, whether the 'co-education' (or 'integration') was not a crucial factor of the program's success. (This is hard to decide, as the factor of 'integration' could not be controlled by an appropriate control group.)

The 'enrichment program' in the restricted sense consisted in the following activities:

1) *Auxiliary lessons.* These were given in preparatory summer camps, as well as during the scholastic year.

2) *Extra-curriculum courses*† in music, sculpture, drawing, drama, psychology, astronomy, folklore, etc., were provided in abundance.

3) *Social group activities*, consisting in weekly meetings of

---

†The following extra-curricular activities were offered in the Jerusalem Boyer Boarding School in 1980: Drama, dance, listening to music, psychology, wood crafts, drawing, yoga, chess, aviation, scouting, sport of all types. Seminars on the 'Quality of Life', on 'Oriental Studies' and on the 'Holocaust'. Lectures on Middle East Problems and Smoking.

small groups with a group instructor, dedicated to discussion of politics, adolescent problems, etc.

4) *Self Government.* Students were encouraged to elect representatives to student councils and committees dealing with various aspects of their life at the boarding school.

5) *Voluntary activities*,† which consisted in sending the boarders to tutor elementary school children in an immigrant quarter, to do volunteer work for the fire brigade, to help blind and invalid people, etc.

It needs not be emphasized, that the program provided guidance and counselling, and that again 'close educators' in the form of devoted headmasters, teachers and group leaders played an important role.

The results of a comprehensive evaluation study of the 1966 cohort including a 10 year follow up, are convincing. In order to view the findings in correct perspective, some baseline data will briefly cited. Although the experimental population was considered to be 'gifted', 40% had a manifest IQ below 100 at the initial examinations, as assessed by the MILTA (a Hebrew version of the Lorge-Thorndike test constructed by Ortar and Murieli, 1965). Only 23% scored above 110. Background variables of experimental and control groups were as follows: 75% of fathers had elementary education or less, 63% of them were either unemployed, unskilled or semiskilled workers, 77% of families had four children or more.

The major findings can be summarized as follows. *The drop-out rate* of the experimental group was 26%, conspicuously lower than that in other secondary and high school settings with similar

---

†List of voluntary activities carried out by pupils of the Jerusalem Boyer Boarding School during the scholastic year 1980/81: 1) Active participation in educational and recreational programs offered to inpatients in the Hadassah Hospital. 2) Tutoring physically handicapped children and adolescents in the Hospital for Spastic Children, Alyn. 3) After taking courses in First Aid, active duty as nursing assistants at the Central First Aid Station in Jerusalem. 4) Tutoring elementary school children with learning disabilities. 5) Searching for and locating old people in the community who are in urgent need of help and social assistance. 6) Assistance in the maintenance of Jerusalem's Botanic Gardens. (Information based on personal communication, Tsvi Gal'On, Director, Boyer Boarding School, Jerusalem.)

populations, where drop-out rates ranged from 38 to 67%.

Success at matriculation examinations was 87%, somewhat higher than the success rate of the middle-class classmates, which was 83%. However, the more pertinent findings was the success of the experimentals when evaluated within ability ranges, as measured by the IQ level. Within the IQ level ranges below 89, 53% of the experimental completed 12 grades as against 22% of controls; 32% succeeded at the matriculation examinations as against 13% of the controls. Within IQ level range 90–99, 86% experimentals completed 12 grades as against 49% of the controls, and 66% graduated as against 38% of the controls. (All differences significant beyond the .05 level). Above the IQ level of 100, these differences vanished, which actually means, that although the population was defined as 'gifted', those with an intelligence level below 100, i.e. with manifest average and low average intelligence essentially profited from the program. Experimental effects on subjects scoring above 100, on the other hand, were negligible. It may be asked, whether the designation 'gifted' did not serve more the purpose of 'an expectation' than being an objective description of the target population.

The follow up data revealed that 63% of the experimentals studied at a university and 40% held a BA degree in 1971, as against 36% university students and 16% BA graduates in the control group.

A second follow up study on 556 graduates from six boarding schools participating in the fostering program during the years 1964-1973 was carried out in 1977-78 by Marbach and Zahavi (1980). The follow-up questionnaire was returned by 50% of the boys and 40% of the girls, the proportion of the sexes being about equal in the original sample. Background data are again typical for disadvantaged populations, namely:

1) *Father's occupation*: 4% on welfare; 66% unskilled labour; 32% skilled workers; 2% professionals.

2) *Father's education*: 17% no education; 57% elementary education of eight years or less; 26% post-elementary education of nine years and more; 20% no information.

3) *Number of siblings*: Mean = five; 28% of families more than seven; only 15% families of one to two children.

As to level of intelligence as measured by a combined score of the MILTA, Minnesota and Arithmetics Tests (see above), the population of the follow-up sample scored 6.43 stanines (Guilford, 1956) however 7% had stanines under fives, i.e. had intelligence levels in the lower range of 'normality', the normative standard sample being the total population of disadvantaged preselected and referred as candidates for the project of Boarding School Fostering.

Because in Israel, high school students join the Army immediately after graduation, it was of interest to evaluate the military career of the boarding schools graduates.† It turned out that only 7% remained enlisted men, whilst 24% attained the rank of commissioned officers and about 50% the rank of non-commissioned officers. In the light of the extremely stringent standards of the Israeli Army, such a high proportion of military promotion reflects not only intellectual skill, but also emotional steadiness, prosocial conduct, efficient leadership and last but not least, a considerably high level of tolerance of physical and psychological stress.

The academic career of the boarding school graduates is not less impressive. Seventy-eight percent were enroled in universities throughout the country as well as in the Haifa Technological Institute, most of these institutions being of internationally recognized high academic level. The rest studied in teacher colleges, schools of nursing and technological undergraduate courses.

As to the academic status in 1978, 45% were undergraduates, 34% hold BA degrees, 16 were engaged in their graduate studies, 6% had received their MA diploma and 3% (i.e. seven subjects) had been awarded the title of PhD.

Forty-eight were married at the time of the follow up. When asked, whether they would recommend that their siblings should enrol in the program of Boarding School Fostering, 92 replied 'Yes'. Ninety-one percent stated that they had never experienced any discrimination during their involvement in the program.

Smilansky's program is nowadays an integral part of the Israeli high school system. Its undeniable success should, however, not

---

†Reported follow-up data refer to boys, as most girls being religious were exempted from military service.

divert our attention from the fact that its target population is a selected minority among the thousands of disadvantaged post-adolescents, whose educational problems have not yet been solved. It seems, however, that one of the basic principles of Smilansky's method of re-education, separation from the home and the boarding school system (eventually without 'integration') is worthy of replication with 'less gifted' and more extremely disadvantaged and underprivileged youngsters.

CHAPTER 12

The Curriculum of Contextual Learning Units

The Curriculum of Contextual Learning Units (Kohen-Raz and Barl-Lev, 1980) is another attempt to deal with the educational and rehabilitational problems of post-adolescent drop-outs in Israel. It was designed and prepared in part in the context of basic research on the relationships between physiological maturation and development of higher forms of reasoning in disadvantaged adolescents (Kohen-Raz, 1973), in part upon the request of the Ministry of Labour in the light of the failure of all hitherto available teaching programs and curricula to show any palpable effect on the scholastic progress of disadvantaged adolescents placed in Semiskilled Apprentice Schools (see Chapter 3, p. 60) and their motivation to stay and to learn in class during the one day per week allotted to what may be called their 'last chance of scholarization'. In designing and implementing this program, great efforts were invested to take into consideration the psychodynamics of culturally disadvantaged adolescents, as described in Chapter 3, as well as the sources of failure of the regular curriculum to meet their educational needs, as outlined in Chapter 8.

Thus, the Curriculum of Contextual Learning Units was based on the following principles:

1) The method was supposed to differ from the routine teaching programs in form and content, the traditional classroom situation being one which the disadvantaged adolescent associated with frustration, failure and humiliation. This was achieved first of all by avoiding the use of methods and teaching materials, originally prepared for lower grades and superficially adapted for disadvantaged adolescents, because of lack of alternative programs. Thus the *content* of the new curriculum was based on subject

matter likely to impress the disadvantaged adolescent as being similar to assignments which would be challenging to High School students and adults. Examples are: the application of laws of elementary physics (such as the law of beams, wheel transmission, temperature transformations, etc.); questionnaires in history and geography; scientific crossword puzzles; mathematical and geometric problems; decoding of telegrams; rules of First Aid, and so on.

2) The second principle of the curriculum is its format, most of its exercises being set in the form of game-like paper and pencil quizzes, questionnaires and work sheets, including instructions and exemplars. Thus, every pupil may work independently and individually with minimal assistance on the part of the teacher. This type of classroom activity in the form of individual assignments differs fundamentally from the oral-frontal method of the teacher prompting a class of pupils and expecting their responses.

3) The third principle is the sequential order of exercises, within each 'learning unit', by ascending level of difficulty, whilst their content and external form remain similar. Within each such sequence the range of difficulty is very wide, the simplest tasks being at the first grade and even preschool level, whilst the ceiling can be deliberately raised to intelligence levels of normal adults. As an example we cite the learning unit of 'Bus Lines', which seeks to discover by logical exclusion the terminal station of a number of bus lines, while the destinations are only given in part either directly or indirectly (see p. 181). The simplest exercise of this unit would be: 'Two buses, Line A and Line B, go to Market Place and Park Side. Line A goes to Market Place. Where does bus B go?' A problem with 7 buses and 7 terminals, including statements such as 'No. 6 and No. 7 go neither to X nor to Y and Z', would be difficult enough to be included in a test for High School Graduates.

It is possible in principle to extend the sequence *downwards* by adding exercises based on concrete manipulation of palpable objects. In the above example this would be the use of toy buses to be moved from one place to another. By such concretization it is possible to use the same unit also with mentally retarded subjects.

The advantage of this format is the possibility of using the same unit of content 'area' in classes or groups with heterogeneous mental and scholastic level, i.e. each pupil is given exercises according to his ability, while the class as an entity is engaged in an overall homogeneous set of assignments. It is well known that the 'easy way out' to handle heterogeneous groups is to give simple tasks to the weaker pupils, which often take the form of 'busy work'. The records of our observations demonstrate that such practice is resented as humiliating. Some of our weak youngsters reported that solving the problems of the Contextual Learning Units gave them, for the first time, the feeling that they were 'doing' what the rest of the class 'was doing'. The fact that they were actually not doing exactly the 'same thing' is irrelevant, as contentwise and 'difficulty-level-wise' the challenge was subjectively perceived as similar, by both the advanced and the more retarded pupils.

It was also demonstrated by follow-up (Kohen-Raz, 1981), that disadvantaged post-adolescents interviewed two years after they had left the Semiskilled Apprentice Schools stated clearly that more efforts should be invested to prepare special teaching programs, which would meet the individual needs of the 'gifted' as well as of the 'retarded' pupils, who according to their reminiscences were 'neglected' by the traditional curriculum.

In this context the reader should be reminded of the findings reported above (p. 42) demonstrating the heterogeneity of mental level in disadvantaged post-adolescents. It seems that the adolescents themselves are well aware of the discrepancies in mental and scholastic abilities within their classroom groups, as the above reported interviews indicate.

Obviously, the principle of the traditional curriculum to focus on 'the average pupil' is not appropriate. In the case of disadvantaged populations, it misses the concentrations of the 'better' and 'weaker' pupils, at the two ends of the distribution who then tend to drop out. The former because of boredom and the latter because of being unable to cope. This is what happens in reality. The flexible and the graded format of the Contextual Learning Units promises to tackle this problem, as evaluation and follow-up indicate (Kohen-Raz, 1979, 1980, 1981a).

4) The fourth principle of the curriculum is the presentation of

problems in familiar contexts (hence the designation of the method as Curriculum of Contextual Learning). Actually, most of the learning units are directly or indirectly related to themes and subject matter belonging to the Life Space of the disadvantaged pupil. This principle is based on a conceptualization of mental development, which somewhat deviates from the Piagetian model, in that it emphasizes that *context* is a most important, if not crucial, factor determining *level* of mental performance (see Chapter 7).

In practice this would mean that disadvantaged pupils manifest low levels of mental performance not because of delayed or deficient crystallisation of mental schemes, but chiefly because they are required to deal with problems in unfamiliar contexts. If this obstacle is removed by giving them opportunity to handle familiar situations, their mental level and the quality and level of their intellectual proficiency should improve. Thus, they should be even able to perform 'formal operations' provided that they are embedded in contexts reflecting their experiences. This, in fact, has been borne out by our experiments. (Kohen-Raz, 1973, 1979, 1980), and exercises have been designed accordingly, the level of their structural complexity rising systematically and gradually from preoperational to formal thought.

Viewed from a different angle this actually represents a way of training higher levels of *practical intelligence* in the sense of Rey's model (see Chapter 4).

5) The fifth principle of the Curriculum is its openness and adaptability, i.e. the teacher is free to change the content of the subject matter or central theme, he wishes to teach. Actually, the learning units can be used as an 'auxiliary curriculum' to supplement and to structure any existing teaching program and to adapt it to the low motivational level of the disadvantaged student. In other words, the original form of the learning units can serve as a paradigm according to which the teacher himself designs and prepares new units, as and when they may be needed in order to enrich and to extend the basic curriculum. Examples of easily adaptable units are crossword puzzles, analogies, sentence and story completion, classifications, and coding (see pp. 160–163). An example of a more complex amplification and adaptation of the curriculum of contextual learning units is the effort made by the

headmaster of one school to create units for a learning program of cooking and housekeeping.

TABLE 12

Specimen of quiz items prepared by disadvantaged pupils
in a youth prison apprentice school

Subject: The functioning of automobile engine

What is the function of the oil in the engine?
a) To soften the mobile engine parts.
b) To restrict the friction of the engine parts.
c) To increase the friction of the engine parts.
d) To prevent the engine from drying up.

What is the function of the carburator?
a) To produce a mixture of essence and oil.
b) To produce a mixture of oil and air.
c) To produce a mixture of essence and air.
d) To produce a mixture of essence and soler.

How does the water cool off in the radiator?
a) Because of concentration of water in the radiator.
b) Because of increase of contact of the engine with air.
c) Because of freezing of the pipes leading to the radiator.
d) Because of removing hot air by means of a special device.

6) The sixth principle is an extension of the fifth in that the pupils themselves are invited to invent learning units and to adapt them to contents and contexts which they choose. As an example we cite a school located in a youth prison, where the inmates who specialize in automechanics constructed closed questionnaires and quizzes with sophisticated distractors on problems related to the functions of an automobile engine and its various components (see Table 12). The fact that the system of contextual learning units is 'open' and enables pupils to design their own tasks and assignments adds important dimensions to the program namely:

a) It stimulates creative thought.
b) It serves a convenient framework for peer teaching.
c) It enhances the contrast between the traditional 'frontal methods' of instruction and the 'correctional scholastic experience'

which the curriculum of contextual learning is intended to provide to the disadvantaged post-adolescent.

d) By assuming the role of a 'tutor' and 'curriculum constructor' the disadvantaged youngster is given the opportunity to correct his negative self-image as a rejected, retarded and unsuccessful pupil.

Overviewing the basic principles of the Curriculum of Contextual Learning Units, it can be seen that they converge on a common aim, which is the rehabilitation of the disadvantaged post-adolescent's deteriorated *motivation* to learn and to study. It is obvious, that without such an effect on motivation, any program of rehabilitation and re-education of the disadvantaged will be doomed to failure, whatever its structural, technical and methodological sophistication.

CHAPTER 13

The Structure and Content of the Curriculum of Contextual Learning Units

Having outlined the principles of the Curriculum of Contextual Learning Units we shall now describe its structure and content, explaining the rationale and purpose of the individual units and exercises, and their linkage to the theoretical background presented in the first part of this book. The material is organized according to the following principle: 'Learning Units' supposed to stimulate similar functions (such as language, spatial orientation, concrete operations, etc.) are grouped into 'Subject Areas'. In turn, each Learning Unit is composed of various Exercises, each characterized by its peculiar technique (such as quiz, questionnaire, puzzle, game, drawing). Within each Exercise there are series of items, arranged in ascending order of difficulty, but identical in content and form (see p. 154). Some Learning Units or Exercises fit into more than one Subject Area and the teacher is free to choose in which context he prefers to use them. As example: The Exercise 'Writing Telegrams' belongs to the Unit 'Elaboration and Organization of Verbal Expression', in the Area of 'Language and Communication'. It can, however, also be conveniently used in the Subject Area 'Citizenship', Learning Unit 'Use of Public Services, Post Office'.

1. Subject Area: Language and Communication

Given the paucity of language and communication skill of the disadvantaged, the focus of this subject area is first of all the stimulation and development of language skills in everyday use, putting emphasis on social communication in the community, understanding and passing on instructions at work, enrichment of vocabulary (including abstract concepts) and the development of a more differentiated and elaborated style of verbal expression.

The units of this subject area were not designed to train directly and explicitly reading and writing skills, assuming

1) that the reading problems in this target population are predominantly rooted in general language deficits (see p. 136) and thus would be indirectly attacked by the linguistic training.

2) emphasis on remedial reading would evoke negative associations with previous adverse scholastic experiences. These qualifications do not limit the option to use the exercises of this unit in the content of remedial reading or writing, if the teacher knows how to adopt them, and to integrate them within his remedial program and is sure that the pupils will profit from these techniques.†

In line with the general principles of the curriculum, the units were designed in such a way as to optimally motivate the students to use more elaborate and complex language. This was achieved mainly by using formats of quiz and riddles, inserting humorous elements, evoking curiosity through non-conventional content and creating situations necessitating exact and differentiated verbal formulations.

The following Learning Units in the Subject Area 'Language and Communication' have been used:

Enrichment of Vocabulary

This unit comprises (a) exercises of sentence completion (b) crossword puzzles. The *missing words in the sentences* are not only nouns and verbs but also adjectives, adverbs, prepositions, and conjunctions. The correct use of the latter stimulates the understanding of relationships between coordinated and subordinated sentences such as: 'I took the umbrella . . . it was not yet raining

---

†In order to tackle the problem of specific learning disabilities in culturally disadvantaged post-adolescents a special program using adaptations of various learning units will be launched at the beginning of the scholastic year 1981–82.

(although)' as well as purpose and special order, 'I came . . . he left (before)'. At the more advanced level, abstract concepts have to be filled in, such as 'As he saw the suffering of the people, he was filled with . . . '.

Crossword puzzles can be designed in extremely simplified form by using only two words crossing by one letter, as shown in the example:

```
       g
     rain
       t
       e
```

The didactic efficacy in the use of crossword puzzles consists in the systematic choice of type of vocabulary to be guessed. Obviously, we start with concrete nouns, but gradually it is possible to use semi-abstract and fully abstract concepts, verbs, adjectives, prepositions and adverbs. Another principle is to organize the vocabulary around a certain subject in the context of the general teaching program or around a topic of current interest, such as an important political event, an innovative invention, a motion picture, a TV show or bestseller which has recently attracted the pupils etc.

An important aspect of the crossword puzzle technique is the definition (or circumscription) of the guessed words. The same word can be so clearly defined that it must not be guessed. It can, however, also be defined in abstract terms so that it cannot be found without considerable mental effort. If we take, for example, the word 'dog', writing 'a domestic animal which barks' is too easy even for first graders. 'A domesticated mammal, generally not used as food or to provide food and not withdrawing the nails of his paws (which excludes the cat)' is an awkward but didactically useful circumscription. It can be seen that the difficulty of the crossword puzzle can be graded not only by content, type and level of abstraction of the words to be inserted but also by way of presenting the information necessary to arrive at the correct solution. Still more effective are exercises requiring the pupils to construct crossword puzzles themselves. It will be convenient to start with a simple structure and a small number of words. In this case, the didcatic objective changes. What was originally designed as an exercise to enrich the vocabulary turns into a technique to teach concept formation and definition.

Obviously, there is ample opportunity to discuss the content area, represented by the crossword's vocabulary, to analyze erros of definition and to focus on differences in connotations between similar words, synonyms and homonyms which naturally come up in the course of administering this exercise. It will also be noted, that problems of ambiguity will arise by designing vague descriptions. This is an important training ground as the disadvantaged show difficulty in tolerating ambivalence and ambiguity, do not like to clarify doubts and to admit misunderstandings (see Chapter 5, p. 85).

Refinement of Connotations and Use of Meaningful Sentences

Although refinement of connotation is implicit in training sentence completion and crossword puzzles, it has been put in the focus of this learning unit, which mainly consist in the formation of antonyms, synonyms and invention of story completions. As these types of exercises are well known, we shall only describe some peculiar features which have been added.

Lists of antonyms and synonyms comprise not only nouns, but verbs and adjectives, which again range from the concrete to the abstract. A special list of 'double antonyms' has been constructed such as 'which is the opposite of a *chilly evening*'. In this case there are three answers '*warm* evening', '*warm morning*' and 'chilly *morning*'. The elucidation of the differential connotations of these double antonyms is a fruitful basis for discussion, especially when in certain cases contradictions 'in adjecto' will emerge such as 'sunny day': 'clouded night', 'clouded day', '*sunny night*'. Possibly some pupils will suggest that summer nights at the north pole are sunny.

Story completion, besides training the use of meaningful sentences naturally, also stimulates fantasy and gives opportunity for creative writing. This type of exercise has been made more attractive by letting pupils not only invent 'the end of the story' but also its 'beginning' and 'its middle part', the rest of the plot being given. Another variation of this type of exercise is the invention of anachronistic stories. Pupils are asked to tell or to write up a biblical episode as if it happened in the technological era, the actions to be dramatized by the use of modern inventions. Or, the other way round, to imagine a current event, such as a school trip or a football match, as if it would occur in ancient times, without all the commodities of modern life. It will be remembered that paucity of imagination and lack of communication with the unconscious is considered, according to Frankenstein's model, an important factor of cognitive deficit (mainly weak abstraction) in the disadvantaged. These exercises in verbal creativity and construction of meaningful sentences are supposed to help overcome this weakness.

Verbal Abstraction

Exercises in verbal abstraction are of various types. '*Encircling categories*' is an exercise in classification of words, which are scattered on a sheet of paper. The pupil is supposed to encircle those 'which belong together', on the basis of perceptual, functional or conceptual similarity. The words (about 6 to 8 for each item) are selected in such a way that some of them may be assigned to two or three 'overlapping' categories. For example, son-daughter-father-mother-aunt-uncle. Son together with daughter is of the class 'children', son together with father and uncle is of the class 'males'.

To mark more clearly the overlap different colors may be used for each demarcating circle. Another exercise consists in defining *similarities between word pairs*, a traditional device to test and to train verbal classification. This technique, however, can be applied to more difficult material such as finding the odd element in groups of four occupations or activities such as: a man plays ping-pong, a woman phones, a man wrestles, a life-guard watches on the beach. Or: a volunteer, a man donating blood, the receiver of an army medal, an army doctor. Here a considerable level of abstraction is required to find the oddity. In both examples the criterion must be defined in semi-abstract terms. In the first case, an activity involving responsibility, in the second case, not volunteering.

Another more sophisticated exercise in categorization is the *Library Catalogue*. The pupils are given lists of books, preferably those which are known to them, and are asked to classify them according to themes, such as 'adventures', 'science fiction', 'fairy tales', etc. In a similar way, motion pictures or types of cinema heroes can be classified.

Constructing these exercises, attention was again given to the use of not only nouns, but also verbs and adjectives as elements of classification. Also, a more than one-way classification was introduced, because of the fact that this 'multidimensional' mental activity is a decisive step in the transition from pre-operative to operational thought. It should be born in mind, that the ability to carry out at least a *two way* classification is a prerequisite of school readiness. Administering these items to disadvantaged post-adolescents we touch a sore point of their mental development, as this function may have suffered from the typical resistance of the 'externalized' individual to view the same object or situation from two different angles (see p. 134).

Acquisition of Syntactic Rules. Elaboration and Organization of Verbal Expression

The 'restricted code' of verbal expression of the disadvantaged, being the result not only of their poor vocabulary but also of their limited knowledge of syntax and grammatical rules, has been extensively described and discussed in psychological and psycholinguistic literature. The aim of this learning unit is to stimulate these deficient syntactic functions using somewhat 'non-conventional' techniques, especially designed to evoke and to strengthen motivation to use differentiated, and clear cut language to express thoughts, impressions, feelings and intentions.

Scrambled Sentences is a simple technique, presenting a sentence of varying length and complexity, the words being out of their syntactic order, scattered in random fashion. The pupil has to reconstruct the correct word sequence. This exercise offers a good opportunity to teach laws of syntax as well as grammatical rules related to inflexions and conjugations. The same technique is employed in a more complex, but also more amusing format, called *mixed-up telephone conversation*. Pupils are presented protocols of two dialogues between persons talking on the telephone. They are told that the 'lines crossed' and one dialogue was mixed up with the other, yielding absurd and comical sequences of questions and answers. The pupil is required to disentangle the two conversations. Here, in addition to the reconstruction of sentences, the pupil is trained to decode messages and to differentiate and to evaluate two and eventually four different points of view. Again an exercise in 'ego mobility'. (For an example, see Table 13.)

Writing and Decoding Telegrams. The structure of this exercise needs no special explanation. The pupils are given 'real telegram

TABLE 13

Mixed-up telephone conversation

= Bicycle with knobs, but I don't know how to ride it.
= What was the gift you received?
= Good bye, Chagit.
= Rami, Shalom, this is Ammi.
= And at home, have you looked for it?
= Of course, come on, I am waiting for you. See you, Ammi.
= I looked for it at home, everywhere, and there is no watch. I am really afraid to tell mother.
= Hallo Nurith. This is Chagit.
= An electric train.
= Nurith. Thank you for comforting me. I shall you call later, to tell you how my parents took it.
= Hallo Chagit. How are you?
= Hi Ammi. I almost could not get up this morning.
= Of course I remember. With a red chain.
= Chagit, you have to tell them and they surely will understand. This can happen to everyone.
= Shalom Rami. I am coming immediately.
= Nurith, I am sorry of waking you up so early, but something sad happened to me.
= So Rami, you want me to come over to see the gifts, which you received for your Bar Mitzva?
= Do you remember the watch which I received on my birthday?
= This train really runs? What else have you got?
= Listen, Yesterday, when I came back from the swimming pool, I realized that it was gone. I asked all the people and the cleaning women, but nobody knew.
= What happened to you, Chagit?
= Yes, I received a lot of gifts.
= I too, but it was wonderful yesterday at the Bar Mitzva Party.

forms' and a lengthy description of an urgent situation, involving two partners who are supposed to send each other several telegrams in order to solve a problem. Pupils are rewarded for optimal brevity of the telegraphic message. Obviously, things can be made more complicated by 'scrambling' two sets of telegraphic dialogues, as in the preceding exercise. The technique can be inverted, by describing a whole sequence of dramatic events in the form of an exchange of telegrams. The pupil has to decode the whole set and to tell the story in well-elaborated 'belletristic' style. If the technical conditions permit, telephone and telegraph sets can be used for these exercises.

Pupils can also be sent to the post office to send and to receive 'real' telegrams. To teach the practical use of the telephone, a special unit has been designed belonging to the Subject Area of Citizenship (see below).

Secret Message. Tasks involving 'secrets' and 'coding techniques' in association with detective and espionage stories naturally have highly motivating effects on children and adolescents. Envisaging this advantage the following technique was designed: A secret message has to be embedded in a sequence of regular, unobtrusive sentences, optimally making sense and giving the impression of an innocent letter. The manner of embedding the words is the code, such as putting three words between each word of the message (not counting the first three). Here is an example:

The message: *Send new papers*

The coded text: You promised to *send* by mail your *new* book and recent *papers* published by you.

The syntactic skill required to encode the message is evident.

It is of course easy to organize a 'play' of detectives and secret agents belonging to groups each supposed to detect the other's secrets and strategies.

Telecommunication of Displays. This exercise requires the description of apparently simple displays of spatially arranged objects as exactly as possible, so that the receiver of the message will be able to reproduce the display by receiving the sender's verbal instructions. For this purpose, sender and receiver each have in front of them identical material to construct the display and must sit at separate tables either with a screen between them, or far apart, even in separate rooms linked by a telephone line. Obviously, the communication by telephone is the most interesting and actually does not involve any technical difficulty. Here is an example of a display: 'A pencil is placed to the left of a book parallel to its longer edge at a distance of 2 cm. An inverted cup is on the top of the book on its mid point, the handle facing the pencil'. It is surprising that these tasks are not easy even for well-educated adults. However, by virtue of their motivating effect the disadvantaged are eager to participate in these exercises. Plays involving competitions between two pairs of senders-receivers can be arranged, and watched by 'onlookers' through closed circuit television.

Imagination of Dialogues. Pupils are presented cut-outs from illustrated newspapers depicting people talking to each other. They are asked to imagine the dialogues.

Red Screen. Pupils are shown specimens of words or sentences written in red pencil, while some parts of them are lightly redrawn in blue. The blue parts form a new word or sentence which becomes recognizable only after red transparent (celluloid) paper is put over the writing, so that the red parts disappear. The now emerging words or sentences may represent an answer to the original sentence which was a question, or some humorous allusion associated with the original words. Here are two examples: (Note that the capital letters are the blue ones remaining after the rest disappears under the red screen.)

who IS behInd the DOoR?
(ISIDOR)

who is the teAcher iN this clASS
(AN ASS)

When *writing* instead of printing letters (like in the above specimen) there is much more leeway to camouflage the hidden message, as letter parts may be used to emerge under the red transparent as independent letters, such as parts of an H becoming an I, an M turning into an N, B into an R, etc.

This technique can of course be used to write messages or short stories, hiding the outcome under the red screen. It is also most suitable to stimulate creativity and very useful for peer teaching. Its motivational effect is excellent.

Interpretation of Fables and Proverbs

The difficulty of disadvantaged populations in grasping the meta-phoric meaning of proverbs and fables is rooted in their exter-nalized style of life, which focusses on the concrete, haveable and immediate (see Chapter 10 p. 135). To understand the double sense of metaphors requires considerable detachment, inner distance and internalization which is quite problematic for exter-nalized individuals.

The exercises of this learning unit consists essentially in the presentation and discussion of the metaphors, fables and proverbs. The difficulties encountered in teaching this material demonstrate clearly the intimate link between impoverished abstraction, inhibited symbol formation, inability to grasp metaphorical meaning and lowered intellectual ability in the disadvantaged. Thus the exercise, sometimes more than stimulating the pupil, provides the teacher with valuable insight as to the problematic cognitive dynamics of his students.

Teaching the Alphabet

This unit deals with a somewhat banal issue, i.e. difficulties of disadvantaged pupils to use the alphabet effectively and rapidly. Exercises to train this skill, which is normally 'overlearned', are the following;

a) *Organizing the 'telephone registry'.* Pupils receive a scrambled list of imaginary names of persons and the towns in which they live. The names, for each town have to be arranged in strict alpha-betical order according to the 'inner alphabet' i.e. Smith before Swift, etc.

b) *Coding words.* In this exercise a code is agreed upon consisting in shifting the whole alphabet one letter forwards, i.e. a becomes b, b becomes c . . . and z becomes a. Words are then encoded and decoded accordingly. The code of course can be varied: two letters forward, one letter backward, etc. Inverting the task yields a kind of puzzle, in that a word is written in an unknown code and its definition is added. The code has to be guessed. For example: The capital of the US is VZRGHMFSNM (Washington). The code is one letter backward.

2. Subject Area: Orientation in Space

The learning units in this functional area have been constructed for three main purposes:

1) To facilitate the post-adolescent's spatial orientation in everyday life such as required for reading a town plan, travelling to an unfamiliar place, searching an address in an unknown quarter, finding the way when lost in a strange environment, etc.

2) To stimulate basic cognitive functions, intimately linked with space perception, namely *overcoming egocentricity* which is an important component of operational thought manifest in the correct perception of directions from diametrically opposed points of view (Piaget, 1956); the *conception of the euclidian space*, which is not only the basis for geometry, but also related to the visual representation of logical relationships and mathematical functions; and finally the *perception of temporal sequences* also linked with operational thought as well as with reading ability (McGee, 1979; Kohen-Raz, 1978; Frank and Levinson, 1976).

3) To help the post-adolescent to acquire basic knowledge in technical drawing, so that he might be able to understand designs of instruments, engines, etc. as well as to grasp the functions of machines and modern technological systems.

In the light of this rationale, the following learning units were designed, most of them based on traditional methods of training and assessing spatial abilities.

Overcoming Egocentricity

The exercises belonging to this Learning Unit are related to the 'Spatial Orientation Factor', based on 'the recognition of objects from different angles; the comprehension of the arrangement of elements within a visual stimulus pattern' (McGee, 1979). The simple and straightforward training of this ability consists in *Left-Right Discrimination* from the subjects point of view, as well as from the point of view of a partner who faces him. More attractive exercises are the following:

Playing Traffic Police, (an exercise which also fits into the subject area 'Citizenship'). The simplest form of this game is to mark crossroads on the playground and to let one pupil play the policeman, who is supposed to organize and to control 'the traffic' represented by other pupils who 'drive' in various directions. The Policeman and the drivers have to define which way they go, which forces the 'policeman' to detach himself from his point of view. The more sophisticated items of this exercise require the analysis of 'traffic accidents', which are described in detail by written 'police reports' and depicted on an attached road map. The pupils have to decide who is guilty and why, which of course demands verbalization and differentiation of directional relationships.

Description of Room Corners is a task, requiring a pupil sitting in the center of a room to point to the 'left upper anterior' . . . 'right lower posterior', etc. corner of the room. The task becomes complicated if a partner is seated at angles of 90, 180 and 270 degrees relative to the subject, who has to point to the corners as defined before, but as seen from the partner's point of view.

Walking on the Checker Floor. The 'checker floor' is a large checker board painted on the floor of a gym or a playground, its squares being approximately 30 x 30 cm. Pupils representing 'figures' are instructed by 'players' to move so many steps to the right, to the left, forward, backward, etc., until arriving at a definitive square.

This technique can be employed to organize competitive plays of two small groups playing one against the other using the rules and rationals of various games normally played on a checkerboard.

Landscapes are the well-known Piagetian tasks, consisting in the presentation of a model of three hills, which the examinee has to visualize by correct selection of photos depicting this landscape from a given angle (Piaget and Inhelder, 1959). In our learning units, simple and schematic top views of landscapes, composed of a tree, a house and a water tower, are shown to the subject who is asked to draw them from the point of view of an imaginary observer standing on the ground and viewing them from the north, south, east and west respectively. As this exercise turned out to be rather difficult, a similar form of *Visualizing Flats and Buildings* has been designed. Again, top views, but of flats and buildings are presented, delineating exactly the position of windows and doors on each of the four external walls. The task is to sketch the view of the flat or building from outside as if standing on the ground in front of each of the four walls (see Figure 9).

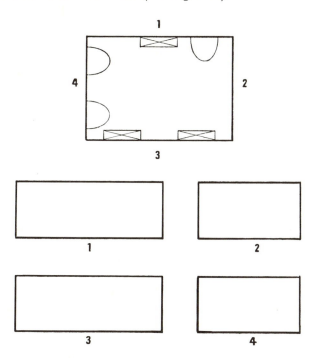

FIGURE 9   *Visualizing flats and buildings.* Upper rectangle is top view of a flat to be visualized from outside from the point of views as designated by numbers. Arches are doors, crossed rectangles are windows.

Interpretation of Maps and Plans

The rationale of this learning unit is self-explanatory. One type of exercise is based on the use of the *checker floor* already described in that pupils have to walk on it according to a pre-designed plan. In this context it is also possible to organize information chains, i.e. one pupil holds the plan, reads it out to another pupil over a telephone, the latter 'gives orders' to a third pupil standing on the checker floor supposed to carry out the 'operation'.

Another exercise is *Searching for the Treasure*. Pupils get plans of their immediate surroundings, such as the school building, its adjacent streets, playgrounds, etc. On a certain place marked on the plan a 'treasure' is hidden. They have to find the treasure using solely this information. A competitive game can be organized in that two or three groups of pupils are given the same plan, or by timing the duration of the search.

As can be easily seen, the range of items in this exercise is wide, from simple hiding games within the classroom to sophisticated 'quasi-military' manoeuvres. *Labelling the Streets* is an exercise, training simultaneously space orientation, citizenship and vocabulary. The pupils are presented a plan of an imaginary town, showing streets and squares without any designations. They are told, for example, that all the streets leading to a certain square called, say, Flower Square have to be given names of flowers. Or all the streets going southwest should be named after famous politicians, etc. The houses along each street are then given even numbers in ascending order on the right side and odd numbers in ascending order on the left side of an imaginary pedestrian walking in a given direction. It can also be asked, in which direction do the four walls face of house number x on y street.

Finally *mazes* of all types can be used in the context of this learning unit.

Mirror Writing and Reading

Mirror writing and reading is self-explanatory. For an example of a set of 'mirror' exercises see Figure 10.

Cuts in Folded Papers

This exercise is a popular game. It consists in guessing the patterns of cuts made in a folded paper after it is unfolded or vice versa.

Unfolding Surfaces of Geometrical Bodies

This Learning Unit is supposed to train the ability to construct a geometrical body (such as a pyramid, prism, cube) from the

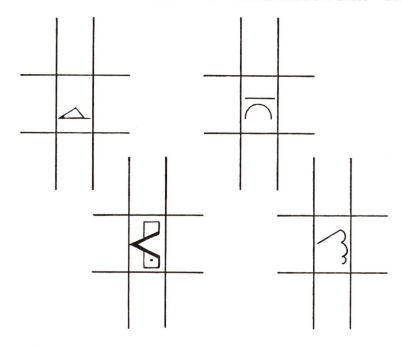

FIGURE 10   *Complex mirror images.* Mirror image of form in center has to be drawn as if mirrors were placed vertically at each of the four edges of the central square.

two dimensional areas which represent its surface, and vice versa, to unfold a geometrical body and to present its surface in two-dimensional format. This is actually a basic skill in technological education comparable to the three R's at the elementary grades. Essentially, it is a mental transfer between two and three dimensional spatial representations, which requires considerable 'ego mobility'. We are thus confronted again with a weak point in the mental structure of the disadvantaged, which crucially limits his eligibility for many skilled vocations, especially those linked with technological problems. Rehabilitation and re-education of this functional area is thus of great importance because, if successful, it will change considerably the disadvantaged youth's prospects of attaining higher vocational and socio-economic status.

The exercises are of three types:

1) Manipulation of concrete geometrical bodies and their respective surfaces.

2) Matching pictures of geometrical bodies with pictures of their unfolded surfaces.

3) Measuring surfaces of bodies and comparing them to their volume.

Basic Training in Technological Drawing

The rationale of this Learning Unit is similar to that of the preceeding one, i.e. training a basic technological skill. One type of exercises is the *use of coordinates.* Pupils are required to find various points on a grid of x/y coordinates, their location being defined by their distance from the x and y axes respectively. If the points are correctly placed on the grid, and afterwards connected by solid lines, a picture or inscription will emerge. The exercise is then reversed. Pupils are asked to draw a picture, a geometrical form or letter on the grid to define the drawing by the coordinates of its contours, and then let other pupils reproduce the original from the coordinates. Other exercises are traditional tasks of *technological drawing,* made more attractive by letting pupils first invent objects or utensils, eventually in absurd form (a wagon with triangular wheels) and then elaborate their technological design.

Drawing of arrays is an exercise which demands the visualization of arrays of geometrical bodies of the same type (such as prisms of varying height and width) put one behind the other, in a straight line.

From different points of view the prisms will cover each other in different ways. In addition to overcoming egocentricity it is necessary to reproduce exact juxtapositions such as a higher prism covering the height of a lower one behind, but leaving its width visible because the latter is thinner.

A variation of this exercise are *arrows of tents* to be depicted from different angles, it being given that the tents are of different size and form.

3. Subject Area: Time Perception

The rationale of this subject area is similar to that of Spatial Orientation, in that three aspects must be considered:

1) *A pragmatic aspect.* The estimation and appreciation of long, short and minute stretches of time in everyday life. The value of punctuality. Planning of time schedules and the establishment of temporal priorities.

2) *A theoretical aspect.* The mathematical aspects of time, as involved in logical and logistic problems.

3) *A vocational aspect.* The role of temporal variables in the process of industrial production, i.e. coordination of time on the production line, deadlines for orders, keeping appointments, etc.

Four Learning Units have been hitherto elaborated in this subject area. But it is relatively easy to develop more along the outlines described below.

Timetables of Bus Lines

Given the travel time of a bus line between its terminals and between its stations all along the route, the pupils have to make up timetables. Exercises differ as to the elements missing in the given data. For example, the first bus leaves the terminal at 6.50 and arrives at the other terminal at 7.45. The second one arrives at station X at 8.15 and arrives at the second terminal at 8.45. If station X is the only station on the route, the full timetable of any bus leaving at any time its first terminal can be calculated. For more difficult items calculations of delayed departures and arrivals can be added.

Temporal Sequences of Events

The principle of this Learning Unit is similar to picture arrangement tests used in traditional mental test batteries. However, for the purpose of 'vocational training' picture, arrangements of technological material are added. For example, phases of an ignition, explosion or leakage. The sequence of events leading to a traffic accident is a suitable item in this context. It has an obvious additional educational effect and can be used also in the subject area of 'Citizenship'.

Airplanes

This Learning Unit consists in the calculation of timetables of airplanes, flying in different directions around the globe. The hours of their departure and arrival must be calculated in local time. The difficulties involved in this type of exercise are evident.

Absurd Time Sequences

Absurd stories involving impossible orders of events, or paradoxical manipulation of time, are presented. The pupil has to detect the error. A well-known example is one of Binet-Simon's test items: 'Johnny was always late for school. One day he decided to put the school clock one hour ahead, in order to be on time.' An airplane leaving Paris at 12.00 pm arrives at Zurich at 11.55. Is it possible? (The answer is yes, when France has shifted to summer time and Switzerland is still on winter time.)

Subject Area: Concrete Operations

The rationale of this subject area is based on the model of 'movement representations', described in detail elsewhere (Kohen-Raz, 1965). According to this model, there is a close link between the attainment of concrete operational thought and the ability to imagine two independent internalized actions. Thus, several exercises have been designed to stimulate the imagination of realistic, coordinated and directed movements. Other Learning Units are based on more traditional exercises of concrete operations.

Movement Representations

The exercise *Knights Move* requires the pupil to imagine the moves of the knight chess figure, which according to chess rules, advances in a zig-zag manner, one square straight, one square diagonally, or vice versa. On checkerboards of various sizes two or three knights are placed in random order. The pupil has to find the square on which the two (or three) knights can meet.

The number of required moves by each figure to arrive at the 'meeting square' is not limited and numbers of moves of different figures need not be equal. Theoretically it is possible to design items requiring equal numbers of moves for each figure, but they are rather difficult, even for subjects with average and above average intelligence. The range of difficulty of this exercise can be extended downwards, by letting pupils move concrete figures on a checkerboard. It can, however, also be extended upwards, not only by increasing the number of knights but by asking the pupil to define the positions of the figures on their moves from start to target solely by defining the checkerboard coordinates (a,4; b,5; etc.).

Practice has shown that there is no problem in teaching disadvantaged post-adolescents the 'knight move', besides which a high percentage of boys in our samples knew how to play chess.

Due to the great flexibility of the exercises a wide range of performance level can be observed providing valuable insight as to the critical stage of transition from intuitive to operational thought in the disadvantaged. As a diagnostic tool, the 'knights move' is also sensitive to the differential diagnosis between 'organic' and 'environmental' retardation, as the former have greater difficulties with the imagination of two moves. The latter, on the other hand, are able to learn to master the task. Actually, subjects who cannot combine two independent movements are mentally functioning at a pre-school level and, in spite of their advanced age, will have great difficulties in elementary school (Kohen-Raz, 1965).

Number Runs. In this exercise, instead of a checker board, a matrix of mixed one-digit numbers is used (see Table 14). The pupil choses a number on the base line of the matrix. He advances in an upward vertical, diagonal or horizontal (never

TABLE 14

Number runs

1	2	3	4	5	6	7	8	9	x
2	3	4	5	6	7	8	9	1	2
3	4	5	6	7	8	9	1	2	3
4	5	6	7	8	9	1	2	3	4
5	6	7	8	9	1	2	3	4	5
6	7	8	9	1	2	3	4	5	6
7	8	9	1	2	3	4	5	6	7
8	9	1	2	3	4	5	6	7	8
9	1	2	3	4	5	6	7	8	9
1	2	3	4	5	6	7	8	9	1

downwards vertical) direction as many steps as indicated by the number from which he started. He arrives at a new number, which again determines the number of his next step. He is supposed to reach a target (the 'x') at the upper edge of the matrix, but is not allowed to 'overshoot'. If he misses the target he has to start again from a different base. The exercise can be made more difficult by limiting the time of each 'run'. Another variation, complicating the task, is to instruct the pupil, to add or to subtract a constant to or from each number on which he happens 'to step'. It is easy of course to let pupils compete, giving credit for the time and number of successful runs. Although this exercise requires only a one-tracked movement representation, the calculation of steps (eventually complicated by the manipulation of constants) provides a second dimension to be simultaneously considered, which requires a mental act on the level of concrete operations.

Coin Constellations. This is another task requiring the combination of two independent actions. The basic operation is to change the 'head-tail' pattern of an array of three coins, by turning over the left and the middle one and hereafter transferring these two to the right of the remaining coin which remains as it was. Each such operation is 'one step'. Pupils are presented two triads of coins and asked how many steps must be carried out to change the 'head-tail' pattern of the first triad into the pattern of the second one. If the 'mental operation' is too difficult, pupils are allowed to perform the task by step-wise manipulation of real coins.

Two and Three Way Classifications

Techniques to train two- or three-way classifications of concrete objects (such as cubes, buttons, paper slips of different color, form and size) are well known and need no further explanations. In the framework of our curriculum a paper and pencil exercise, called 'Classification of Forms' was used. In this exercise a column of four, eight or 12 graphic forms are presented which differ in size, color pattern, direction, etc. and adjacent to it, empty parallel columns are provided. In each column the pupil marks crosses *vis a vis* those forms which have a common feature and represent a class (see Figure. 12). In each of the columns marked

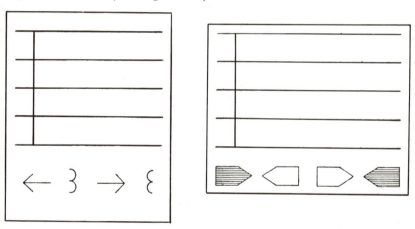

FIGURE 12   *Two-way visuo-spatial classifications.* Examinee marks in columns next to figures which items are similar and in which respect. (Form x Direction, Colour x Direction respectively.)

with crosses, he has to define verbally the criterion he has used to classify the data. Obviously, the classes will overlap as the same object has at least two different characteristics, each representing a different categorical dimension.

As the items of this exercise have a considerable range of

difficulty, it can be administered to groups of pupils with hetero-geneous mental and scholastic level.

Two-Way Seriations

According to Piaget (1952) the ability to consider an element simultaneously as a member of a class and as occupying a fixed position in a sequence is not only a reliable criterion that the level of concrete operations has been attained, but also a prerequisite to the study of elementary arithmetic. The mastery of seriation is thus not less important than the mastery of classification. However, while multi-dimensional classifications are included in almost every pre-school enrichment program, as well as represent-ed in many test batteries (the Raven test is a case in point) little attention has been paid to the training of *two-way seriations.*

Such exercises have been designed, using two-dimensional 4 x 4 matrices. The matrices consist of various forms, which change *quantitatively* along two dimensions (see Figure 13). Or: A circle with a dot inside: the circle increases in size in the horizontal direction of the matrix while the number of dots inside the circle increases in the vertical direction.

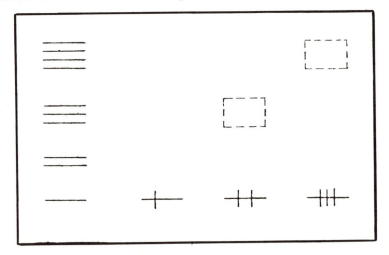

FIGURE 13   *Two-way seriation.* Appropriate item to be inserted into dotted frame.

By interpolation of the two-way seriations the correct missing elements of the matrix have to be inserted. Easy and difficult items have been elaborated. No correlational data on the relationship between the ability to perform two-way seriations and concrete operational reasoning are yet available.

4) *Absurd Sentences and Stories*

This Learning Unit consists in series of absurd sentences, and short stories ranging from simple to more sophisticated ones. The context plays a decisive role here, especially in absurd stories. Concrete logical reasoning is required to detect the absurdity. The advantage of this type of presentation of problems is the motivating effect of the 'funny' material.

5. Subject Area: Formal Reasoning

The rationale of this Subject Area is the presentation of problems of formal reasoning in contexts which are *familiar* to disadvantaged populations, as described in detail below:

Syllogisms

The method of syllogisms *per se* does not need to be explained. From the point of view of the general objectives of the curriculum, the important aspects are thus the familiar contexts. The two exercises described below are based on experiments designed by Donaldson (1963). In the 'Bus Line' exercise, a number of bus lines are presented as well as equal numbers of destinations. A limited number of relations between individual bus lines and their respective destinations is given (sometimes in negative form, such as: bus number three *does not go* to destination x). The rest of the relations have to be found by formal deduction. By augmenting the number of relationships and the number of negative statements, the items become increasingly difficult. On the other hand, very simple items, actually below the level of formal reasoning can be designed for weak pupils, such as: There are two buses and two destinations. Bus 1 goes to x, where does bus 2 go to?

The exercise 'Schools' has exactly the same format, instead of buses and their destinations, individual pupils, defined by their first names have to be matched with individual schools, given that there is not a single case of two pupils going to the same institution.

Absurd Relationships (also taken from Donaldson) are exercises which are aimed (a) to motivate the pupil by their humorous content (b) to train the ability — extremely underdeveloped under conditions of externalization — to reach a logically correct conclusion which, content-wise, is absurd and empirically impossible. Actually, these exercises focus on one important aspect of formal reasoning, which is the complete divorce of form from content. Here is an example: 'If the biggest things were the most flexible which would be the most flexible among the five: a rubber, a tyre, a pencil, a spring, a tower. Another example: if winter would be called summer, which of the four statements would be necessarily true. In summer people would not go to swimming pools. In summer the Lake of Tiberias would freeze. In summer the days in our country would be shorter than in winter. In winter people would wear thin clothes. It should be noted that the last statement is called 'directional' distractor, because it would be plausible, if the basic assumption was inverted: if summer would be called winter. (As found by Donaldson, these directional distractors are sensitive to transitional stages from concrete to formal reasoning). Other types of syllogisms are characterized by improbable, humorous content, closely linked with the real experience of the pupils. For examples (see Table 15).

Family Relations

Exercises of this type have been abundantly used in literature, in various mental tests and in psychological experiments. They have been recently elaborated at high levels of complexity by Feuerstein (1979). The central function, trained by these exercises, is the awareness of the *directionality* and *reciprocity* of *relationships* which is an important component of higher mental functions.

On the other hand, considerable 'ego mobility' is required to

TABLE 15

Syllogisms in familiar contexts

Following the premises, which statement is necessarily true.

THERE IS NO TOWN IN ISRAEL WITHOUT A SWIMMING POOL.
RAMLEH IS A TOWN IN ISRAEL.
a) The inhabitants of Ramleh go to the sea to swim
b) The new swimming pool in Ramleh can be filled with water
c) Many inhabitants in Ramleh don't know to swim
d) In Ramleh it is hot in summer

INFANTS DON'T KNOW HOW TO TALK. RAFI IS AN INFANT.
a) Rafi will be talking when he grows up
b) Rafi cries when he is hungry
c) Rafi likes to be taken for a promenade
d) Rafi does not know how to say what he wants.

NO PERSON UNDER THE AGE OF 16 EVER ENTERED THE CINEMA
ORION ON SATURDAY NIGHT. JOSI IS 15.
a) Josi tried to break into the cinema.
b) Josi never walked to the *Orion* cinema.
c) Josi was at home on Saturday night.
d) Josi did not see the cinema hall of *Orion* cinema on Saturday night.

Note: These items are intentionally based on premises which are negations.

understand that concepts, such as mother, father, brother, etc.,
which originally designate most concrete and personally meaningful human beings, are now treated as abstract concepts which
represent personally meaningless relationships in the context of
hypothetical problems, such as 'The son of the brother of
mother's mother is mother's . . . ' Actually, it may be argued that
problems dealing with family relations are more exercises in ego
mobility than exercises in formal reasoning, which of course does
not change their basic objective, i.e. the fostering of higher mental
functions in disadvantaged populations.

Guessing Numbers

This Learning Unit is based on a popular game played both by
children and adolescents. Normally it is played by two partners,

one chosing a number of two to three digits. The other one guesses systematically the unknown number, receiving from his partner three kinds of feedback: 'Full hit', if the guess contains a digit which appears in the target and in addition has the right decimal position. 'Half hit', if the digit is correct, but not its position. 'Miss' if the guess is utterly wrong. Systematic searching obviously requires formal reasoning as each feedback provides a basis for a set of hypotheses which have to be tested by the next guess. By simple hit and miss techniques it is hardly possible to find the solution.

In the frame of our curriculum, this game has been adapted and transformed into a paper and pencil task. The simplest items consist of two or three pairs of two digit numbers, representing guesses and their respective feedback. They are sufficient to find the target number. Here is an example: 42 = Half Hit; 28 = Miss; 31 = Full Hit. The target number is 34. The strategy: four or two are in the target, but at inverse decimal positions: two is excluded, thus four is correct and occupies the right decimal position. Given 31 being a 'Full Hit', the solution is 34.

In this form the exercises can be administered to groups, each pupil working on his own tasks. Obviously, the range of difficulty can be extended upwards by adding exercises with three or four digits. It will be noted, that the commercially available game 'Master Mind' is based on similar principles.

Naturally, in this game pupils can be invited to construct items and exercises and then let other pupils find the solution. It can also be easily used for competitions, by timing the performance.

6. Subject Area: Arithmetics

The main purpose of this subject area is to present arithmetic problems in familiar contexts and in an attractive form. Due to the focus on content most of the exercises can be also used in connection with the subjects to which they refer. As example, 'Money Exchange' can be linked with 'Citizenship', 'Transformation of Centigrades' with 'Physics', and so on.

Number Crosswords

This Learning Unit consists in various types of 'cross-numbers', i.e., instead of words, numbers have to be inserted into the matrix. Squares are not defined by coordinates, but by consecutive letters of the alphabet. The numbers are either verbally described, such as the number of days in August, or else the result of a given calculation, e.g., 3 x 7. Finally, some squares have to be filled in with the result of an operation based on other squares, which obviously have to be calculated first. As example: Square *f* is three times *t* minus one third of *g*.

It can be easily seen that this method motivates the pupils to perform a considerable number of arithmetic operations within a wide range of difficulty and complexity, which they would be very reluctant to carry out, were the material to be presented in traditional format.

Roman Numbers

Pupils are required to perform arithmetic operations with Roman Numbers. The task needs no further explanations. Again, the rationale of this technique is the motivating effect and the flavour of aristocracy associated with the Roman culture.

Transformation of Centigrades

The relatively simple formula to transform centigrades into Fahrenheit and vice versa is taught. Hereafter, the pupils get lists of statements and have to decide whether they are plausible or absurd. (It must be added, that Israeli pupils have never encountered temperatures expressed in Fahrenheit. For example: Mother gave Jimmy some soup which was 35 degrees Fahrenheit. Jimmy said he could not eat it because it was too hot.)

Calculations of Journeys

The exercises of this unit consist in calculations of speed and duration of travel, the content of the problems being somewhat unusual and stimulating. Examples of problems are: How long would it take to walk from Jerusalem to Paris? How many years would it take to make a bicycle trip to the moon? Is it more worthwhile travelling to town x by car, bus or train, it being given that there is no direct train, the auto-route makes a detour, etc.

Foreign Exchange

Pupils are given the exchange rates of various currencies and are asked whether 'it is a bargain' to buy a certain merchandise in a foreign country, knowing its local price.

7. Subject Area: Citizenship

The purpose of this Subject Area is evident: familiarization of the disadvantaged post-adolescent with vital tasks and problems of everyday life. Simultaneously, an attempt made to train 'practical intelligence' (in the sense of Rey's theory) in the context of these everyday problems. The area is wide and the priority of subjects to be taught will depend on local circumstances as well as on the amount of knowledge and experience which the adolescent has already developed. This is also a subject area which has been extensively treated by the normal and special education learning and enrichment programs, so that abundant material is available which can be adapted to the principles and techniques of our curriculum. In the following sections, the main Learning Units, presently in use, will be described.

Communication

The importance of modern communication media is obvious. The most vital among them is the *telephone*. Therefore, a whole set of exercises has been designed to teach the disadvantaged how to use it. (Our experience has shown that the ignorance and awkwardness in this practical domain is amazing, and not only in disadvantaged populations). The exercises cover the following tasks and activities:

dialling, discrimination and interpretation of dial tones, knowledge of area codes; how to answer the phone, how to formulate and to take on telephone messages, and finally the organization of the telephone directory. Pupils train with real telephones, which in the beginning are not connected. Hereafter, internal lines (within the school) are used, one pupil phoning another in a different room. Finally, pupils undertake calls which normally are made by the administrative personnel of the school. For example, pupils have learned to order by telephone all the services required to organize a school trip, such as travel agencies, bus services, food, hostels. Naturally, there is a good opportunity to refine oral language (construction of clear and concise sentences, intonation, pronounciation, etc.). Another area implicitly involved in the telephone exercises, is social contact, i.e. the awareness of the other's reaction to the way we speak, the importance of certain manners which differentiate between polite, civilized conversation and rude, inconsiderate egocentric talk.

The telephone exercises were also introduced in normal Elementary and High Schools where teachers realized the necessity of teaching regular pupils these routine skills of our times. Encoding and decoding *telegrams* is an important exercise in communication which has already been described in the Language Area (see p. 165). 'Post Office' exercises deal with writing and reading letters, putting the correct amount of stamps, dispatching and receiving registered letters, money orders, etc. Arithmetics as well as language can be trained in this context.

Newspaper

This Learning Unit has several purposes. It teaches pupils to read the newspaper, it provides information on current events and widens the horizon of general knowledge. It stimulates 'meaningful' reading and abstraction ability, and also enriches the vocabulary. The tasks are simple: in one type of exercise, two or three short newspaper articles or reports are cut into two parts and the parts are mixed. The pupils have to find the corresponding parts and put them together. In a similar fashion, headings which have been separated from their respective columns, have to be correctly matched. The difficulty of the exercises can be gradually increased by separating headlines from columns which themselves are cut into more than two parts, and by chosing more and more complex passages with unfamiliar content. Besides administering these exercises, the teacher should use this opportunity to explain the structure of the newspaper, its various parts, sections and columns and how each is dedicated to a particular topic. Obviously, this Learning Unit offers a large basis for discussion of everything appearing in the news, i.e. political events, the life histories of persons making the headlines, cultural programs, and last but not least, traffic accidents and criminal acts.

Safety and First Aid

The content of this Learning Unit does not need to be explained. Its form has been made attractive by designing crossword puzzles, sentence completions, matching exercises, and open and closed questionnaires, which focus on problems of dressing wounds, resuscitation, prevention of poisoning, dealing with electrical instruments, using safety devices with industrial machinery, and so on. Experience has shown that in this domain pupils are eager to invent units and exercises. As there is a high ego involvement in these problems, and some of them provoke anxiety, the teacher should dedicate considerable time to discussions and ventilation of inner tensions.

4) Finally there are miscellaneous exercises which represent a Learning Unit of *General Information.* These exercises include information on agricultural products and their origin, evaluation of different types of transportation, and explanations of the function and competency of various public services. Some exercises are based on questions of the type, 'What do you do, if you have lost your identity card?' 'Which service or governmental department is supposed to deal with the following problems: insufficient water supply; prevention of spreading of infectious disease; granting a driver's licence; ensuring school attendance.'

Another type of exercise deals with the definition of the administrative power and competency of officers, directors, officials and other persons working in public services. There are also questionnaires focussing on the description of occupations and professions.

There is a whole group of units which focusses on the main school subjects, namely Geography, History, Physics, Bible and Biology. Except in content, the techniques of the Learning Units of these subject areas are the same as those used in the area of Citizenship, already described. In this part of the curriculum, much is left to the teacher as he alone can decide which content should be taught and to what extent, and which cognitive function could be most conveniently trained in the context of the general teaching program he wishes to implement.

There is another Learning Unit which remains to be described, which fits into a Subject Area not yet developed in the Curriculum of Contextual Learning Units, namely 'Social Relations'. This Learning Unit, 'Imagination of Characters' has been specially designed to train disadvantaged adolescents to differentiate social responses. The exercise consists in the presentation of two persons, who differ in their characters. The pupil has to imagine how they will behave at home, as children at the Elementary School, at High School, as adults at work in the army, as marriage partners and as parents of their own children. The simplest items deal with two opposite characters: a good, intelligent boy/a wicked, stupid boy. (Such an item is easy for the disadvantaged as he is used to judging persons as either extremely positive or extremely negative.) The tasks become complicated when the characters are ambiguous: a generous, strong, stupid boy/an intelligent, weak, miserly boy.

Naturally, this Learning Unit will stimulate discussions. It can be made more interesting by using role play to dramatize the life histories of the two different 'characters'.

CHAPTER 14

Evaluation of the Program of Contextual Learning Units

The curriculum of contextual learning units was introduced in Semi-skilled Apprentice Schools by the Israeli Ministry of Labour in 1975. It has been expanded since then, and during the scholastic year 1980-81 it was being used in 27 schools involving a population of about 2500 pupils.

General observations on the program's impact indicate that it has been widely accepted by teachers and educators. At present, educational systems and settings for which this curriculum was not originally designed are also interested in using it, namely Vocational High Schools, Institutions for Delinquents, Army Vocational Rehabilitation Centers for mentally retarded and disturbed youngsters exempted from military service, and Transit Hostels for wayward youth. The reason for the rapid and spontaneous acceptance of the method by educational personnel seems to be, on the one hand, the failure of existing programs to motivate the disadvantaged post-adolescent drop-outs to return to school and, on the other hand, the immediate intensive involvement of the pupils who are eager to cooperate. Another general observation made by educators is a conspicuous change in 'time on task', i.e. the time the pupils are ready to concentrate on their assignments. Teachers report increases from of 1 to 10 minutes before the introduction of the program up to concentration spans of one hour and more during and after the experimental period.

Furthermore, teachers as well as pupils are eager to 'invent' new teaching units (see Table 12, p. 157).

In addition to these general impressions and observations, some results of systematic evaluations are available. These results are based on two evaluation studies which refer to controlled experiments in two representative schools out of the 20 involved in the program during the scholastic years 1977–78 and 1978–79 respectively (Kohen-Raz, 1979, 1980). In addition, in 1980 a follow-up study on one of the schools of the 1977–78 experiment was carried out, i.e. two years after the pupils had left the Semi-skilled Apprentice School (Kohen-Raz, 1981). The central criteria of evaluation were the following:

a) Changes in mental level between pre- and post-tests in experimental and control groups.

b) Comparison of the rate and type of 'drop-out' from experimental and control groups.

Before reporting the findings, the criterion of 'drop-out' has to be qualified. As evident from the follow-up, and as will be described in detail below, a not negligible number of pupils left the Semi-skilled Apprentice School in order to enrol in higher level 'Skilled' Apprentice Schools — eventually to join a Kibbutz or some other institution providing formal education. In such cases it seems appropriate to speak of 'upwards move', or 'upward moving pupils'†, reserving the term 'drop out' to those youngsters who leave school and drift, lose contact with educational settings and services and eventually become wayward and delinquent.

In the first evaluation study an attempt was made to use the Milta Verbal Intelligence Test†† and the Raven Matrices (Raven, 1962) to assess change in mental level. However, many pupils refused to be examined with the Milta, which is a group test, involving reading and writing.

This happened in several schools and thus must be considered as a reaction of the disadvantaged to unpleasant reminiscences of classroom examinations, requiring language skill and literacy where they apparently experienced failure and frustration.

On the other hand, they responded well to the Raven Matrices, which besides being non-verbal does not bear any resemblance to scholastic assignments and examinations.

Comparison of pre-test and post-test scores in experimental and control groups, obtained with this instrument, revealed experi-

---

†Starr and Kahane (1978) speak of 'Legitimate Leavers', (See Chapter 3, p. 62).
††A Hebrew Version of the Lorge-Thorndike Test elaborated by Ortar and Murieli, 1965.

mental effects significant at the .05 level (Kohen-Raz, 1979). As already mentioned before (see Chapter 2, p. 43), the mental level of disadvantaged populations tend to be bi-modally distributed. It seems, therefore, plausible to analyze separately experimental effects in the 'retarded' and 'normally intelligent' subgroups of the samples. Chosing a cutting point of a Raven score of 30, which is one SD below the mean of normal Israeli adolescents at the age of 15, two groups emerged: one within normal range of mental level, and the other in the range of mild and borderline retardation. Separate data elaboration within these two subpopulations showed significant experimental effects in the group of the retarded and borderline†, while the 'normal' actually did not show any improvement.

An important aspect of the findings is the fact, that the experimental effect operates across schools, classes and teachers (see Table 16). It will be noted that in order to avoid Hawthorne Effects, all teachers taught in experimental as well as in control groups.††

As to the second evaluation criterion (drop-out and upwards move), it turned out that the 'normal' experimentals had an overall higher percentage of 'school leavers' than normally intelligent controls, while in the retarded group school leaving rates were not significantly different in experimentals and controls. Follow-up revealed that 32% of the school leavers from the experimental groups had entered regular skilled apprentice schools (i.e., were upwards moving), as against 4% in the control groups (p = .001). As evident from follow-up data after two years, most of the 'upwards moving' pupils were able to finish one to two years of systematic vocational training in the regular schools which they had joined, before enlisting in the army at the age of 18/19.

These results were carefully checked for bias, such as IQ

---

†Eventual effects of regressions towards the Mean were carefully investigated and found to be irrelevant (Kohen-Raz, 1979).
††Actually it can be seen (Table 16) that one teacher (number 4) seems to have been ineffective in most of the classes assigned to her. Thus, the negative results obtained in her experimental groups could well be due to her personal approach rather than the result of the teaching method. (These data highlight the importance to control the teacher variable, which is so often neglected in educational experiments.)

TABLE 16

Mean difference between pre- and post-tests (Raven) in 12 experimental and seven control groups (classes) sampled from two schools and taught by four different teachers. First evaluation study (1977/78)

		Experimental	Control
School I	Teacher 1	+ 0.2 (4)* + 3.3 (3) + 6.5 (2)	− 3.0 (2) − 5.0 (1)
	Teacher 2	+ 7.0 (3)	− 2.0 (3) + 1.5 (2)
School II	Teacher 3	+ 9 (1) + 1 (1) + 1.3 (3) + 2 (1)	− 3.5 (2)
	Teacher 4	− 9 (1) − 5.4 (5) − 0.2 (5) + 1 (3)	− 2.1 (8) − 3.3 (4)

	Experimental	Control
+	9	1
−	3	6

p = .05

*Numbers in brackets are numbers of Ss in each class for whom pre- and post-test data were available.

differences between experimental and controls, Hawtorne Effects, and teacher involvement in the transfer to higher level schools. None of these suspected factors turned out to have affected the significantly higher incidence of 'upwards moving pupils' in the experimental groups, i.e.:

a) There was no difference in the initial mental level between program participants and controls.

b) the 'upwards moving' came from different schools, different classroom groups taught by different teachers, who each had been teaching experimental as well as control groups during the experimental period. As already stated, this procedure had been established from the beginning of the study in order to control Hawthorne Effects.

TABLE 17

Distribution of 'upwards moving' pupils as per class, teacher, experimental and control groups (follow-up data)

	Teacher A				Teacher B				
	Exp.		Co.		Exp.		Co.		
Class[a]	I	II	III	X	VI	VII	VIII	XII	Total
Upwards moving	3	0	2	0	5	1	1	0	12
Not upwards moving	7	10	6	4	5	7	9	5	53

[a] Classes IV, V, IX and XI not tabulated, because including only girls (see footnote on p. 195).

TABLE 18

Distribution of mental scores[a] (Raven) in 'upwards moving' pupils as compared to rest of experimentals and controls (follow-up data boys only)[b]

		Mental level			
	N	Mild m. ret.	Borderline	Normal	
Raven score		-20	$21-30$	$31-40$	$41+$
Moved upwards	12	3 (25%)	2 (17%)	3 (25%)	4 (33%)
Rest of exp.	42	11 (26%)	13 (31%)	14 (33%)	5 (12%)
Controls[c]	11	3 (27%)	4 (36%)	3 (27%)	1 (9%)

[a] Pretest
[b] See footnote on p. 195
[c] None of the controls of the follow-up sample 'moved upwards'

c) The teachers were entirely ignorant as to what happened to the school leavers after they had left. It was the school counsellor who selected the pupils for transfer to 'better' schools, and she on her part had no knowledge as to the assignment of subjects to experimental or control groups.

Tables 17 and 18 show data of the follow-up study, involving one school, two teachers and eight male classes (six experimentals and two controls.† It will be noted (Table 18) that there is a relatively high incidence of experimental subjects (5) whose pretest mental level is borderline, in part even within the range of mild mental retardation, who nevertheless succeeded in adjusting to skilled apprentice schools. On the other hand, not a single subject of similar low mental ability in the control group of the follow-up sample 'moved upwards'.

Although no objective measures on pre- and post-experimental reading level are available (as already stated, pupils refused to take tests associated with reading skills), teacher evaluation of reading achievements at the end of the scholastic year (i.e. after the experimental intervention) in the follow-up sample of the 1977–78 experiment, indicate that reading level seems to play a decisive role in the 'upwards move' to higher level schools. That is, it turned out, that those pupils who were able to enter and complete vocational courses in skilled apprentice schools, in spite of functioning on a *low mental level*, were evaluated as *moderate or good readers*, while low intelligence controls, as well as a small group of experimentals of similar low intelligence, who absconded from class throughout most of the experimental period (none of them 'moving upwards') were considered to *read very poorly*. The difference in reading achievements was significant at the .01 level (Kohen-Raz, 1981a). Unless we assume that in spite of the random assignment of the 12 classes to eight experimental and four control groups, there was a covert bias in the experimental group in that initially it included a selected group of low intelli-

----

†As no girls in the follow-up sample had registered in skilled apprentice schools, only boys are tabulated on Tables 17 and 18. As revealed by the follow-up study (Kohen-Raz, 1981a), most girls, after leaving the semi-skilled apprentice school at the age of 17/18, got involved in relatively permanent jobs in nursing, welfare, office work and hotel services. Some of them married between the ages 18 to 20 and became housewives.

gence but reasonably good at reading, it is plausible to propose the hypothesis, that the program may improve the reading ability in disadvantaged post-adolescents of low and borderline mental level which in turn increases their chances to be accepted and to succeed at skilled apprentice schools.

It is obvious that this hypothesis cannot be supported by our present data, as no pretest scores on reading performance are available. However, it would not be difficult to test it in the context of future evaluations. In view of present findings and in the light of the high incidence of illiteracy in the population of disadvantaged 'unskilled' apprentices (the estimated percentage is 15 to 50%) specially adapted versions of the Program of Contextual Learning Units are to be used as a technique of remedial teaching.

In a second evaluation study (Kohen-Raz, 1980) two schools with a relatively low drop-out rate were chosen. On the other hand, principals did not agree to split each class into an experimental and control sub-group, which prevented the control of the teacher variable. Another obstacle was a drastic reduction of the experimental period to three months due to a prolonged teacher strike during the first two months of the scholastic year.

A larger battery of tests, routinely used by the Vocational Guidance Service of the Ministry of Labour was used.† Again, no experimental effects on mental achievements were observed in the normally intelligent groups, but on the other hand there were definitive gains on the tests of verbal instructions and technical problems in the *retarded* classes. No effects were obtained on tests of matrices, coding, arithmetics and visual acuity. Although experimentals and controls had equal intelligence levels at the beginning of the evaluation study, 'drop outs' from the experimental groups had a significantly higher intelligence than those from the controls. Again, it seemed as if the curriculum 'pushed' the normally intelligent pupils out of the semiskilled apprentice school. Although the follow-up on the populations of this second study is as yet incomplete, preliminary data indicate that 'upwards moving pupils' belong exclusively to the experi-

---

†This battery included the following tests: verbal instruments, matrices, coding, technical reasoning, arithmetic problems and visual acuity.

mental groups. On the other hand, among the drop-outs from the control groups, four became delinquent as against none among the experimentals.

Summing up the results of hitherto available systematic evaluations the following tentative conclusions can be drawn:

1) The program is rapidly being accepted and implemented by teachers and educators.

2) Disadvantaged post-adolescents, who hitherto did not respond to any form of teaching programs become quickly motivated and involved in the Curriculum of Contextual Learning Units.

3) Teachers, as well as pupils respond well to the incentive built into the program to invent and to create by themselves new exercises and learning units.

4) The mental level in the population of disadvantaged post-adolescent drop-outs tends to be bi-modally distributed, so that two sub-groups can be differentiated: a sub-group of borderline and mildly retarded youngsters, and a sub-group within the normal range of mental ability. The scholastic failure of the latter has thus to be attributed chiefly to environmental and educational neglect, as well as to the inadequacy of the general curriculum. (See Chapter 8.)

5) The program of the contextual learning units seems to improve the manifestly low mental level of the 'retarded' sub-groups, but has no tangible effect on the intellectual performance of the 'normals'.

6) On the other hand, it appears to stimulate the 'upwards move' of normally intelligent, as well as of low and borderline intelligent, disadvantaged adolescents to leave semiskilled apprentice schools and to enrol successfully in higher level skilled apprentice schools. Reading level seems to represent an important factor in this process, especially in the lower intelligence subjects. The suspected impact of the program on reading ability remains to be demonstrated by further evaluation of specially designed intervention methods.

Concluding Remarks

After having presented the various theoretical and pragmatic aspects of education and rehabilitation of disadvantaged post-adolescents we are aware that we are facing a problem which is still far from being resolved.

Neither the theoretical framework nor the practical approaches can be considered as being wholly satisfactory and comprehensive.

One basic difficulty lies in the insufficient differentiation of the various types of 'culturally disadvantaged' pupils, whose development diversifies increasingly as they pass through late childhood and adolescence. We have seen, that some of the disadvantaged function at normal intellectual levels, and a not negligible number among the latter even within the upper range of intelligence. Some others seem to be 'secondarily' retarded, in that their ability for abstract thought is inhibited and distorted as a result of 'externalization'. But there appears also to be a considerable percentage of those functioning at and below the boundaries of normal mental level, whose retardation seems to be only partly reversible. Finally, it must not be forgotten, that due to 'biosocial' interaction of social deprivation and (sometimes mild) CNS damage, as well as due to the great physical and mental stress to which the disadvantaged family is exposed, we find in each 'random' 'normal' sample of disadvantaged children and adolescents a higher incidence of psychopathology than in non-disadvantaged strata.

This is specially true for mild and medium brain dysfunction, behavior disorders, deep personality disturbances and various types of 'multiple handicap', etc. No satisfactory theory can thus be developed without taking into account these different types, and no comprehensive system of rehabilitation can be developed without being equipped with instruments of differential diagnosis and specialized programs of intervention properly designed to confront the variety of problems of these 'variations' of the 'disadvantaged'.

It seems that the theories of Rey and Frankenstein are best available approximations to a 'general theory of disadvantaged post-adolescence'. Rey, by virtue of his meticulous analysis of 'basic mechanisms' of intelligence and by virtue of the instruments and clinical methods of testing he has designed. Frankenstein has created a psychodynamic model, which serves as an alternative to classical 'psychodynamics', to explain the emotional, social and intellectual maladjustment of the disadvantaged person as being interdependent and manifest in syndromes of 'externalization'. He has also provided a differential diagnosis of various types of mental retardation, including 'secondary' retardation, as the most prominent in disadvantaged populations and from the point of view of rehabilitation, also the most promising.

It can also be seen why psychoanalysis and neo-psychoanalysis as well as the Piagetian 'structural approach' are 'out of context' when to be applied to problems of cognitive development of disadvantaged persons. This does not mean, that these very important theoretical frameworks should not be applicable to the problem area of underpriviledged youth. However, considerable efforts have yet to be made to adapt these models to suit the peculiar needs of these populations, as well as in order to provide a basis for pragmatic research which would yield findings operative in educational situations. In this respect Wason's and Johnson-Laird's lucid experiments on the role of context in higher cognitive functions seem to offer valuable contributions.

Overviewing the four projects which have been presented, we gain an overall impression that they complement each other to a certain extent. First, they seem to deal, in descending order, with 'a continuum' of disadvantaged types, from the 'gifted' to the 'retarded'. The Boarding School Fostering being on the top, hereafter Frankenstein's Rehabilitative Teaching. Contextual Learning Units are on the other, lower end of the continuum, attempting to cope with the marginal, drop out post-adolescents. Feuerstein's Instrumental Enrichment takes an in between position, which is difficult to define. His target population is of a great variety, but is definitively not 'gifted', and on the other hand, does not comprise youngsters, whose school attendance is sporadic, irregular and loosely controlled, which is typical for participants in the Contextual Learning Program. Frankenstein, dealing with the impairment of higher symbol formation, verbal-linguistic backwardness and restricted abstraction ability complements Feuerstein, who focusses on formal reasoning in visual-spatial contexts. The Curriculum of Contextual Learning Units covers the 'content areas' which Feuerstein intentionally avoids, in order to concentrate on 'pure' structure formation. Smilansky and Frankenstein, both have designed potent intervention methods to deal with parent/post-adolescent dynamics, which are not in the focus of Instrumental Enrichment and Contextual Learning. Finally, Frankenstein and Smilansky present two complementary experiences on integration.

There are, however, also important common points which might serve as basis for a theory and practical design for rehabilitation methods for disadvantaged post-adolescents:

1) All programs postulate the reversibility of the disadvantaged post-adolescent's mental retardation, and all four of them have proved it to varying degrees, and with different statistical rigor, Smilansky's project being the most convincing.

2) All projects focus on the rehabilitation of motivation and re-establishment of positive attitudes towards school and work as well as on the improvement of the self-image.

3) In all projects techniques have been designed to foster higher forms of reasoning, including higher concept formation and formal reasoning.

4) The role of the 'close educator' is evident in all programs.

5) All projects show a 'snowball' effect of being increasingly applied throughout the country, each in the section of disadvantaged youth which had been chosen as target population.

Thus, in spite of the fact, that we are confronted with a difficult and vital problem of modern post-technological society, still facing failure and difficulties in our attempts to cope with all the various and pressing needs of disadvantaged post-adolescents, the overall picture is optimistic. The problem is there, but it can be tackled by integrating sound and appropriate theories with well intended and well designed systematic, practical efforts.

References

Abernethy, E.M. Relationship between mental and physical growth. *Monographs of the Society for Research in Child Development.* 1, Serial No. 7 1936.

Adler, A. *Problems of Neurosis.* New York: Harper and Row 1964.

Ainsworth, M.D.S. and Bell S.M. Mother-infant interaction and the development of competence. In *The Growth of Competence* (Conolly, K. and Burner, J.). London, Academic Press, 1974.

Anastasi, A. *Differential Psychology.* New York: MacMillan, 1958.

Arbitman-Smith, R., Haywood, H.C. and Bransford, D. Assessing cognitive change. In *Learning and Cognition in the Mentally Retarded*, (McCauley, C.M., Sperber, R. and Brooks, P., eds.). Baltimore: University Park Press, in press.

Arthur, G.A. *A Point Scale Performance Test.* Clinical Manual. New York: Commonwealth Fund, 1930.

Ausubel, D. and Ausubel, P. Cognitive development in adolescence. *Review of Educational Research*, 36, 4, 403—413, 1966.

Ausubel, D. *Educational Psychology, A Cognitive View.* New York: Holt, Rinehart and Winston, 1968.

Bachman, J.G., O'Malley, P.M. and Johnston, J. *Youth in Transition.* Vol. 6. Ann Arbor: I.S.R. University of Michigan, 1978.

Bandura, A. The stormy decade. Fact or fiction? *Psychology in the Schools.* 1, 224—231, 1964.

Barker, R.G. Ecology and motivation. Nebraska Symposium on Motivations, 8, 1—50, 1960.

Beard, R.M. The nature and development of concepts. *Educational Review*, 13, 12—26, 1960.

Benedict, R. Continuities and discontinuities in cultural conditioning. In *The Adolescent* (Seidman, J.M.). New York: Dryden, 1953.

Berlyne, D.E. *Conflict, Arousal, Curiosity.* New York: McGraw-Hill, 1960.

Bernfeld, S. Uber eine typische From der mannlichen pubertät. *Imago*, 9, 1923.

Bernstein, B. *Class, Codes and Control.* London: Routledge and Kegan Paul, 1975.

Bernstein, B. Language and social class. *British Journal of Sociology*, 11, 271—276, 1960.

Bidwell, C.E. and Kasarda, J.D. School district organization and student achievement. *Amer. Sociological Review*, 40, 55–70, 1975.

Binswanger, L. *Grundformen and Erkenntnis des menschlichen Daseins.* Zürich: Niehaus, 1942.

Bloom, B. *Stability and Change in Human Characteristics.* New York: Wiley, 1964.

Blos, P. *On Adolescence.* Glencoe, Ill.: Free Press, 1962.

Boyd, P.R. Drug abuse and addiction in adolescents. In *Modern Perspectives in Adolescent Psychiatry*, (Howell, J.G. ed.). New York: Bruner-Mazel, pp. 290–328, 1971.

Brittain, C.V. Adolescent choices of parent-peer cross pressures. *American Sociological Review*, 28, 385–391, 1967.

Brittain, C.V. A comparison of rural and urban adolescents with respect to peer *vs.* parent compliance. *Adolescence*, 4, 57–68, 1969.

Buber, M. *I and Thou.* New York: Charles Scribner and Sons, 1958.

Bühler, Ch. *From Birth to Maturity.* London: Kegan Paul, 1947.

Buxton, C.E. *Adolescents in School.* New Haven: Yale Universities Press, 1973.

Castarède, M.F. *Les Adolescents d'Aujourdhui. Psychosexualité Adolescente en 1976.* Unpublished Ph.D. Thesis. University of Paris V. 1978.

Cazden, C.B. Subcultural differences in child language. In *The Disadvantaged Child*, Helmuth J. (ed.). Vol I. Seattle: Special Child Publications, 1967.

Chen, M. Levi, A. and Adler, Ch. Process and Outcome in Education. Evaluation of the Comprehensive Secondary School System in Israel (Hebrew). Jerusalem: Tel-Aviv University and Hebrew University, 1978.

Cherry, F.F. and Eaton, E.L. Physical and cognitive development in children of low-income mothers working in the child's early years. *Child Development*, 48, 158–166, 1977.

Chronique, O.M.S. *Le suicide chez les jeunes.* 29, 214–218, 1975.

Claxton, G. *Cognitive Psychology. New Directions.* London: Routledge, Kegan and Paul, 1980.

Clinard, M.B. *Anomie and Deviant Behavior.* New York: Free Press, 1964.

Cogner, J.J. Sexual Attitudes and Behavior of Contemporary Adolescents. In *Contemporary Issues in Adolescent Development*, (Cogner, J.J.). New York: Harper and Row, 1975.

Constantinople, A. An Erikson measure of personality development in college students. *Developmental Psychology*, 1, 357–372, 1969.

Cronbach, L. Five decades of public controversy over mental testing. *American Psychologist*, 30, 1–14, 1975.

Cull, J.G. and Hardy, R.E. *Problems of Disadvantaged and Deprived Youth.* Springfield, Ill.: Thomas, 1975.

Davidson, F. and Choquet, M. Etude epidemologique du suicide de l'adolescent. *Revue Epid. et Santé Publique*, 24, 11–26, 1976.

Deutsch, C.P. The development of auditory discrimination; relationship to reading proficiency and social class. Washington, D.C. U.S. Office of Education. Final Report. Project No. 6-3034, 1972.

Deutsch, H. *Psychology of Women.* New York: Grune and Stratton, 1945.

Deutsch, M. *The Disadvantaged Child.* New York: Basic Books, 1967.

Donaldson, M. *A Study of Children's Thinking.* London: Tavistock, 1963.

Douglas, L.W.B. and Ross, J.M. Age of puberty as related to educational ability, attainment and school leaving age. *Journal of Child Psychology and Psychiatry*, 5, p. 185–196, 1964.

Dreikurs, R. *Fundamentals of Adlerian Psychology.* New York: Greenberg, 1950.

Dulit, D. Adolescent thinking à la Piaget. The formal stage. *Journal of Youth and Adolescence*, 1, 281–301, 1972.

Dunphy, D.C. The social structure of urban adolescent peer groups. *Sociometry*, 26, 230–240, 1963.

Edwards, D. Social relations and early language. In *Action, Gesture and Symbol*, (Lock, A. ed.). London: Academic Press, 1978.

Eibl-Eibesfeldt, I. *Ethology: The Biology of Behavior.* New York: Holt, Rinehart and Winston, 1970.

Eisenstadt, S.N. The new youth revolt. (Hebrew). *Megamoth*, 9, 95–102, 1958.

Eliram, Y. *Variables in Differential Diagnosis of Delinquency Proneness in Disadvantaged Children.* Unpublished Ph.D. Thesis. Jerusalem: Hebrew University, 1979.

Elkind, D. Children's discovery of the conservation of mass, weight and volume. *Journal of Genetic Psychology*, 98, 219–227, 1961.

Elkind, D. Adolescent cognitive development. In *Understanding Adolescents*, (Aram, J.E.). Boston: Allyn and Bacon, 1968.

Elkind, D. Egocentrism in adolescence. In *Studies in Adolescence*, (R.E. Grinder, ed.). New York: MacMillan, 1969.

Ennis, R.H. Children's ability to handle Piaget's propositional logic. *Review of Educational Research.* 45, 1–41, 1975.

Ennis, R.H. Conceptualization of children's logical competence: Piaget's propositional logic and an alternative proposal. In *Alternatives to Piaget, (Siegel, L.S. and Brainerd Ch. J.).* New York: Academic Press, 1978.

Epstein, H.T. Phrenoblysis. Special brain and mind growth periods. *Developmental Psychology*, 7, 207–224, 1974.

Erikson, E.H. *Youth, Change and Challenge.* New York: Basic Books, 1963.

Erikson, E.H. *Identity, Youth and Crisis.* New York: Norton, 1968.

Erikson, E.H. *Childhood and Society.* Harmondsworth: Penguin, 1972.

Evans, J.H. and Wason, P.V. Rationalisation in a reasoning task. *British Journal of Psychology*, 67, 479–486, 1976.

Eysenck, H.J. *The Measurement of Personality.* Baltimore: University Park Press, 1976.

Fay, W.H. *Temporal Sequences in the Perception of Speech.* The Hague: Mouton, 1966.

Ferguson, E. The mind's eye. Non verbal thought in technology. *Science*, 197, 4306, 827–836, 1977.

Ferron, O. The test performance of 'colored' children. *Educational Research*, 8, 42–57, 1965.

Feuerstein, R. The dynamic assessment of retarded performance. *The*

Learning Potential Assessment Device. Baltimore: University Park Press, 1979.

Feuerstein, R. *Instrumental Enrichment.* Baltimore: University Park Press, 1980.

Finch, F. *Kuhlman-Finch Tests. Junior High School Test.* Minneapolis: American Guidance Service, 1957.

Fischbein, S. Heredity-environment influences on growth and development during adolescence. In *Twin Research,* Vol. 3, Part B., 211–226, (Gedda, L., Parisi, P. and Nance, W.E., eds.). New York: Alan Liss, 1981.

Florida, Dale County Public Schools, Department of Research and Information. *A Study of Drop-Outs.* Dale County Miami: Florida Public Schools, 1960–1963.

Frank, J. and Levinson, H.N. Compensatory mechanisms in cerebellar-vestibular dysfunction, dysmetric dyslexia and dyspraxia. *Academic Therapy,* 12, 1–14, 1976.

Frankenstein, C. A new type of juvenile delinquency. (Hebrew). *Megamoth,* 9, 237–249, 1958.

Frankenstein, C. *Psychopathy.* New York: Grune and Stratton, 1959.

Frankenstein, C. The school without parents. In *Scripta Hierosolymitana,* Vol. 13, Studies in Education. Jerusalem: Magnes Press, 1963.

Frankenstein, C. *The Roots of the Ego.* Baltimore: Williams and Wilkins, 1966.

Frankenstein, C. *Psychodynamics of Externalization.* Baltimore: Williams and Wilkins, 1968.

Frankenstein, C. *Impaired Intelligence.* New York: Gordon and Breach, 1970a.

Frankenstein, C. *Varieties of Juvenile Delinquency.* New York: Gordon and Breach, 1970b.

Frankenstein C. *They Think Again.* New York: Van Nostrand, 1979.

Freud, A. *The Ego and the Mechanisms of Defense.* New York: International University Press, 1953.

Freud, S. *Totem and Taboo.* New York: Random House, 1948.

Fromm, E. *Psychology and Religion.* New Haven: Yale University Press, 1950.

Gedda, L., Parisi, P. and Nance, W.E. (eds.). *Twin Research,* Vol. 3, Part B. New York: Alan Liss, 1981.

Gewirtz, J.L. and Baer, D.M. Deprivation and satiation of social reinforcers as drive conditions. *Journal of Abnormal Social Psychology,* 56, 165–172, 1958.

Goldman, A.R. and Herman, J.L. Studies in vicariousness. The effects of immobilisation on Rorschach responses. *Journal of Projective Techniques,* 25, 164–165, 1961.

Gough, H.C. and Domino, C. The D-48 test as a measure of general ability among grade school children. *Journal of Consulting Psychology,* 27, 344–349, 1963.

Guhl, A.M. The social order of chickens. *Scientific American,* 194, 42–62, 1956.

Guilford, J.P. *Fundamental Statistics in Psychology and Education.* New

York: McGraw-Hill, p. 503, 1956.

Guilford, J.P. *The Nature of Human Intelligence.* New York: McGraw-Hill, 1967.

Guttman, L. and Schlesinger, I.M. *Development of Diagnostic Analytical and Mechanical Ability Tests Through Facet Design and Analysis.* Jerusalem: Israel Institute of Applied Social Research, 1966, 1967.

Hall, G. St. *Adolescence.* New York: Appleton, 1908.

Halper, J. *Ethnicity and Education.* Ann Arbor Michigan University Microfilms, No. 7812903, 1979.

Halpern, L. Studies on the neurobiological effects of colors. In *Problems of Dynamic Neurology,* (Halpern, L. ed.). Jerusalem: Hebrew University Hadassa University Hospital, 1963.

Havighurst, R.J. *The Public Schools of Chicago.* Chicago: Board of Education, 1964.

Holinger, P.C. Adolescent suicide. An epidemological study of recent trends. *American Journal of Psychiatry,* 135, 6, 754—756, 1978.

Horney, K. *Neurosis and Human Growth.* New York: Norton, 1950.

Hunt, D.E. Person environment interaction. A challenge found wanting before it was tried. *Review of Educational Research,* 45, 209—230, 1975.

Hunt, J. Motivation inherent in information processing and action. In *Motivation and Social Interaction,* (Harvey, O. ed.). New York: Ronald, 1963.

Inhelder, B. and Piaget, J. *The Growth of Logical Thinking from Childhood to Adolescence.* New York: Basic Books, 1959.

Jensen, A. How much can we boost IQ and scholastic achievements. *Harvard Educational Review,* 39, 1—123, 1969.

Johnson-Laird, P.V., Legrenzi, P. and Legrenzi, M. Reasoning and a sense of reality. *British Journal of Psychology,* 63, 1972.

Jung, C.G. *Psychologie und Alchemie.* Zürich: Rascher, 1952.

Jung, C.G. *Man and His Symbols.* New York: Doubleday, 1964.

Jung, C.G. *Symbols of Transformation.* Princeton: Princeton University Press, 1974.

Kantner, J.F. and Zelnik, M. Sexual experience of young unmarried women in the U.S. *Family Planning Perspectives,* 4, 9—18, 1972.

Karmel, B.Z. Contour effects and pattern performance in infants. *Child Development,* 45, 39—48, 1974.

Karplus, R. Education and formal thought — a modest proposal. In *New Directions in Piagetian Theory and Practice,* (Sigel, I.E., Brodzinsky, D.M. and Golinkoff, R.M. eds.). 285—314. Hillsdale, N.J.: Lawrence Erlbaum, 1981.

Katz, P. and Zigler, E. Self image disparity. *Journal of Personality and Social Psychology,* 5, 186—195, 1967.

Kaufman, I., Makkay, E.S. and Zilbach, J. The impact of adolescence on girls with delinquent character formation. *American Journal of Orthopsychiatry,* 29, 130—143, 1959.

Keating, D.P. Thinking processes in adolescence. In *Handbook of Adolescence,* (Adelson, J. ed.). New York: Wiley, 1980.

Keniston, K. Youth as a stage of life. In *The Adolescent as Individual: Issues and Insights*, (Guardo, C.J.). New York: Harper and Row, 1975.

Kitsis, I. *The Israeli Adolescent in the Apprentice School: His Personality and Educational Problems*. Unpublished Ph.D. Thesis. Jerusalem: Hebrew University, School of Education, 1974.

Kohen-Raz, R. Movement representations and their relations to the development of conceptual thought at early school age. In *Scripta Hierosolymitana*. Vol. 14, Studies in Psychology, Jerusalem: Magnes Press, 1965.

Kohen-Raz, R. *The Child from 9–13. The Psychology of Pre-adolescence and Early Puberty*. Chicago: Aldine-Atherton, 1971.

Kohen-Raz, R. *From Chaos to Reality. An Experiment in Re-education of Emotionally Disturbed Immigrant Youth in a Kibbutz*. New York: Gordon and Breach, 1972.

Kohen-Raz, R. *Growth and acquisition of formal reasoning in disadvantaged adolescents as related to physiological maturation*. Final Report. Dallas, Texas: Zale Foundation, 1973.

Kohen-Raz, R. Special education needs at adolescence. In *Adolescent Psychiatry*, (Feinstein, S.C. ed.). Vol. V. New York: Aronson, 1977a.

Kohen-Raz, R. *Psychobiological Aspects of Cognitive Growth*. New York: Academic Press, 1977b.

Kohen-Raz, R. *YIFTACH: A Program of Contextual Learning Units*. (Hebrew). Annual Research Progress Reports. Jerusalem: Ministry of Labour and Social Affairs, 1979, 1980, 1981a.

Kohen-Raz, R. and Bar-Lev M. *YIFTACH. A Program of Contextual Learning Units*. (Hebrew). Jerusalem: Ministry of Labour and Social Affairs, 1980.

Kohen-Raz, R. The impact of twin research in developmental studies on models of human development. In *Twin Research*, Vol. 3, Part B., p. 251–254, (Gedda, L., Parisi, P. and Nance, W.E., eds.). New York: Alan Liss, 1981.

Kohen-Raz, R., Russel, A. and Ornoy, A. Early assessment and prevention of socio-cultural deprivation in infants. *Mental Health and Society*, 2, 11ᴱ -123, 1975.

Kohlberg, L. *Stages in the Development of Moral Thought*. New York: Holt, Rinehart and Winston, 1969.

Kohlberg, L. Moral stages and moralisation. The cognitive development approach. In *Moral Development and Behavior. Theory, Research and Social Issues*, (Lickone, T. ed.). New York: Holt, Rinehart and Winston, 1976.

Kohlberg, L. and Gilligan, C. The adolescent as a philosopher. The discovery of self in a post-conventional world. *Daedalus*, 100, 1051–1086, 1971.

Kohlberg, L. and Kramer, R. Continuities and discontinuities in childhood and adult moral development. *Human Development*, 12, 93–120, 1969.

Kriesberg, L. *Mothers in Poverty: A Study of Fatherless Families*. Chicago: Aldine, 1970.

Kuhlen, R.G. *The Psychology of Adolescent Development*. New York: Harper and Brothers, 1952.

Lane, B.A. The relationship of learning disabilities to juvenile delinquency:

Current Status. *Journal of Learning Disabilities*, 13, 425—434, 1980.

Leissner, A. *Street Club Work in Tel-Aviv and New York*. London: Longmans, 1969.

Levin, D.E. *The Predication of Academic Performance*. New York: Russell Sage Foundation, 1965.

Levine, D. and Linn, M.C. Scientific reasoning ability in adolescence. *Journal of Research in Science Teaching*, 14, 371—374, 1977.

Linn, M.C. and Rice, M. A measure of scientific reasoning. The spring task. *Journal of Educational Measurement*, 16, 55—58, 1979.

Ljung, B.D. *The Adolescent Spurt in Mental Growth*. Uppsala: Almquist, 1965.

Lorenz, K. *Studies in Animal and Human Behavior*. London: Methuen, 1970.

Lunzer, E. Problems of formal reasoning in test situations. In *European Research in cognitive development, Monographs of the Society for Research in Child Development*, (Mussen, P.H., ed.). Vol. 30, No. 2 1965.

Maier, H.W. *Three Theories of Child Development*. New York: Harper and Row, 1969.

Manaster, G.J., Saddler, C.D. and Williamson, L. *The Ideal Self and Cognitive Development in Adolescence*. Austin: University of Texas, Austin, (mimeo), 1976.

Manaster, G.J. *Adolescent Development and the Life Tasks*. Boston: Alyn and Bacon, 1977.

Marans, A.E. and Lourie, R. Hypotheses regarding the effects of child rearing patterns on the disadvantaged child. In *The Disadvantaged Child*, (Hellmuth, J. ed.). Vol. 1. Seattle: Special Child Publications, 1967.

Marbach, S. and Zahavi, P.A. *Follow-Up Study of Graduates from Boarding Schools of the Israel Society for the Advancement of Education*, 1964—1973, (Hebrew). Jerusalem: Publication of the Israel Society for the Advancement of Education, 1980.

Marcia, J.E. Developmental validation of ego identity status. *Journal of Personal and Social Psychol.*, 3, 551—558, 1966.

Marcia, J.E. Ego identity status. *Journal of Personality*, 35, 118—133, 1967.

Matheny, A.P. and Dolan, A.B. Persons, situations and time. A genetic view of behavioral change in children. *Journal of Personality and Social Psychol.*, 32(6), 1106—1110, 1975.

McGee, M. Human spatial abilities. *Psychol. Bulletin*, 86, 5, 889—918, 1979.

McLaughlin, M.M. Survivors and surrogates. In *History of Childhood*, (De Maise, L. ed.). New York: The Psycho-history Press, 1974.

Montgomery, K.C. Explorative drive in learning. *Journal of Comparative and Physiological Psychology*, 47, 60, 1954.

Muchov, H.H. *Jugend und Zeitgeist*. Hamburg: Rohwolt, 1962.

Musgrove, F. *Youth and the Social Order*. London: Kegan-Paul, 1964.

Mykelbust, H. *Progress in Learning Disabilities*, Vol. IV., New York: Grune and Stratton, 1978.

Nisbet, J.D. and Illsley, R. The influence of early puberty on test performance at the age of eleven. *British Journal of Educational Psychology*, 33, 176—196, 1963.

Odom, R.D., A perceptual-salience account of decalage relations and developmental change. In *Alternatives to Piaget*, (Siegel, L.S. and Brainerd, Ch. J.). New York: Academic Press, 1978.

Ortar, G. Examination of the validity of the eighth grade screening test. (Hebrew). *Megamoth*, 10, 209—221, 1960.

Ortar, G. and Murieli, A. *MILTA. A Group Intelligence Test for Grades 1—12*. (Hebrew). Jerusalem: Hebrew University, School of Education, 1965.

Parsons, T. and Bales, F. *Family, Socialization and Interaction Process*. Glencoe, Ill.: Free Press, 1955.

Passow, H.A., Golberg, M. and Tannenbaum, A.J. *Education for the Disadvantaged*. New York: Holt, Rinehart and Winston, 1967.

Passow, H.A. *Opening Opportunities for Disadvantaged Learners*. New York: Teacher's College Press, 1972.

Peel, E.A. *The Pupil's Thinking*. London: Oldbourne, 1960.

Perkal, M. *Assessment and Analysis of Class Atmosphere in Comprehensive Secondary Schools in Israel*. Unpublished M.A. Thesis. Jerusalem: Hebrew University, School of Education, 1980.

Piaget, J. *The Child's Conception of Number*. London: Routledge and Kegan Paul, 1952.

Piaget, J. *The Child Concept of Space*. London: Routledge and Kegan Paul, 1956.

Piaget, J. *Les Mechanisms Perceptifs*. Paris: Presses Universitaires de France, 1961.

Piaget, J. *Biology and Knowledge*. Chicago: Univ. of Chicago Press, 1971.

Piaget, J. Intellectual evolution from adolescence to adulthood. *Human Development*, 15, 1—12, 1972.

Poeck, K. and Huber, W. To what extent is language a sequential activity? *Neuropsychologia*, 15, 359—363, 1977.

Rahamim, R. *Social Distance and Perception of Parents in Regular and Disadvantaged Elementary School Pupils* (Hebrew). Unpublished M.A. Thesis. Jerusalem: School of Education, Hebrew University, 1979.

Raven, J.C. *Progressive Matrices*. London: Lewis, 1962.

Rey, A. *L'Intelligence Pratique Chez L'Enfant (Observations et Experiences)*. Paris: Alcan, 1935.

Rey, A. *Etude des Insuffisances Psychologiques*. Neuchâtel: Delachaux and Nestlé, 1947.

Rey, A. *Techniques Inedites pour L'Examen Psychologique*. Neuchâtel: Delachaux and Nestlé, Vol. 1—5, 1968, 1969.

Riessman, F. *The Inner City Child*. New York: Harper, 1976.

Rourke, P. Reading, spelling and arithmetic disabilities. A neuropsychological approach. In *Progress in Learning Disabilities*, (Myklebust, H. ed.). New York: Grune and Stratton, 1978.

Rousseau, J.J. *Emile*. London: Dent, 1969.

Rutter, M. and Madge, N. *Cycles of Disadvantage*. London: Heinemann, 1976.

Rutter, M., Graham, P., Chadwick, O.F.D. and Yule, W. Adolescent turmoil. Fact or fiction? *Journal of Child Psychology and Psychiatry*, 17, 35—56,

1976.
Rutter, M. and Yule, W. Specific reading retardation. In *The First Review of Special Education*, (Mann, L. and Sabatino, D. eds.). Philadelphia, Pennsylvania: Butterwood Farms Inc. JSE Press Series in Special Education, 1973.
Salzstein, L., Diamond, R.M. and Belenky, M. Moral judgement level and conformity behavior. *Developmental Psychology*, 7, 327–336, 1972.
Scarr-Salapatek, S. An evolutionary perspective on infant intelligence. In *Infant Intelligence*, (M. Lewis, ed.). New York: Plenum, 1976.
Silberberg, N. School achievement and delinquency. *Rev. of Educational Research*, 41, 17–33, 1971.
Silberman, C.E. *Crisis in the Classroom*. New York: Random House, 1970.
Slovin-Ela, S. and Kohen-Raz, R. Developmental differences in primary reaching responses of young infants from varying social backgrounds. *Child Development*, 49, 132–140, 1978.
Smilansky, M. *Gifted Students in Schools for the Disadvantaged. Their Assessment and Training*. Jerusalem: Szold Foundation, 1966.
Smilansky, M. and Nevo, D. *The Gifted Disadvantaged*. New York: Gordon and Breach, 1979.
Smilansky, S. *The Effect of Sociodramatic Play on Disadvantaged Preschool Children*. New York: Wiley, 1968.
Smith, T.E. some bases for parental influence upon late adolescents: an application of a social power model. *Adolescence*, 5, 323–338, 1970.
Sorenson, R.C. *Adolescent Sexuality in Contemporary America. Personal Values and Sexual Behavior, Ages 19–13*. New York: World Publishing, 1973.
Staats, A.W. Intelligence, biology and learning. In *Socio-cultural Aspects of Mental Retardation*. (H.C. Haywood ed.). (Proceedings of the Peabody-NIMH Conference.) New York: Appleton-Century-Crofts, 1970.
Starr, L. and Kahane, R. Holding power. An analysis of school leaving and drop out from the technological system in Israel. Jerusalem: Hebrew University, N.C.J.W. Research Institute, (mimeo), 1978.
Stoddard, G. *The Meaning of Intelligence*. New York: MacMillan, 1951.
Strang, R. *The Adolescent Views Himself*. New York: McGraw-Hill, 1957.
Sundberg, N.D. *Assessment of Persons*. Englewood Cliffs, New Jersey: Prentice Hall, 1977.
Sullivan, H.S. *Interpersonal Theory of Psychiatry*. New York: Norton, 1953.
Talmon-Garber, Y. Mate selection in collective settlements. *Amer. Soc. Review*, 29, 461–508, 1964.
Tanner, J.M. *Growth at Adolescence*. Springfield, Ill.: Thomas, 1962.
Tanner, J.M. Early maturation in man. *Scientific American*, 218, 21–27, 1968.
Thurstone, L.L. and Ackerman, L. The mental growth curve for the Binet tests. *Journal of Educational Psychology*, 20, 569–583, 1929.
Thurstone, T.G. S.R.A. *Primary Mental Abilities Test*. Chicago: Science Research Associates, 1962.
Tinbergen, N. *The Study of Instinct*. Oxford: Clarendon, 1955.

Tomlinson-Keasey, C. and Keasey, C.B. The mediating role of cognitive development and moral judgement. *Child Development*, **45**, 291–298, 1974.

Tulkin, S.R. Mother-child interaction in the first year of life. *Child Development*, **43**, 31–41, 1972.

Vener, A.M., Steward, C.S. and Hager, D.L. Adolescent sexual behavior in America revisited, 1970–1973. *Journal of Marriage and the Family*, **36**, 728–735, 1974.

Wapner, S. and Werner, H. *Perceptual Development*. Worcester, Mass.: Clark University Press, 1957.

Wason, P.C. Hypothesis testing and reasoning. *British Journal of Psychology*, **60**, 47–80, 1969.

Wason, P.C. and Johnson-Laird, P.N. *Psychology of Reasoning: Structure and Content*. London: Batsford, 1972.

Wason, P.C. and Evans, J.H. Dual processes in reasoning. *Cognition*, 3, 141–154, 1975.

Weisbroth, S.P. Moral judgement, sex and parental identification in adults. *Developmental Psychology*, 2, 396–402, 1970.

Wessmann, A.E. and Ricks, D.F. *Mood and Personality*. New York: Holt, Rinehart and Winston, 1966.

Willerman, L. Biosocial influence on human development. *American Journal of Orthopsychiatry*, **42**, 452–462, 1972.

Wilson, R.S. Twins: Mental development in the preschool years. *Developmental Psychology*, 10, 580–588, 1974a.

Wilson, R.S. Twins: Patterns of cognitive development measured on the WIPPSI. *Developmental Psychology*, 11, 126–134, 1974b.

Wilson, R.S. Synchronized developmental pathways for infant twins. In *Twin Research*, Vol. 3, Part B, 199–209, (Gedda, L., Parisi, P. and Nance, W.E. eds.). New York: Alan Liss, 1981.

Witkin, H.A. Individual differences in ease of perception of embedded figures. *Journal of Personality*, 19, 1–15, 1950.

Wortis, H., Bardach, J.L. Child rearing practices in a low socio-economic group. *Pediatrics*, 32, 298, 1963.

Wrigley, E.A. *Population and History*. London: World University Library, 1969.

Author Index

Page numbers set in roman type indicate the entry in the text and page numbers in italic type indicate the entry in the references section.

Abernethy, E.M. 102, *202*
Ackerman, L. 2, *210*
Adler, A. 15, *202*
Adler, Ch. 37, 57, *203*
Ainsworth, M.D.S. 125, *202*
Anastasi, A. 102, *202*
Arbitman-Smith, R. 121, *202*
Arthur, G.A. 129, *202*
Ausubel, D. 16, 35, 36, *202*
Ausubel, P. 16, *202*

Bachman, J.G. 50, *202*
Bales, F. 36, *208*
Bandura, A. 31, *202*
Barker, R.G. 36, 37, *202*
Bar-Lev, M. 53, *207*
Beard, R.M. 18, 22, *202*
Belenky, M. 16, 21, *209*
Bell, S.M. 125, *202*
Benedict, R. 8, *202*
Berlyne, D.E. 113, *202*
Bernfeld, S. 49, *203*
Bernstein, B. 112, 114, *202*
Bidwell, C.E. 36, *202*
Binswanger, L. 23, *202*
Bloom, B. 2, *203*
Blos, P. 1, 26, 30, 38, *203*
Boyd, P.R. 41, *203*
Bransford, D. 121, *202*

Brittain, C.V. 29, *203*
Buber, M. 24, *203*
Bühler, Ch. 47, *203*
Buxton, C.E. 36, *203*

Castarède, M.F. 31, *203*
Cazden, C.B. 112, *203*
Chen, M. 37, 57, *203*
Cherry, F.F. 125, *203*
Chronique, O.M.S. 13, *203*
Claxton, G. 108, *203*
Clinard, M.B. 112, *203*
Cogner, J.J. 32, *203*
Constantinople, A. 22, 23, *203*
Cronbach, L. 122, *203*
Cull, J.G. 3, *203*

Davidson, F. 13, *203*
Deutsch, C.P. 115, *203*
Deutsch, H. 32, *203*
Deutsch, M. 1, 2, 21, *203*
Diamond, R.M. 16, 21, *209*
Dolan, A.B. 16, *208*
Domino, C. 131, *205*
Donaldson, M. 181, 182, *203*
Douglas, L.W.B. 4, 94, *203*
Dreikurs, R. 50, *204*
Dulit, D. 17−19, 22, 46, 106, *204*
Dunphy, D.C. 28, *204*

Eaton, E.L. 125, *203*
Edwards, D. 112, *204*
Eibl-Eibesfeldt, I. 83, *204*
Eisenstadt, S.N. 38, *204*
Eliram, Y. 41, *204*
Elkind, D. 21, 106, *204*
Ennis, R.H. 16, 87, 106, *204*
Epstein, H.T. 102, *204*
Erikson, E.H. 8, 21–5, 41, 50, 113, *204*
Evans, J.H. 108, 109, *204*
Eysenck, H.J. 61, *204*

Fay, W.H. 15, *204*
Ferguson, E. 75, *204*
Ferron, O. 122, *204*
Feuerstein, R. 3–4, 14, 16, 22, 36, 42–3, 45–6, 48, 67, 76–7, 79, 114, 121–32, 141, 182, 200, *204*
Finch, F. 131, *204*
Fischbein, S. 16, 104, *204*
Florida Study 37, *205*
Frank, J. 115, 169, *205*
Frankenstein, C. 3–4, 8, 14–16, 21–4, 26, 36, 38, 41–2, 46, 54, 63, 83–9, 107, 112–14, 130, 133–44, 199–200, *205*
Freud, A. 15, *205*
Freud, S. 38, *205*
Fromm, E. 37, *205*

Gedda, L. 15, 104, *205*
Gewirtz, J.L. 125, *205*
Gilligan, C. 16, 20, *207*
Goldman, A.R. 105, *205*
Gough, H.C. 131, *205*
Guhl, A.M. 83, *205*
Guilford, J.P. 2, 151, *205*
Guttman, L. 95, *205*

Hager, D.L. 31, *210*
Hall, G.St. 11, *205*
Halper, J. 2, 42, 50, 114, 116, *206*
Halpern, L. 105, *206*
Hardy, R.E. 3, *203*
Havighurst, R.J. 36–7, *206*

Haywood, H.C. 121, *202*
Herman, J.L. 105, *205*
Holinger, D.C. 13, 26, *206*
Horney, K. 15, *206*
Huber, W. 115, *209*
Hunt, D.E. 122, *206*
Hunt, J. 113, *206*

Illsley, R. 94, *208*
Inhelder, B. 3, 16, 46, 70, 107, 170, *206*

Jensen, A. 76, *206*
Johnson-Laird, P.V. 4, 46, 106, 108–10, *206*
Johnston, J. 50, *202*
Jung, C.G. 15, 88, *206*

Kahane, R. 14, 40, 43, 61–2, 191, *210*
Kantner, J.F. 31, *206*
Karmel, B.Z. 67, *206*
Karplus, R. 4, 17–19, 46, 70, 87, *206*
Kasarda, J.D. 36, *202*
Katz, P. 27, *206*
Kaufman, I. 30, *206*
Keasy, C.B. 20, *210*
Keating, D.P. 43, 106, *206*
Keniston, K. 7–8, 10–12, *206*
Kitchis, I. 2, 40, 42, 48, 50–2, 61–2, *206*
Kohen-Raz, R. 1, 2, 4, 16, 21–2, 28, 30, 36, 41–4, 48–9, 53, 55, 61–3, 76, 91, 94, 102–3, 115, 117, 153, 155–6, 169, 177, 191–2, 195–6, *206*, *207*
Kohlberg, L. 16, 20, 22, 84, *207*
Kramer, R. 16, *207*
Kriesberg, L. 112, *207*
Kuhlen, R.G. 102, *207*

Lane, B.A. 43, *207*
Legrenzi, M. 109, *206*
Legrenzi, P. 109, *206*
Leissner, A. 35, *207*

Levi, A. 37, 57, *203*
Levin, D.E. 36, *207*
Levine, D. 17, 110, *207*
Levinson, H.N. 115, 169, *205*
Linn, M.C. 4, 17, 46, 110, *207*
Ljung, B.D. 4, 102, *207*
Lorenz, K. 83, *207*
Lourie, R. 112, *208*
Lunzer, E. 16, 46, *207*

Madge, N. 1, *209*
Maier, H.W. 25, *207*
Makkay, E.S. 30, *206*
Manaster, G.J. 7, 16, 21, 36−7, *208*
Marans, A.E. 112, *208*
Marbach, S. 146, *208*
Marcia, J.E. 22, 41, *208*
Mattheny, A.P. 16, *208*
McGee, M. 69, 114, 169, *208*
McLaughlin, M.M. 9, *208*
Montgomery, K.C. 113, *208*
Muchov, H.H. 8−11, *208*
Murieli, A. 146, 149, *208*
Musgrove, F. 32, *208*
Myklebust, H. 43, *208*

Nevo, D. 145−52, *209*
Nisbet, J.D. 94, *208*
Odom, R.D. 107−8, *208*
O'Malley, P.M. 50, *202*
Ornoy, A. 115, *207*
Ortar, G. 145, 149, *208*

Parsons, T. 37−8, *208*
Passow, H. 1, *208*
Peel, E.A. 18, 22, *208*
Perkal, M. 16, 37, 57, *208*
Piaget, J. 3, 16−19, 22, 46, 67, 69, 70, 83, 106−7, 160−70, 180, *209*
Poeck, K. 115, *209*

Rahamim, R. 54, *209*
Raven, J.C. 78, 191, *209*
Rey, A. 42, 67−82, 122−4, 127, 129, 186, 199, *209*
Rice, M. 4, 17, 46, *207*

Ricks, D.F. 23, *210*
Riessman, F. 1, *209*
Ross, J.M. 4, 94, *203*
Rourke, P. 114, *209*
Rousseau, J.J. 11, *209*
Russel, A. 116, *207*
Rutter, M. 1, 29, 43, *209*

Saddler, C.D. 16, 27, *208*
Salzstein, L. 16, 21, *209*
Scarr-Salapatek, S. 16, 83, *209*
Schlesinger, I.M. 95, *205*
Silberberg, N. 43, *209*
Silberman, C.E. 36, *209*
Slovin-Ela, S. 115, *209*
Smilansky, M. 4, 42, 43, 56, 63, 145−52, 200, *209*
Smilansky, S. 114, *210*
Smith, T.E. 30, *210*
Sorenson, R.E. 31, *210*
Staats, A.W. 68, *210*
Starr, L. 14, 40, 43, 61−2, 191, *210*
Steward, C.S. 31, *210*
Stoddard, G. 84, *210*
Strang, R. 7, *210*
Sullivan, H.S. 15, 23−4, 41, *210*
Sundberg, N.D. 122, *210*

Talmon-Garber, Y. 39, *210*
Tanner, J.M. 9, 11, 102, *210*
Thurstone, L.L. 2, *210*
Thurstone, T.G. 131, *210*
Tinbergen, N. 83, *210*
Tomlinson-Keasey, C. 20, *210*
Tulkin, S.R. 125, *210*

Vener, A.M. 31, *210*

Wapner, S. 105, *210*
Wason, P.C. 4, 46, 106, 108−10, *210*
Weisbrot, S.P. 21, *210*
Werner, H. 105, *210*
Wessman, A.E. 23, *210*
Willerman, L. 42, 94, 113, 115, *210*
Williamson, L. 16, 27, *208*
Wilson, R.S. 2, 16, 104, *211*

Witkin, H.A. 131, *211*
Wortis, H. 112, *211*
Wrigley, E.A. 9, *211*

Yule, W. 43, *209*

Zahavi, P.A. 146, *208*
Zelnik, M. 31, *206*
Zigler, E. 26, *206*
Zilback, J. 30, *206*

Subject Index

Abstract attitude 197
  thought 198
Abstraction ability 46—7, 85, 86, 200
  definition of 43, 45
  verbal abstraction 131
    exercises 163
    and formal reasoning 48
    and higher mental ability 123
    and visual-spatial training 128
Absurd relations
  as exercises in picture stories 129
  in premises of formal reasoning 17
  in sentences and stories 181
  in syllogisms 182
  in time sequences 176
Academic career 12
  of disadvantaged high school graduates 151
Academic high school see School
Achievement need 60
Adolescence
  definition of 7—9
  historical aspects of 9—13
  lower class adolescents 42—3, 48—9, 53, 69
  mid-adolescence 20—1, 23, 25, 28, 55
  middle class adolescents 8, 10, 21, 23, 25—6, 28—9, 32, 38, 49—50
  post-adolescence
    definition of 1, 8—9

  general characteristics of 13, 14
  pre-adolescence 30, 50
  proper 8
  simple adolescence 49, 53, 63
  unrealized 63
Adult status 8
Adulthood 26
Affective reactions 138
Alienation 29
Ambiguity 25, 162
Ambivalence 162
Androgens 8
Anomy 112
Antonyms 162
Apprentice school see School
Arithmetics 184—6
Army
  Adjustment of the disadvantaged to 131, 151
  artisan workshop 60
  career 39
    of disadvantaged postadolescents 151
  intelligence screening test 131
  rejectee 51
  service 147, 151
    exemption from 51
  vocational rehabilitation centers 190
Atomic bomb
  fear of 12
Auditory perception 115

Authoritarian discipline 29
Automatisms (of cognitive functions)
   67—9, 77, 123—4
Auxiliary lessons
   in boarding school program 148

Behavior genetics 15, 16
Bimodal distribution 43—5, 197
Block construction exercises 80, 129
Brain dysfunction 198
Branching as a method of rehabilita-
   tive teaching 137—8
Breakdown
   academic 35
   psychotic 26

Cerebral dysfunction 68
Child labour 10—11
Citizenship as learning units 186
Class atmosphere 37, 57
Classification 179
Classroom dialogue 137
Cliques 28, 30
Close educator see Educator
CNS damage 133, 198
Co-education 148
Cognitive growth 15
   process as separated from emo-
      tions 135
Collective unconscious 88
Combinatorial system 16
Communication 159, 186
   verbal 124
Concentration 190
Concept formation 46, 162
Concrete operations
   acquisition of in normal children
      17
   assessment of 124
   in "beans and can" problem 107
   in conservation tasks 106
   exercises in 176—81
   and ideal self 21
   and Jensen's level II intelligence
      76
   juxtaposed to formal operations
      46, 70

and practical intelligence 69,
   71—2
   stagnation at level of 14
   and two types of reversibility 17
Concretistic thinking 135
Concretisation 154
Conservation tasks 106—8
Content — structure interference 130
Context
   in "bean and can" problem 108
   in crossword puzzles 161
   in curriculum design 110
   familiar 110—11, 128, 183
   familiar to disadvantaged appren-
      tices 157
   in formal reasoning 17, 117
   in "four card" problem 109
   its general role in mental develop-
      ment 4, 105—11, 156, 199
   non-verbal 48, 57
   in practical intelligence 70
   in rehabilitative teaching 138
   unfamiliar 109
Contextual learning units 4, 153—89,
   199
Contraception 32
Contraceptive
   devices 33
   pill 32
Counselling
   educational 13
   vocational 13
Creative thought 157
Criminal code 14
Crisis
   at adolescence as positive learning
      experience 146
   precipitated by examination
      failure 140
   of post-adolescence 26
Crossword puzzles exercises 161
Cultural disadvantage
   definition of 40
   typology of 42—3, 48—9
Cumulative deficit 89
Cumulative effects 1
   of early deprivation 21

causing decrease in verbal intelligence 48

Curriculum 2—3, 36—7, 43, 57, 110—18, 139, 153, 156, 197
extra-curricular activities 37, 148

Deadlock (at adolescence) 26—8, 38, 41

Décalages 106
in formal reasoning 19
as related to stimulus saliency 107

Decoding telegrams as exercise 165

Delinquency
in control groups of contextual learning program 197
in disadvantaged youth 41
and drop-out from compulsory education 10, 191
female adolescent delinquency 30, 35
and fixation to peer group 30
increase at post-adolescence 13
institutions for delinquents 190
and learning disability 43
in middle-class adolescents 38
and peer group pressure 28—9
proneness 2
and street corner gang 35
and threshold of adult criminal law 14

Directionality 182

Disadvantaged see Cultural disadvantage

Domino test 131

Dramatic play 114

Drop-out
from apprentice school 61—2
from boarding school program 149
from compulsory education 10
of disadvantaged adolescents 50—3, 116, 153
in experimental groups of contextual learning program 192, 194, 196—7
factors related to 61

as general phenomenon at post-adolescence 13
at high school 26, 142
at higher grades of elementary school 56
drop-outs as "legitimate leavers" 60—2
return of drop-outs to school 190
from vocational school 61—2

Drug addiction 41

Dyslexia 42

Economic independence 32

Education
compensatory 2
compulsory 2, 10
formal 40

Educational system
for the disadvantaged 55

Educational personnel 61

Educator
close educator 34—6, 117, 200
definition of 34—5
for disadvantaged populations 53
foremen and employers as 62
as mediator 123—4, 126, 132
in rehabilitation processes 55
social worker as 35
semi-professional 62
turnover of educators 116

Ego autonomy 22, 28, 31, 54
definition of 83

Ego defense mechanisms 49
development 16, 22—7
in disadvantaged post-adolescents 49—53
distortion of 133
plasticity of 121
exhaustion 53
functions impaired by externalization 141
involvement 23, 46, 188
mobility 69, 86
strength 88

Egocentric attitudes 135

interest 46
Egocentricity 83
    exercises to overcome it 169
    overcoming of 125
Eighth grade screening examinations
    145
    Embedded figures test 131
Emotional disturbance 43
    maturity 23
Enrichment programs 1, 2
Examination failure 140
Existential despair 26
    enrichment 38
    expansion 11, 14, 37—9, 63, 147
    modus 23—5, 31, 50
Explorative drive 117
Externalization see also Externalized
    style of life 1, 198
    definition of 84
Externalized style of life
    description of its dynamics 84—9,
        199
    and disadvantaged adolescents 8
    and egocentricity 47
    and existential expansion 63
    and its impact
        on mental functions 84—9
        on social adjustment 84—9
    and intimacy 51
    and language development 114
    and parent-adolescent relationship
        54
    and plural mode of existence 23
    and traditional curriculum 112
Extra-curricular activities see curri-
    culum
Extraneous stimulation 105

Family of origin 34
Family relations as learning units
    in instrumental enrichment pro-
        gram 128
    in contextual learning program
        182
Father
    absence 112

failure to identify with 50
    weakness of 63
First aid as learning unit 188
Formal operations
    assessment of 76, 124
    with concrete objects 70
    definition of 16—17
    as determinants of moral judge-
        ment 24
    in different domains 18—20, 106
    in different populations 18—20,
        106
    and ego mobility 86
    and emotional maturity at post-
        adolescence 25
    exercises in 130, 181—4
    under conditions of externaliza-
        tion 89
    in "four card problem" 109—10
    in numerical context 128
    and personality variables 20—1
    and practical intelligence 73
    and physiological maturation
        90—104
    and rehabilitation programs 200
    and spatial orientation 114
    variations in competency of 46
    and low verbal abstraction 47
Formal reasoning see formal opera-
    tions
Four card problem 109—10
French revolution 10
Frontal method of teaching 117,
    154, 157
Future time perspective 53, 61, 87

Generation gap 30
Gifted disadvantaged 43, 49, 145—52
Grace Arthur Test 124
Growth
    deceleration 8
    intellectual 2
Growth spurt
    mental 91, 102, 103
    physical 8, 42, 91
Guidance services 2

Guttman-Schlesinger Analytical Test 95—101

Hawthorne effect 192—4
Heterogeneous groups 155
Heterogeneous mental level 56
Homework 61
Homosexuality see Sex
Hormonal disequilibrium 1
Human figure drawing 131
Hyperactivity 42
Hyperfatiguability 76

Identity 8, 22—3, 25, 28, 31
   confusion 32, 41, 49—50
   crisis 21, 53
   struggle for 50
Illiteracy 2, 126
Incest taboo 38
Individual instruction 154
Industrial revolution 10
Information theory 122, 138
Instincts 134
Instrumental enrichment 36,
   121—32, 199
Integration (in education) 37, 56,
   143, 148
Intelligence
   practical 3, 70—5
   quotient 22, 192
   sensori-motor 75
   tests 22, 46
   critical evaluation of 122
   verbal 61, 70, 131, 136, 141, 143
Intellectual growth deceleration see
   Growth
Intercourse see Sex
Intimacy 23—5, 50

Juvenile delinquency see Delinquency

Kibbutz 36, 38—9, 63, 191

Labelling 122
Language development 131—2, 141
   skills 159

Learning disability 43, 113
   experience 36
   potential assessment 122—4
Legitimate leavers see Drop-out
Life experience 35, 38
   in principles 25—6
   space 17, 37
Linguistic communication 114, 136
   restricted code of 114
Love 31—2, 34
   object 33

Mainstreaming 2
Maladjustment 121
Marriage 24, 31—2, 195
   age of 32
   in pre-technological society 9
   partner 39
   status of disadvantaged high school
      graduates 151
Mass media 12, 31
Mathematics
   achievement of disadvantaged
      students 57
Mediating learning experience 124
Menarche 8, 11
Menarcheal age 96—8
Mental development 4, 67, 83
   at post-adolescence 22
   psychobiological aspects of
      91—104
   stagnation of 14
Mental differentiation 136
   effort 68
   energy 88
   equilibrium 19
   field 68, 77, 123
      training to widen it 127
   functions 43, 48—9, 68, 124
   growth 90, 105, 106
   heritage 38
   incompetency 51
   inferiority 16
   maturation 4.
   level 21, 27, 51, 193
      heterogeneous 155

performance 156
    in the disadvantaged 76
plasticity 2
potential 2
process 77
retardation 42, 195, 199, 200
    environmental 177
    mild 197
    at post-adolescence 22
    primary 133, 135
    reversibility of types of 90
    secondary 135
schemata 4
sickness 29
structures 106, 111
    as trained by instrumental
        enrichment 130
Metaphors 168
Mid-adolescence see Adolescence
Milta Verbal Intelligence Test 146,
    149, 191
Minimal CNS dysfunction 113
Minnesota Test 151
Moral education 34
    judgement 20, 22, 24, 47, 49, 87,
        143
        post-conventional level of 20,
            84
Morality 16
Moratorium 8, 10, 21, 23, 32, 49—51
Mortality
    of children 9
    of women at childbirth 9
Mother-child relationship 125
Motherhood 32—3
Motivation 158, 200
    to stay at school 56
    to study 57
Movement representations 177

Neutralizing affective reactions 138
Non-inductiveness 137
Number crossword exercises 185
Number runs exercises 177
Numerical progressions exercises 128

Oculomotor responses 67

Oedipal conflict 10, 33, 49
    fairy tales 87
    impediment of intellectual func-
        tions 88
    involvement 54
    stage 50
Organization of dots technique
    78—80, 126
Ossification
    of epiphyses 8

Parent 27—30, 112
    adolescent relations 28—9
        under conditions of external-
            ization 139—40
    child interaction 139
    as partner 139
    peer dialectics 27—30
    separation from 147
        in boarding school program
            147
Parental
    conflict 54
    figures 87
    identification 21
    involvement in school 112—13
Paternal role 49
Peer
    conformity 20, 49
    group 28—30, 54
        instable relation to 54
    relationship 37
    teaching 126, 157
Peers 27—30
    vs parents 28—30
Perceptual
    ability 107
    mechanisms 69
Personality
    development 112
    disturbances 198
    growth 23
    test differences in disadvantaged
        post-adolescents 52—3
Phobia 28
    of school 28
Physical development

at adolescence 91—4
Physical growth *see* Growth
Physiological maturation
    at adolescence 90—103, 153
Post-adolescence *see* Adolescence
Post-adolescent crisis 26
Post-technological era 11
Posture test 131
Pre-adolescence *see* Adolescence
Pregnancy out of wedlock 32, 33
    and unconscious motivation 33
Prepositional logic 16—17, 107
Pre-technological era 9
    society 9
Primary Mental Ability Test 131
Procreation 31
Promiscuity 31
Proverbs 168
Psychiatrist 35
Psychoanalysis 87
    neo-psychoanalytical theory 41
Psychobiological studies 3, 90—104
Psychodynamic theory
    of cognitive development 83—9
    of adolescence 21—5
Psychologist 35
Psychopathology 198
Psychosocial development 83, 132
Psychotechnical tests 75
Psychotherapy 14, 118, 138
Psychotic
    borderline type 43
    breakdown *see* Breakdown
Puberty 1, 2, 7 *see also* Adolescence
Pubic hair growth 99
Pupil status 37

Rape 30
Raven Matrices Test 93—101, 124,
    131, 191, 196
Reading
    ability 196—7
    level 195
    problems 160
    remedial reading 160
Reciprocity 17, 182

Regression
    to lower stages of moral judge-
        ment 20
    in the service of the ego 20, 54
Rehabilitative teaching 133—44, 199
Remedial
    reading *see* reading
    teaching 196
Retarded disadvantaged adolescents
    57—8, 91—101, 192
Reversibility
    exercises to train 127
    in mental operations 17

Scholastic experience 160
School
    academic high school 40—1, 50,
        58, 62, 141—4, 145—52, 154,
        187
    apprentice school 40, 48, 50—1,
        60
    attendance 2
    boarding school fostering 145—52,
        199
    failure 2, 50, 113, 122, 197
    industrial school 48, 58
    junior high school in Israel 56—8,
        133
    reform in Israel 55—7
    semi-skilled apprentice school in
        Israel 60, 153, 155, 190—1,
        196—7
    skilled apprentice school 58—9,
        196
    system
        elementary 2
        European 20
        high school 16, 36—7, 151
        Israeli 55
    vocational high school program 50
    vocational school 40, 42, 48,
        50—1, 58, 190
Scrambled sentences exercise 164
Secondary retardation syndrome 135
Secular trend 11
Self 22

concept 27
government in boarding school 149
ideal self 21, 27
image 16, 37, 49, 126, 143, 158, 200
Sensitivity training of teachers 126
Sensory-tonic theory 105
Separation
  anxiety 54, 147
  from home 152
Sequential
  memory 77, 123
  order of exercises 154
Seriation 180
Sex 32
  education 33, 34
    by social worker 140
  and love 31—2
Sexual freedom 12, 31
  heterosexual relations 30
  homosexual fixation 30
  intercourse 31—4
    collective 30
  partner 24, 29, 38
  potency 32
  precocious sexual life 32
  psychosexual development
    in disadvantaged boys 54
    in disadvantaged girls 55
  reproduction 7, 38
  unisexual clique 30
Social
  group activities 148
  development 57
  environment 124
    proximal 125
  roles 7
  status of pupils 16
  work 118
  worker 36, 141, 147
    intervening in parent-adole-
      scent relations 140, 143
    intervening in street corner
      projects 35
Socialization process 28, 30, 35, 37

Spatial
  imagination 79, 81
  orientation, organization 48, 69, 123, 169
    exercises 127, 169
  relations 114
Special class 56, 58, 121
Stencil design technique 129
Street corner gang projects 35
Structural approach 105, 199
Suicide 13, 26
Syllogisms 17, 130
Symbol
  formation 113, 168, 200
  understanding 135
  system 69, 87
    secondary 136
Symbolic
  interaction 113
  modes of communication 113
  play 88
Symbolization 114
Synkinetic movements 76
Synonyms 162
Syntax 164

Teacher
  academic level of 57
  authority 134
  high school 35
  higher qualification of 57
  as interpreter 137
  as mediator 125—6
  pupil dialogue 139
  pupil interaction 37, 140
    disruption of 122
  substitute teacher 116
Technological drawing exercises 174
Telencephalisation 68
Temporal
  orientation 128
  sequences 48, 115, 176
    exercises 175
Test
  performance observation 123
  situation 76, 122

Time
    perception 175
    on task 190
Traumatic childhood experiences 26
Turmoil at adolescence 8, 15, 121
Twin studies 103—4

Urge to travel
    at post-adolescence 25

Value system
    change in 12
Verbal
    abstraction *see* Abstraction
    communication 82
    intelligence *see* Intelligence
Virginity 32, 34
Visual perception 48
Visual-spatial
    abilities 69, 75
    relations 130
        trained by verbal instructions

            129
    tests 78
Vocabulary
    enrichment exercises 160
Vocational
    school *see* Schools
    training 192
        centers 133
Voluntary activities in boarding
    school program 149

Wanderjahre 25
Waywardness 29—31, 35
Wechsler Intelligence Test 45
Womanhood 32
Women soldiers as teachers 60, 62
World War 8, 11—12, 38

Youth
    middle-class 54
    prison apprentice school 157
    wayward 60

DATE DUE

DEMCO 38-297